THE BIG BOOK
of BIBLE
ANSWERS

RON RHODES

HARVEST HOUSE PUBLISHERS
EUGENE, OREGON

THE BIG BOOK OF BIBLE ANSWERS
Copyright © 2013 by Ron Rhodes
Published by Harvest House Publishers
Eugene, Oregon 97402
www.harvesthousepublishers.com

Library of Congress Cataloging-in-Publication Data

Rhodes, Ron.
  The big book of Bible answers / Ron Rhodes.
    p. cm.
  Indexes.
  ISBN 978-0-7369-5140-1 (pbk.)
  ISBN 978-0-7369-5141-8 (eBook)
  1. Bible–Miscellanea. I. Title.
BS612.R43 2013
220–dc23

2012026966

To my beloved son, David

Acknowledgments

Through the years I've received countless letters and e-mails from people around the world asking a variety of interesting questions about the Bible. I'm happy to say that many of these questions have found their way into this book. A special thanks to each of you for taking the time to write. You have continued to challenge my thinking!

I also continue to be profoundly thankful to our gracious God for the wondrous gift of my family—Kerri, David, and Kylie. Without their endless love and support, my work of ministry would truly be an impossible task.

Heartfelt appreciation also goes to the entire staff at Harvest House Publishers. It's been a pleasure working with you these many years! Your professionalism and commitment to truth are shining examples among Christian publishers.

Contents

My Interest in Strong Bible Answers

I remember it as if it were just yesterday. Back in 1990, when I worked at the Christian Research Institute, I was asked to become a "regular" on the *Bible Answer Man* call-in radio broadcast. I was initially very resistant. Who in his right mind wants to go on national radio, with millions of people listening, and get asked hard questions for an hour each day?

After a while, though, I became quite comfortable and even grew to enjoy the challenge of responding to these tough questions on live radio. A side benefit of doing that show was that it forced me to give thoughtful (and *biblical*) attention to issues I'd really not thought that much about. And the more I wrestled with these issues, digging through the Scriptures each day for answers, the more I came to see that the Bible really does provide wisdom and insight on a plethora of relevant issues.

Over the years that I was on the *Bible Answer Man*, I noticed that many questions seemed to come up quite regularly. In fact, over time, I developed a detailed listing of the most frequently asked questions. Since my days on the *Bible Answer Man*, I've continued doing countless other call-in radio shows where I've answered a plethora of challenging questions, and I've continued to supplement my list of frequently asked questions. The book you're holding in your hands is largely the fruit of that list. I've also supplemented the list with the "best of the bunch" in terms of questions people have sent me via mail or e-mail.

I need to mention at the outset that this book does not attempt to provide an exhaustive treatment of every Christian doctrine. This is not a theology textbook. My goal in this book is simply to answer common questions people are asking about some of these doctrines. If you want a fuller treatment of individual doctrines, you might be interested in reading some of my other books, such as *The Wonder of Heaven, Angels Among Us,* and *Christ Before the Manger.*

As you read this book, you'll notice that I answer some questions very briefly, while others are allocated more space. This is by design. The fact is, some questions are easily answered, while others require more detail.

My prayer as you read this book is that *you* will become truly comfortable in answering questions people ask you about the Bible. You will find that God will open many doors of opportunity for you to engage in dialogue with others *if you make yourself available to Him.*

Dig in! And by all means, as you go through this book, look up some of the Scripture references I cite. Like the ancient Bereans, we should make a regular habit of testing all things against Scripture (Acts 17:11; see also 1 Thessalonians 5:21). If you do this consistently, you'll soon become a formidable warrior of the Word, or, as I jokingly used to say among my apologetics colleagues, an Apolo-Jedi Master.

—Ron Rhodes, Frisco, Texas, 2012

Part 1
Questions About the Bible

Scripture: From God to Us
The Trustworthiness of the Bible
The Books That Belong in the Bible
All About Bible Translations
Interpretation of Scripture: Sense and Nonsense

1
Scripture: From God to Us

What does it mean to say that the Bible is "inspired"?

Inspiration does not mean the biblical writer just felt enthusiastic, like the composer of "The Star-Spangled Banner." Nor does it mean the writings are necessarily inspiring to read, like an uplifting poem. The biblical Greek word for *inspiration* literally means "God-breathed." Because Scripture is breathed out by God—because it *originates* from Him—it is true and inerrant.

Biblical inspiration may be defined as God's superintending of the human authors so that, using their own individual personalities—and even their writing styles—they composed and recorded *without error* His revelation to humankind in the words of the original autographs. In other words, the original documents of the Bible were written by men who were permitted to exercise their own personalities and literary talents but wrote under the control and guidance of the Holy Spirit. The result was a perfect and errorless record of the exact message God desired to give humankind.

In what way did the biblical authors use their own writing styles?

The writers of Scripture were not mere writing machines. God did not use them like keys on a typewriter to mechanically reproduce His message. Nor did He dictate the words, page by page.

The biblical evidence makes it clear that each writer had a style of his own: Isaiah had a powerful literary style. Jeremiah had a mournful tone. Luke's style had medical overtones. John was very simple in his approach.

The Holy Spirit infallibly worked through each of these writers, through their individual styles, to communicate His message to humankind without error.

To what extent were the biblical writers controlled by the Holy Spirit as they wrote?

In his second letter, Peter provides a key insight regarding the human-divine interchange in the process of inspiration. This verse informs us that "no prophecy [or Scripture] was ever produced by the will of man, but men spoke from God as they were carried along by the Holy Spirit" (2 Peter 1:21). The phrase "carried along" in this verse literally means "forcefully borne along."

Even though human beings were used in the process of writing down God's Word, they were all literally "borne along" by the Holy Spirit. The human wills of the authors were not the originators of God's message. God did not permit the will of sinful human beings to misdirect or erroneously record His message. Rather, "God *moved* and the prophet *mouthed* these truths; God *revealed* and man *recorded* His word."[1]

Interestingly, the Greek word for "carried along" in 2 Peter 1:21 is the same as that found in Acts 27:15-17. In this passage the experienced sailors could not navigate the ship because the wind was so strong. The ship was being *driven, directed,* and *carried along* by the wind. This is similar to the Spirit's driving, directing, and carrying the human authors of the Bible as He wished. The word is a strong one, indicating the Spirit's complete superintendence of the human authors. But just as the sailors were active on the ship (though the wind, not the sailors, ultimately controlled the ship's movement), so the human authors were active in writing as the Spirit directed.

Were the New Testament writers aware that their writings were inspired by God and therefore authoritative?

Yes, no doubt about it. In 1 Corinthians 2:13 the apostle Paul said he spoke "in words not taught by human wisdom but taught by the Spirit." In this passage Paul (who wrote nearly half the books in the New Testament) affirmed that his words were authoritative because they were rooted not in fallible human beings but infallible God (the Holy Spirit). The Holy Spirit is the Spirit *of truth* who was promised to the apostles to teach and guide them into all the truth (see John 16:13).

Later, in 1 Corinthians 14:37, Paul said, "If anyone thinks that he is a prophet, or spiritual, he should acknowledge that the things I am writing to you are a command of the Lord." In 1 Thessalonians 2:13 Paul likewise said, "We also thank God constantly for this, that when you received the word of God, which you heard from us, you accepted it not as the word of men but as what it really is, the word of God, which is at work in you believers."

Again, Paul's words were authoritative because they were rooted in God, not in man. God used Paul and other biblical writers as His instruments to communicate *His* word to man.

What are some of the incorrect views of the inspiration of Scripture?

At least seven incorrect views of inspiration are circulating today:

First, the Dictation Theory says that God raised men up, prepared the men *and* their vocabularies, and then dictated to them the very words which they would put down in the Scriptures. Second, the Natural Inspiration Theory says that the writers of Scripture were simply men of great genius. Nothing supernatural was involved. These were men with talent similar to that of Shakespeare. Third, the Mystical Theory says that the writers of Scripture were simply Spirit-filled and Spirit-guided believers, like any believer may be today.

Fourth, the Neo-orthodox Theory says that the Bible is a fallible and often unreliable "witness" to the Word of God. In a fallible way, it points to Christ. Fifth, the Concept Inspiration Theory holds that the concepts, but not the very words of Scripture, were inspired. So, for example, the concept of salvation in Christ may be inspired, but the words used to communicate this concept are not inspired and therefore may have mistakes.

Sixth, the Inspired Purpose Theory says that although the Bible contains many factual errors and insoluble discrepancies, it still has "doctrinal integrity" and thus accomplishes God's purpose for it. The Bible's infallibility is carefully limited to the main purpose or principle emphasis of the Bible—that is, salvation.

And seventh, the Partial Inspiration Theory says that certain parts of the Bible are inspired—that is, the portions that would otherwise have been unknowable (creation, prophecy, salvation by faith in Christ, and so forth).

This is the correct view of inspiration: God superintended the human authors so that they used their own personalities and styles to record without error (in the original manuscripts) God's word to humankind.

Objections to Inspiration and Inerrancy

Some critics question the Bible's reliability by arguing that the Gospel writers were biased. How can we respond to this?

Some critics say the four Gospel writers were biased in the sense that they had theological motives. Their intent was to convince readers of Jesus' deity, we are told, and therefore their historical testimony is untrustworthy.

The fallacy here is to imagine that to give an account of something one believes in passionately necessarily forces one to distort history. This is simply not true. In modern times some of the most reliable reports of the Nazi Holocaust were written by Jews who were passionately committed to seeing such genocide never repeated.[2]

The New Testament is not made up of fairy tales but rather is based on eyewitness testimony. In 2 Peter 1:16 we read, "We did not follow cleverly devised myths when we made known to you the power and coming of our Lord Jesus Christ, but we were eyewitnesses of his majesty." First John 1:1 affirms that the apostles proclaimed "that which was from the beginning, which we have heard, which we have seen with our eyes, which we looked upon and have touched with our hands, concerning the word of life."

Why did God allow four Gospels into the Bible that have apparent contradictions?

First of all, while the Gospels may have some *apparent* contradictions, I do not believe they have *genuine* contradictions. There are differences, yes. But actual contradictions? No.

Second, keep in mind that inspiration and inerrancy are, strictly speaking, ascribed only to the original autographs of Scripture—that is, the original documents penned by the actual biblical authors. Certainly I believe that the copies we have of the original autographs are extremely accurate. But theologians have been very careful to say that the Scriptures, in their *original autographs* and *properly interpreted,* will be shown to be *wholly true* in everything they teach.

Third, if all four Gospels were the same, with no differences, critics would be screaming "collusion" all over the place. The fact that the Gospels have differences shows there was no collusion. They represent four different (but inspired) accounts of the same events.

One should not assume that a *partial* account in a gospel is *a faulty* account. In Matthew 27:5, for example, we are told that Judas died by hanging himself. In Acts 1:18 we are told that Judas burst open in the middle and all his entrails gushed out. These are both partial accounts. Neither account gives us the full picture. But taken together we can easily reconstruct how Judas died. He hanged himself, and sometime later the rope loosened and Judas fell to the rocks below, thereby causing his intestines to gush out. As one probes into alleged contradictions, one consistently sees that they are all explainable in a reasonable way.

Is science the judge and jury of the miracles in the Bible?

No. Let's keep in mind that science depends upon observation and replication. Miracles, such as the incarnation and the resurrection, are by their very nature unprecedented events. No one can replicate these events in a laboratory. Science therefore cannot be the judge and jury as to whether or not these events occurred.

Besides, the scientific method is useful only for studying *nature*, not *super-nature*. Just as football stars are speaking outside their field of expertise when they appear on television to tell you what razor you should buy, so scientists are speaking outside their field when they address theological issues like miracles or the resurrection.

Can we trust that the biblical miracles really occurred?

Yes. One highly pertinent factor is the brief time that elapsed between Jesus' miraculous public ministry and the publication of the Gospels. It was insufficient for the development of miracle legends. Many eyewitnesses to Jesus' miracles would have still been alive to refute any untrue miracle accounts (see 1 Corinthians 15:6).

One must also recognize the noble character of the men who witnessed these miracles—Peter, James, and John, for example. Such men were not prone to misrepresentation, and they were willing to give up their lives rather than deny what they knew to be true.

There were also hostile witnesses to the miracles of Christ. When Jesus raised Lazarus from the dead, for example, none of the chief priests or Pharisees disputed the miracle (John 11:45-48). (If they could have disputed it, they would have.) Rather, their goal was simply to stop Jesus (verses 47-48). Because so many hostile witnesses observed and scrutinized Christ, a successful fabrication of miracle stories in His ministry would have been impossible.

Are science and the Bible irreconcilable?

Personally, I believe that nature and Scripture, properly interpreted, do not conflict. God has communicated to humankind both by *general* revelation (nature, or the observable universe) and *special* revelation (the Bible). Since both of these revelations come from God—and since God does not contradict Himself—we must conclude that these two revelations are in agreement with each other. While there may be conflicts between one's *interpretation* of the observable universe and one's *interpretation* of the Bible, there is no ultimate contradiction.

We might say that *science* is a fallible human interpretation of the observable universe while *theology* is a fallible human interpretation of the Scriptures. If the secularist challenges the idea that science can be fallible, remind him or her of what science historian Thomas Kuhn proved in his book *The Structure of Scientific Revolutions*: Science is in a constant state of change. New discoveries have consistently caused old scientific paradigms to be discarded in favor of newer paradigms.

Here is the point: *Nature* and *Scripture* do not contradict. Rather, *science* (a fallible human interpretation of nature) and *theology* (a fallible human interpretation of Scripture) sometimes fall into conflict. So the secularist cannot simply dismiss certain parts of the Bible because certain interpretations of nature offered by some scientists may conflict with particular interpretations of Scripture.

How can we respond to the claim that some language in the Bible is scientifically incorrect?

Some critics allege that the Bible is not scientifically accurate in view of its frequent use of "phenomenological" language—that is, the language of appearances. Ecclesiastes 1:5, for example, says that the sun "rises" and "goes down." From a scientific perspective, the sun does not actually rise or go down. But let's be fair. This is the same kind of language weather forecasters use today. "Rising" and "going down" are accepted ways of describing what the sun *appears* to be doing from an earthly perspective. So, the Bible's use of such language does not prove that it contains scientific errors.

2
The Trustworthiness
of the Bible

Scholars say there is strong archeological evidence for the Bible. What is archeology?

Archeology comes from two Greek words: *archaios*, meaning "ancient things," and *logos*, meaning "study of." Archeology is the study of ancient things. More specifically, it is the study of excavated materials, such as art, architecture, monuments, inscriptions, pottery, literature, items related to language, customs, and various other artifacts.

Is archeology a science?

Yes. Archeology is categorized as a science because knowledge is acquired by systematic observation of discovered items, and these items are then classified and cataloged into an organized body of information. Archeology also seeks assistance from other sciences, such as chemistry, anthropology, and zoology.

Why is archeology relevant to the Bible's reliability?

Broadly speaking, archeology helps us to better understand the historical context of the Bible, and it also provides background information about subjects the Bible tells us little about. In many cases it illuminates the meaning of some passages of Scripture. And, of course, it verifies the accuracy and reliability of biblical references to customs, places, names, and events.

Numerous scholars have noted the significance of biblical archeology. For instance, Bible scholar Donald J. Wiseman notes that "today, more than 25,000 sites within [Bible lands] and dating to Old Testament times, in their broadest sense, have been located."[1] These 25,000 sites verify Bible customs, places, names, and events.

Nelson Glueck, a specialist in ancient literature, did an exhaustive study and concluded, "No archaeological discovery has ever controverted a biblical reference."[2] World renowned scholar William F. Albright agrees: "Discovery after discovery has established the accuracy of innumerable details, and has brought increased recognition of the value of the Bible as a source of history."[3]

What have archeologists discovered about cities in Bible times?

In Bible times, a city was often built close to trade routes and good water supplies. Homes and buildings in these cities were generally constructed of bricks, which could be easily knocked down by an enemy, a flood, or an earthquake.

Whenever that happened, those who lived in the city—or, perhaps, new inhabitants—would level the rubble and rebuild atop the old city, using more bricks. Over time, the process repeated itself again and again. City would be built upon leveled city, on and on throughout history.

As this continued, the city eventually took on the appearance of a mound, for it had been built and rebuilt—layer upon layer—many times through the years. Archeologists call these mounds *tells* (Arabic for *mounds*). These tells could rise as high as 75 feet.

Eventually, people might choose to no longer settle there. This might happen, for example, if the water supply dried up, if trade routes changed significantly, or if a threatening enemy settled nearby.

How do archeologists study such cities upon mounds?

When archeologists study such a mound, they first conduct a surface exploration, in which they carefully examine and analyze pottery and various other artifacts on the surface. They seek clues to the history of the mound, and they look for evidence of what might lie beneath the top layer.

Then they construct a contour map of the mound and select one or more sectors on the contour map where excavation will begin. They subdivide the sectors into ten-meter squares so they can properly catalog whatever is discovered beneath the surface of the mound.

Archeologists then proceed to excavate one layer at a time, with each layer representing a certain period of occupation. As they go through each successive layer, they steadily uncover the progressive history of the city. The deeper they go, the more ancient history they uncover.

Is it true that archeological evidence for the Bible is presently fragmentary?

Yes, that is indeed true. The discoveries archeologists have made so far provide incredible evidence in support of the Bible, but they are nevertheless fragmentary. Only a fraction of what was made or what was written in ancient times has survived to the present day. Also, archeologists have not yet surveyed all the available sites, nor have they excavated all the sites they have surveyed. They only examine a portion of an excavated site *in detail*, and they only report and publish a fraction of what they excavate.[4]

Our knowledge in this field of study is therefore incomplete at present. The good news is that Bible scholars are continually making new archeological discoveries (more than 25,000 so far). And the more they discover, the more evidence we have to support the Bible!

What are some examples of archeological discoveries related to Old Testament cities and peoples?

Excavations at Ur, the hometown of Abraham, reveal that this had been a powerful city-state before it finally fell. The fall of Ur may have been one reason Abraham's father, Terah, relocated to Haran (see Genesis 11:31).

Also, critics once considered the Hittites pure myth. Some 10,000 clay tablets found at a ruin of an ancient city in Turkey called Boghazkoy now provide abundant archeological evidence for the existence of the Hittites during the time of Abraham.

Carvings on the wall of an Egyptian temple at Thebes, dated around 1175–1150 BC, portray the Philistines—enemies of Israel—in all their military might. The ruins of ancient Babylon have been extensively excavated in modern Iraq. Among the many discoveries is the palace of King Nebuchadnezzar (see Daniel 4:29). At an archeological site located at the northern section of biblical Jericho, a portion of the lower city wall has been discovered that did not fall as it did everywhere else (see Joshua 6:17-25).

What are some examples of Old Testament archeological discoveries related to false religions mentioned in the Old Testament?

Excavations throughout Egypt have uncovered much information about the false gods the Egyptians worshipped during the time of the Exodus. These false gods could not intervene when the true God, Yahweh, inflicted the ten plagues upon the Egyptians. For example, the Egyptian sacred river god Nilus (considered to be the *lifeblood* of Egypt) could not prevent Yahweh from turning the Nile River into real blood.

Also, excavators have discovered hundreds of stories about Canaanite gods and goddesses recorded on clay tablets at the ruins of ancient Ugarit (modern Ras Shamra). These tablets provide a virtual mother lode of information about false pagan gods and goddesses, such as Baal.

What are some examples of Old Testament archeological discoveries related to language and writing?

Increasing evidence is surfacing that the world, at one time, had a single language, as Sumerian literature often suggests. One clay tablet discovered has remarkable similarities to the account of the Tower of Babel in Genesis 11.

Critics once claimed Moses could not have written the first five books of the Bible because handwriting had not yet been invented. Archeological discoveries of numerous ancient inscriptions over a wide area in the ancient Near East now conclusively prove that there indeed was handwriting during the time of Moses.

The discovery of the Rosetta Stone at Rashid, a harbor on the Mediterranean coast in Egypt, has not only helped scholars unlock Egypt's writing system (known as hieroglyphics) but also has provided rich information on Egypt's history, religion, and culture.

What are some examples of Old Testament archeological discoveries related to ancient culture?

Drawings have been discovered in Egypt depicting Hebrew slaves making bricks for the cities of Pithom and Rameses. Laws regulating slavery have been uncovered at various archeological sites—including at Nuzi, Sumer, Babylonia, Assyria, and Israel. Such laws demonstrate the Bible's alignment with the broader Near Eastern cultural view of slavery, while at the same time pointing to their more humane treatment in Israel.

The Nuzi Tablets, discovered at Nuzi (east of the Tigris River), are 20,000 baked clay tablets that contain an abundance of information on customs, stories, and history that shed light on the book of Genesis. Among them are legal tablets indicating that an infertile wife had the prerogative of giving her maidservant to her husband in order to provide him an heir who could then be adopted by the wife. This sheds light on the biblical account of Abraham and Sarah's maidservant (see Genesis 16).

Also, Saul's fortress at Gibeah has been excavated, and it was discovered that slingshots were among the most common weapons of the day. David used one to slay Goliath (see 1 Samuel 17:49).

What are some examples of New Testament archeological discoveries related to ancient cities?

Nazareth, the hometown of Jesus (see Matthew 2:23; 4:13; Mark 1:9; Luke 1:26-28), has been excavated. Discoveries include olive oil presses and a large number of diverse artifacts from the time of Christ. Bethsaida, the birthplace of Peter, Andrew, and Philip, has been thoroughly excavated (see Matthew 11:21). The ruins at Khirbet Qana are apparently the biblical Cana, the city where Jesus turned water into wine (John 2:1-11).

Also, excavations have uncovered key portions of Damascus, including the remains of a "street called Straight," where Saul once stayed (Acts 9:11). Excavations in Caesarea have uncovered a marketplace, a theater, temples, houses, and streets which may have been traversed by the apostle Peter, who won the Gentile convert Cornelius to Christianity in this city (see Acts 10). Excavations in Philippi have uncovered a number of shrines to pagan gods and goddesses. The apostle Paul, of course, wrote a letter to the church at Philippi.

What are some examples of New Testament archeological discoveries related to famous personalities?

Archeologists have made a number of discoveries corresponding to well-known biblical personalities:

For instance, the ruins of Herod the Great's winter palace have been excavated at Jericho, the city where Jesus met the tax collector Zacchaeus (Luke 19:1-10). Archeologists have also discovered a stone slab at the ruins of Caesarea Maritima that bears the name of Pontius Pilate, who participated in the trial of Jesus (Acts 4:27). The surviving portion has the actual words, "Pontius Pilate, Prefect of Judea."

The ossuary of Caiaphas, the Jewish high priest who officiated at Jesus' trial, has been discovered (see Matthew 26:57; John 18:13-14). On the ossuary are the words "Caiaphas," "Joseph, son of Caiaphas." Inside were the bones of six people, including a 60-year-old (Caiaphas).

A limestone box has been discovered that apparently contains the bones of James, the half brother of Jesus (see Matthew 13:55; Mark 6:3). It bears the words, "James, son of Joseph, brother of Jesus."

What are some examples of New Testament archeological discoveries related to notable locations?

A number of prominent New Testament locations have surfaced:

Near Mount Gerizim, excavators have unearthed Jacob's well, where Jesus spoke with a Samaritan woman (see John 4:1-42). Archeologists have uncovered the pool of Bethesda in the northeast quarter of Jerusalem, where Jesus healed a paralyzed man (John 5:2-11). An excavation at the site of Tell Hum has revealed the ruins of a synagogue in Capernaum, the town where Jesus conducted much of His public ministry (Matthew 4:13; Mark 2:1).

Archeologists have also excavated a site in Capernaum that may have been the location of the apostle Peter's house (see Mark 1:29). Further, part of the Jewish temple of Jesus' day has been excavated, particularly in the area of the south retaining wall (see Matthew 21; Mark 11).

The pool of Siloam, referenced in John 9, has been discovered as well. It is 225 feet long and has a three-tiered stairway that leads down into the pool.

How many New Testament manuscripts have been discovered?

The overwhelming manuscript evidence points to the accuracy and reliability of the Bible. Presently 5,686 partial and complete Greek manuscript copies of the New Testament are known. These manuscript copies are very ancient and are available for inspection now.

If one adds into the mix more than 10,000 Latin Vulgate manuscripts and at least 9,300 other early versions (including Ethiopic, Slavic, and Armenian versions), the total approximates 25,000 manuscripts that cite portions of the New Testament. This far exceeds the number of manuscripts of other ancient documents, most of which have less than ten extant manuscripts each.

Do any early manuscripts contain significant portions of the New Testament?

The Chester Beatty papyrus (P45) is named after a man who obtained a number of biblical manuscripts. The letter *P* refers to papyrus, a durable writing material manufactured from the river plant *cyperus papyrus* in ancient Egypt. The number 45 is an identifying number. This particular manuscript dates to the third century AD, within 150 years of the original New Testament documents. It contains the four Gospels and the book of Acts (chapters 4–17).

Another Chester Beatty papyrus is P46, which dates to about AD 200, obviously quite close in time to the original writing of the New Testament documents. It contains ten Pauline Epistles (all but the pastoral Epistles) and the book of Hebrews.

Yet another Chester Beatty papyrus is P47. It dates to the third century AD and contains Revelation 9:10–17:2.

One very early fragment is P52, also called the John Rylands Fragment. Scholars date this fragment to about AD 117–138 (some scholars date it even earlier). It contains portions of John's Gospel. This is clearly within a generation of the original autograph penned by John.

Do any manuscripts contain all or most of the New Testament?

Yes. One important manuscript that contains the entire New Testament is the Sinaiticus uncial manuscript, which dates to the fourth century. "Uncial" manuscripts were written entirely in capital letters and were commonly used from the third through the eighth centuries AD. This is contrast to "minuscule" manuscripts, which used smaller, cursive letters and date from the ninth to the fifteenth centuries.

The Vaticanus uncial manuscript dates to the fourth century. It contains most of the New Testament except for part of Hebrews, the pastoral Epistles, Philemon, and Revelation.

What about support for the New Testament in the writings of the church fathers?

In addition to the many New Testament manuscripts, more than 36,000 quotations of the New Testament are included in the writings of the early church fathers and several thousand lectionaries (church-service books containing Scripture quotations used in the early centuries of Christianity). In fact, even if we did not have a single manuscript copy of the

New Testament, scholars could still reconstruct more than 99 percent of it (all but eleven verses) from quotations in the early church fathers written within 150 to 200 years from the time of Christ.

How many "variants" are in the manuscript copies of the New Testament?

In the many thousands of manuscript copies we possess of the New Testament, scholars have discovered between 200,000 and 400,000 "variants," depending on who you talk to. This may seem like a staggering figure to the uninformed mind. But to those who study the issue, the numbers are not as serious as they may initially appear. Indeed, a look at the hard evidence shows that the New Testament manuscripts are amazingly accurate and trustworthy.

The large number of manuscript copies of the New Testament reduces the seriousness of the variants.

Many variants occur in the New Testament manuscripts because *we have so many New Testament manuscripts.* New Testament scholars are careful to emphasize, however, that the sheer volume of manuscripts we possess greatly narrows the margin of doubt regarding what the original biblical document said.

New Testament scholar F.F. Bruce puts it this way: "If the number of [manuscripts] increases the number of scribal errors, it increases proportionately the means of correcting such errors, so that the margin of doubt left in the process of recovering the exact original wording is not so large as might be feared; it is in truth remarkably small."[5]

Also, because of the way variants are counted, the 400,000 figure may be misleading. The misspelling of a single word in 2,000 manuscripts counts as 2,000 variants. This fact alone substantially reduces the severity of the variant problem.

What is the real significance of the variants in New Testament manuscripts?

More than 99 percent of the variants hold virtually no significance whatsoever. Many simply involve a missing letter in a word.

Some involve reversing the order of two words (such as "Christ Jesus" instead of "Jesus Christ"). And some may involve the absence of one or more insignificant words.

New Testament scholars conclude that less than 1 percent of the variants are meaningful variants, and they do not affect Christian doctrine in any significant way. J. Harold Greenlee, in his book *Introduction to New Testament Textual Criticism*, assures us that "no Christian doctrine hangs upon a debatable text."[6]

Really, when all the facts are put on the table, only about 40 of the variants have any *real* significance, and no doctrine of the Christian faith or any moral commandment is affected by them. For more than 99 percent of the cases, the original text can be reconstructed to a practical certainty.

How does textual criticism help to assure us of the reliability of the New Testament manuscript copies?

By practicing the science of textual criticism—comparing all the available manuscripts with each other—we can come to an assurance regarding what the original document must have said.

Perhaps an illustration might be helpful: Let's suppose we have five manuscript copies of an original document that no longer exists. Each of the manuscript copies is different from the others. Our goal is to compare the manuscript copies and ascertain what the original must have said. Here are the five copies:

Manuscript #1: Jesus Christ is the Savior of the whole world.
Manuscript #2: Christ Jesus is the Savior of the whole world.
Manuscript #3: Jesus Christ s the Savior of the whole worl.
Manuscript #4: Jesus Christ is th Savior of the whle world.
Manuscript #5: Jesus Christ is the Savor of the whole wrld.

Could you, by comparing the manuscript copies, ascertain what the original document said with a high degree of certainty that you are correct? Of course you could.

This illustration may be extremely simplistic, but a great majority of the 200,000 to 400,000 variants are solved by this methodology.

By comparing the various manuscripts, all of which contain minor differences, it becomes fairly clear what the original must have said.

Does good manuscript support exist for the Old Testament?

Yes! To illustrate, before the discovery of the Dead Sea Scrolls, our earliest Old Testament manuscript was the Cairo Codex, which dates to about AD 895. The word *codex* is a Latin term meaning "book." A codex was a manuscript bound in book form rather than as a scroll. The Cairo Codex contains the latter and former prophets.

The Dead Sea Scrolls, by contrast, provide manuscripts that date a thousand years earlier—from the third century BC to the first century BC. And the two sets of manuscripts are essentially the same, with very few changes. The fact that manuscripts separated by a thousand years are essentially the same indicates the incredible accuracy of the Old Testament's manuscript transmission.

What is an example of a Bible book discovered among the Dead Sea Scrolls?

The book of Isaiah is a good example. Previous to the discovery of the Dead Sea Scrolls, our earliest manuscript copy of the book of Isaiah dated to AD 916. The Dead Sea Scroll manuscript copies of Isaiah date to about 125 BC—a thousand years earlier. The variation between the two sets of manuscripts is less than 5 percent. That shows a remarkable degree of accuracy in the transmission of the biblical manuscripts.

Dr. Gleason Archer personally examined both the AD 895 and 125 BC copies of Isaiah and makes this observation:

> Even though the two copies of Isaiah discovered in Qumran Cave 1 near the Dead Sea in 1947 were a thousand years earlier than the oldest dated manuscript previously known, they proved to be *word for word identical* with our standard Hebrew Bible in more than 95 percent of the text. The 5 percent of variation consisted chiefly of obvious slips of the pen and variations in spelling.[7]

The Dead Sea Scrolls thus *prove* that the copyists of biblical manuscripts took great care in going about their work. These copyists knew they were duplicating God's Word. Therefore they went to incredible lengths to ensure that no error crept into their work. The scribes carefully counted every line, word, syllable, and letter to guarantee accuracy.[8]

Does any biblical basis exist for the idea that God preserves Scripture through the ages?

Yes. I believe that the God who had the power and sovereign control to *inspire* the Scriptures in the first place is surely going to continue to exercise His power and sovereign control in the *preservation* of Scripture.

Actually, the text of the Bible illustrates God's preserving work. By examining how Christ viewed the Old Testament (keeping in mind that He had copies, not the *original* books penned by the Old Testament writers), we see that He had full confidence that the Scriptures He used had been faithfully preserved through the centuries. Bible scholar Greg Bahnsen puts it this way:

> Because Christ raised no doubts about the adequacy of the Scriptures as His contemporaries knew them, we can safely assume that the first-century text of the Old Testament was a wholly adequate representation of the divine word originally given. Jesus regarded the extant copies of His day as so approximate to the originals in their message that He appealed to those copies as authoritative.[9]

The respect that Jesus and His apostles held for the extant Old Testament text is an expression of their confidence that God providentially preserved these copies and translations so that they were substantially identical with the inspired originals.

3

The Books That Belong in the Bible

What is the canon of Scripture?

The word *canon* comes from a Greek word that means "measuring stick." The word eventually came to be used metaphorically of books that were "measured" and thereby *recognized* as being God's Word. When we talk about the canon of Scripture today, we are referring to all the biblical books that collectively constitute God's Word.

Were any of the New Testament books recognized as belonging in the canon when they were written?

Yes indeed. In 1 Timothy 5:18, the apostle Paul joined an Old Testament reference and a New Testament reference and called them *both* "Scripture" (Deuteronomy 25:4 and Luke 10:7). It would not have been unusual in the context of first-century Judaism for an Old Testament passage to be called Scripture. But for a New Testament book to be called Scripture so soon after it was written says volumes about Paul's view of the authority of contemporary New Testament books.

To be more specific, only three years had elapsed between the writing of the Gospel of Luke and the writing of 1 Timothy. (Luke was written around AD 60. First Timothy was written around AD 63.) Yet, despite this, Paul (himself a Jew—a "Hebrew of Hebrews") does not hesitate to place Luke on the *same level of authority* as the Old Testament book of Deuteronomy.

Further, the writings of the apostle Paul were recognized as Scripture by the apostle Peter (2 Peter 3:16). Paul, too, understood that his own writings were inspired by God and therefore authoritative (1 Corinthians 14:37; 1 Thessalonians 2:13). Paul, of course, wrote nearly half the New Testament.

How did the early church know which books belonged in the Bible?

When the church formally recognized which books belonged in the Bible, some key tests were applied. Here are the two most important:

Was the book written or backed by a prophet or apostle of God? The reasoning here is that the Word of God, which is inspired by the Spirit of God for the people of God, must be communicated through a man of God. Deuteronomy 18:18 informs us that only a prophet of God will speak the Word of God. Second Peter 1:20-21 assures us that Scripture is only written by men of God. In Galatians 1 the apostle Paul argued support for the gospel he preached by appealing to the fact that he was an authorized messenger of God, an apostle.

Does the book tell the truth about God as it is already known by previous revelation? The Bereans searched the Old Testament Scriptures to see whether Paul's teaching was true (Acts 17:11). They knew that if Paul's teaching did not accord with the Old Testament canon, it couldn't be of God. Agreement with all earlier revelation is essential. Paul certainly recognized this, for he said to the Galatians, "Even if we or an angel from heaven should preach to you a gospel contrary to the one we preached to you, let him be accursed" (Galatians 1:8).

What other considerations guided the early church on the canon?

There were three secondary tests:

Is the book authoritative? In other words, can it be said of this book as it was said of Jesus, "They were astonished at his teaching, for he taught them as one who had authority, and not as the scribes" (Mark 1:22)? Put another way, does this book ring with the sense of, "Thus says the Lord"?

Does the book give evidence of having the power of God? The reasoning here is that any writing that does not exhibit the transforming power of God in the lives of its readers could not have come from God. Scripture says that the Word of God is "living and active" (Hebrews 4:12). Second Timothy 3:16 indicates that God's Word has a transforming effect. If the book in question did not have the power to change a life, then, it was reasoned, the book couldn't have come from God.

Was the book accepted by the people of God? In Old Testament times, Moses' scrolls were placed immediately into the ark of the covenant (Deuteronomy 31:24-26). Joshua's writings were added in the same fashion (Joshua 24:26). In the New Testament, Paul thanked the Thessalonians for receiving the apostle's message as the Word of God (1 Thessalonians 2:13). Paul's letters were circulated among the churches (Colossians 4:16; 1 Thessalonians 5:27). It is the norm that God's people—that is, the majority of them and not simply a faction—will initially receive God's Word as such.

Why were certain New Testament books doubted as belonging in the canon?

The books that were doubted for a time were Hebrews, James, 2 Peter, 2 and 3 John, Jude, and Revelation.

Hebrews was doubted because the author of the book was unknown. However, the book eventually came to be viewed as having apostolic authority, if not apostolic authorship.

James was doubted because of its apparent conflict with Paul's teaching about salvation by faith alone. The conflict was resolved by seeing the works James speaks of as an *outgrowth* of real faith.

Second Peter was doubted because the style of this book differs from that of 1 Peter. It seems clear, however, that Peter used a scribe to write his first epistle (see 1 Peter 5:12). So a style conflict is not really a problem.

Both 2 and 3 John were doubted because the author of these books calls himself an elder, not an apostle. However, Peter (an apostle) also calls himself an elder in 1 Peter 5:1. So it seems clear that the same person can be both an elder and an apostle.

Jude was doubted because it refers to two noncanonical books—the Book of Enoch and the Assumption of Moses. This objection was eventually overcome because even Paul quoted pagan poets (see Acts 17:28 and Titus 1:12). Moreover, Jude enjoyed early acceptance by most of the early believers.

The book of Revelation was doubted because it teaches a thousand-year reign of Christ. Since a local contemporary cult taught the same, it was reasoned that Revelation must not be true Scripture. However, because many of the earliest church fathers believed in a thousand-year reign of Christ too, this objection was eventually seen as being without merit.

What is the Apocrypha, and why do Roman Catholic Bibles have it?

The Apocrypha refers to 14 or 15 books of doubtful authenticity and authority that the Roman Catholics decided belonged in the Bible sometime following the Protestant Reformation. The Catholic Council of Trent (1545–1563) canonized these books. This canonization took place largely as a result of the Protestant Reformation. Indeed, Martin Luther had criticized the Catholics for not having scriptural support for such doctrines as praying for the dead. By canonizing the Apocrypha (which offers support for praying for the dead in 2 Maccabees 12:44-45), the Catholics suddenly had "scriptural" support for this and other distinctively Catholic doctrines.

Roman Catholics argue that the Septuagint (the Greek translation of the Hebrew Old Testament that predates the time of Christ) contained the Apocrypha. Also, church fathers such as Ireneaus, Tertullian, and Clement of Alexandria used the Apocryphal books in public worship and accepted them as Scripture. Further, it is argued, Augustine viewed these books as inspired.

Why do Protestants reject the Apocrypha?

Protestants point out that even though some of the Apocryphal books may have been alluded to in the New Testament, no New Testament writer ever quoted from any of these books as holy Scripture or gave them the slightest authority as inspired books. Jesus and the disciples virtually ignored these books, something that wouldn't have been the case if they had considered them to be inspired.

Moreover, even though certain church fathers spoke approvingly of the Apocrypha, there were other early church fathers—notably Origen and Jerome—who denied their inspiration. Further, even though the early Augustine acknowledged the Apocrypha, in his later years he rejected these books as being outside the canon and considered them inferior to the Hebrew Scriptures.[1]

The Jewish Council of Jamnia, which met in AD 90, rejected the Apocrypha as Scripture. Combine all this with the fact that the Apocrypha contains clear historical errors (especially those relating to Tobit) and the fact that it affirms unbiblical doctrines (such as praying for the dead). Therefore, these books clearly do not belong in the Bible.

We might also observe that unlike many of the biblical books, no Apocryphal book claims divine inspiration.

Is it true that Mark 16:9-20 does not belong in the Bible?

Mark 16:9-20 is absent from the two oldest Greek manuscripts in our possession—Codex Alexandrinus and Codex Sinaiticus. Also, these verses are absent from the Old Latin manuscripts, the Sinaitic Syriac manuscript, about 100 Armenian manuscripts, and the two oldest Georgian manuscripts. Further, Clement of Alexandria and Origen show no knowledge of the existence of these verses. Eusebius and Jerome attest that the passage was absent from almost all the Greek copies of Mark known to them. Understandably, then, many scholars believe that Mark 16:9-20 does not belong in the Bible. Fortunately, Mark 16:9-20 does not affect a single major doctrine of Christianity.

4
All About Bible Translations

Can we trust English translations of the Bible from the original languages of Hebrew and Greek?

Yes, we can.

As a backdrop, a Bible translation puts the original Old Testament Hebrew and New Testament Greek texts into the English language. An accurate English translation communicates to today's English readers (or hearers) the same meaning that the original author's text conveyed to his original readers (or hearers). Bible scholars often say that the best translation of the Bible remains faithful to the original meaning of the text but uses language that sounds as clear and natural to the modern reader as the Hebrew or Greek did to the original readers (or hearers).

Many of our modern Bible translations succeed marvelously at this. More literal translations include the New American Standard Version and the English Standard Version. An easier-to-read translation is the New Living Translation. The Holman Christian Standard Bible is somewhere in between literal and easy-to-read. Below I'll demonstrate why such translations can be trusted. I'll also demonstrate the wisdom of owning several translations for comparison purposes.

Why do translations differ? Doesn't each Hebrew and Greek word have one essential meaning with an English counterpart?

I wish it were that easy. It would be delightful if all we had to do was line up all the New Testament Greek words on one side of the page and then place similar-meaning English words on the other side of the page, translating fifteen Greek words with fifteen English counterparts. And *voilà*—we would have a Bible translation.

But in reality, Bible translation is not an easy task. In many cases, no direct one-to-one parallel exists between words in the original Hebrew or Greek languages and the English language. For example, Greek has several words that correspond to the English word *love*. Each of those Greek words communicates a different aspect of love, such as friend love or sexual love. For this reason, Bible translators must use their interpretive skills, remaining constantly sensitive to which nuance of meaning the original Hebrew or Greek word is communicating so that they can choose the proper English word to render that meaning.

Is it better to trust a translation done by a single scholar or one done by a committee of scholars?

Some translations have been produced by a single individual. Such translations often have more vibrancy of style than translations done by committees. But there is always the possibility that—whether consciously or unconsciously—the translator might allow too many of his interpretive views to bias or at least influence his translation.

Some translations involve the work of a single individual that was later revised by a committee. For example, the King James Version is heavily based on the prior translation done by the great William Tyndale. The New Living Translation is heavily based on the prior paraphrase done by Kenneth Taylor, The Living Bible.

Most scholars believe doing a translation as a team effort has many benefits. A team of translators not only provides a greater depth of knowledge but also serves as a guard against the personal biases (theological or otherwise) of an individual translator. Committee translations draw on the broader expertise of many scholars (usually several dozen), each of whom can cross-check the work of the others.

Still, some problems can emerge with translations done by committees of Bible scholars. For example, Bible linguists are not necessarily skilled English stylists. But that's not an insurmountable problem.

English stylists are typically brought in to consult with the committee in order to "smooth out" the English.

Because Bible translators are separated from biblical culture by thousands of years, does that make the translation process harder?

Yes indeed. A historical barrier separates the original documents from the translator by thousands of years. In order for translators to best accomplish their task, therefore, they must be thoroughly conversant in both the grammar and the culture of the language they are translating. The more they know about the history of the culture that produced the document, the easier it is to translate.

How are Jewish idioms or figures of speech translated?

Languages typically make use of idioms (or figures of speech) that mean something in the original language but not necessarily in the translated language. Many of these idioms are culturally dependent.

For example, we have quite a number of idioms in the English language. To communicate that something is easy, we might say, "It's a piece of cake." We might exhort someone to do a good job by telling him or her to "break a leg." When we want someone to calm down, we might say, "Chill." When something goes wrong, we might say, "How did the wheels come off this thing?" If we're going on a trip, we might say, "Let's hit the road." Such idioms or figures of speech make little sense to people who come from France or Spain.

Of course, the ancient Jews also used many idioms—hundreds of them—and these are not easy to render into modern English. For example, the Greek idiom "take up souls" carries the idea "keep in suspense" (John 10:24). To "have lifespan" is a Greek idiom that means a person is of age (John 9:21). "All the ones having badly" is a Greek idiom that means "all who were sick" (Mark 1:32). "Having in belly" is a Greek idiom meaning "pregnant" (Matthew 1:18 NLT). Speaking "with a heart and a heart" is a Jewish idiom meaning to speak with a "double heart," or deceitfully (Psalm 12:2). Because most English readers would never "get it" when reading such idioms, most modern translations express the intended meaning of the figures of speech and do not literally translate the idiom.

Did the ancient Jews use euphemisms? How do Bible translators handle these?

A euphemism is a culturally appropriate way of saying something that might otherwise be considered offensive, unpleasant, or perhaps too direct. It is an indirect way of saying something that could be offensive if it is stated directly. For example, people might say that "nature is calling" or that they need "to visit the restroom" when they need to urinate.

People use euphemisms in all languages, including Hebrew and Greek. For example, among the ancient Jews, to "cover your feet" refers to going to the bathroom. To "know" a woman is a euphemism for sexual intercourse. The "way of women" is a reference to a woman's monthly period.

Bible translators handle such euphemisms in one of several ways. The more literal Bible translations render them quite literally and leave it up to the reader to figure out what they mean. More reader-friendly Bible translations leave out the euphemism and describe the action in understandable terms. Some translations might use an alternate euphemism that is known in the receptor language (like English). For example, a translation might render the Jewish euphemism "to cover his feet" as the English euphemism "to relieve himself."

What is an example of a way Bible translators handle poetic features in the biblical text?

A common feature of Hebrew poetry is the alphabetic acrostic. An acrostic is a poem that begins each line with a successive letter of the Hebrew alphabet. Obviously, while this makes great sense to someone who knows Hebrew, it is almost impossible to translate such acrostic forms into English. Most Bibles today simply insert some kind of footnote that clarifies the presence of an acrostic, but they leave the actual acrostic out of the translation.

Why do some translations seem to use more technical theological words, while others use easy language?

Bible translation committees vary regarding their policies on how they handle technical language from the original Hebrew or Greek. Below I will discuss different philosophies of Bible translation (literal versus easy-to-understand). Suffice it to say, translators who subscribe to a literal approach will keep the technical language (such as "justification," "sanctification," and "propitiation"). Translators who subscribe to the easy-to-understand philosophy will utilize user-friendly synonyms.

Why are Bible translations different in how they handle money, weights, and measures?

Money, weights, and measures in the Bible are unique to the Jewish cultural context, so they are not easy to translate into English. Some Bible translations transliterate the Jewish weights, measures, and money—that is, they spell out the Hebrew or Greek term in English letters (for example, monetary units would include shekels, talents, denarii, and minas). Translators typically include a footnote with the modern English equivalent of the term. In other cases, Bible translations insert a modern equivalent, sometimes including a footnote that references the original Hebrew or Greek term. Also, many Bible versions provide tables that make all this more understandable to the English reader.

Do all Bible translations involve a certain amount of interpretation among the translators?

Yes, no doubt about it. Translation without interpretation is an absolute impossibility. At every turn the translator is faced with interpretative decisions regarding grammar, syntax, and a range of possible meanings of the Hebrew or Greek words in question.

To illustrate, I can tell you from firsthand experience that if a Japanese man wants to say, "That person is smart," he might use the phrase *ano hito wa atama ga ii desu.* Those words are literally translated, "As for that person, his head is good." However, in the United States, no one ever says, "As for that person, his head is good." It's just not how we talk! An English person translating from the Japanese must therefore *interpret* this phrase, properly rendering it, "That person is smart."

We must do the same thing when translating biblical manuscripts from the original Hebrew or Greek languages. To put the Greek or Hebrew language into readable English, the translator must decide what each of the terms mean. To do that, he or she must understand what the sentence or phrase meant in the original biblical culture. Sometimes it is difficult to find the exact right word.

What is the formal equivalence philosophy of Bible translation?

This philosophy advocates as literal a rendering of the original text as possible. The translator attempts to render the exact words from Hebrew or Greek into English. This is why the word *formal* is used—the rendering is *form for form* or *word for word*. Formal equivalence translators are careful to choose an English word that accurately conveys the meaning of the original Hebrew or Greek word.

This type of translation philosophy seeks not only to be a word-for-word translation but also to accurately reproduce the grammar and syntax of the original Hebrew or Greek text. If the Hebrew uses an infinitive, the English must use an infinitive. If the Greek uses a prepositional phrase, the English must likewise use a prepositional phrase.

This type of translation is excellent for serious Bible study. But understanding it can be more challenging for many readers who do not have formal training in biblical studies.

The King James Version (1611), the New American Standard Bible (1971—updated in 1995), the Revised Standard Version (1952), and the English Standard Version (2001) all reflect the formal equivalence approach to Bible translation. Such translations beneficially retain the style of the original writers. They also better preserve the original beauty and theological precision of Scripture—that is, they keep theological terminology necessary for a fuller understanding of what God intended to communicate. They maintain the original grammar and sentence structure as much as possible.

We can also trust such translations not to mix too much commentary in with the text derived from the original Hebrew and Greek manuscripts. To clarify, all translation entails *some* interpretation, but formal equivalence translations keep interpretive additives to a minimum.

Does the formal equivalence philosophy of Bible translation have any problems?

Bible translators who hold to the dynamic equivalence philosophy (a philosophy that produces an easy-to-understand translation) often say that a translation can be *so* literal that it does not adequately communicate God's Word to people. They suggest that an English translation, however literal, is not truly accurate if readers cannot understand it. The translation has not done its job if it has not communicated the original meaning intended by the biblical writers to today's English readers. As a result, some scholars reject the formal equivalence philosophy in favor of using easier-to-understand language.

Advocates of the formal equivalence philosophy rebut by saying that God Himself inspired the original Hebrew and Greek words, and human beings do not have the prerogative of using English words not reflected in the original text.

What is the dynamic equivalence philosophy of Bible translation?

If you have purchased a Bible in recent years, you have more than likely purchased a dynamic equivalence Bible. This philosophy advocates a more readable translation that does not provide an exact rendering of the text. Instead, it focuses on communicating the meaning of the text. It is a *thought-for-thought* translation that seeks to produce the same dynamic impact upon modern readers as the original had upon its audience.

The goal is for the translation to sound as clear and natural to the contemporary reader as the original text sounded to the original readers. It is considered successful to the degree that modern English readers respond to the text in substantially the same manner as the readers in Bible times. An example of this type of translation is the New Living Translation.

How do dynamic equivalence translations make the Bible easier to read?

Dynamic equivalence translations generally use shorter words, sentences, and paragraphs. They use easy vocabulary, especially for theological and cultural terminology. They often convert culturally dependent figures of speech into easy, direct statements, and they seek to avoid ambiguity and biblical jargon in favor of a natural English style. Translators concentrate on transferring *meaning* rather than *mere words* from one language to another.

Dynamic equivalence translators seek to provide easier-to-understand equivalents to phrases that one does not hear in common speech today. For example, in our day, we do not use phrases such as "And it came to pass," "Verily, verily, I say unto you," or "Thus saith the LORD" (all literally rendered recurring phrases in the KJV). Such phrases seem unnatural to most people. So in the interest of communication, translators who advocate this philosophy change them into easier equivalents.

Dynamic equivalence translators also seek to clarify cultural customs within the text. For example, most readers don't realize that when Reuben "tore his clothes" upon discovering that his brothers had sold Joseph as a slave (Genesis 37:29), he was expressing a cultural sign of grief. So, some dynamic equivalence translations qualify the statement in Scripture so readers know Reuben tore his clothes "in grief."

Is there any historical precedent in support of dynamic equivalence translations?

Proponents of dynamic equivalence translations believe so. They note that papyri discoveries have helped us to see that the New Testament was written in the language of the common person (Koine Greek). They suggest that we too ought to seek to express our translations in the language of the common person. Dynamic equivalence translations are said to best fit this need.

Are there problems with the dynamic equivalence philosophy of Bible translation?

The dynamic equivalence philosophy has received criticism for making interpretive decisions for the reader and adding commentary into the text. Such translations might unintentionally incorporate personal interpretations of the translators. Therefore, they are less suitable for serious Bible study. If the translators missed the point of the original—intentionally or unintentionally—they will proceed to inaccurately communicate the intended meaning in their translation. A dynamic equivalence translation essentially comprises a translation plus a bit of commentary.

Some critics have alleged that today many seem to have more concern for the *human reader* than the *divine author*. That is, they want the human reader to understand things so much that they do not care enough to accurately translate the divine author. It should be the opposite, they say. We should have more concern to accurately communicate what the divine author said.

Critics also allege that the dynamic equivalence philosophy takes liberties in translating the Bible that we would certainly not permit in other areas of our lives. In certain documents, the exact words are very important—such as legal documents (wills, contracts, and the like). If getting the words right on such human-based documents is important, then how much more important is it that we get the words exactly right when translating God's Word? Such critics claim that to do anything less is "linguistic license."

Can you give an example of how a dynamic equivalence translation might subtly change the meaning of a text?

Consider John 6:27, a verse which speaks of the Father setting His "seal" upon Jesus. The New American Standard Bible (a literal translation, based on the formal equivalence philosophy) renders it this way: "On Him the Father, God, has set His seal." Dynamic equivalence translations render this verse variously. The Contemporary English Version says, "God the Father has given him the right to do so." The

New Living Translation says, "God the Father has given me the seal of his approval." The New English Translation renders it, "God the Father has put his seal of approval on him."

With such widely divergent translations of the same verse, a level of subjectivity evidently exists among dynamic equivalence translations, which can undermine one's confidence that one is truly being given "the Word of God" as communicated by His prophets and apostles. When I say "subjectivity," I am referring to the fact that not enough objective controls govern and guard the translation process.

What is a paraphrase?

A few modern Bibles are not translations at all—they're paraphrases. To paraphrase a statement is to say it in different (and simpler) words than the author used. It involves even more literary license than the "dynamic equivalence" philosophy. In fact, paraphrases often involve more interpretation than translation.

Some paraphrases come from preexisting English translations of the Bible. This was the case with The Living Bible. Other paraphrases are actually derived from the original Hebrew or Greek. This was the case with The New Testament in Modern English, by J.B. Phillips. Most such paraphrases are characterized by a great freedom of expression, a use of contemporary idioms and colloquialisms, and a highly communicative language style.

What is the case for utilizing gender inclusive language in the Bible?

Many say that such language makes our English Bibles clearer and more accurate in terms of the biblical authors' intended meaning. It is suggested that even though masculine-oriented language was heavily used in the Bible, such terminology today can mislead people into thinking that men are the primary focus of God's words. But this is not so. Indeed, the Bible clearly aims its message at both men and women. The Bible is not just communicating to or about the brothers—it is referring to the brothers *and* the sisters.

Gender inclusivity is consistent with the dynamic equivalence philosophy of translation, which is sensitive to how the biblical author might communicate his ideas today. In the ancient world, it was common to say "man" or "he" when speaking of all people. A basic principle of translation theory is to express the ancient text in the thoughts and idioms of modern language. Translations should not be done strictly based on individual Hebrew or Greek words. Rather, they should reflect how those words are used in the context. If the context indicates inclusivity, then the translation should indicate inclusivity.

Gender-inclusive translations include the New Revised Standard Version, the Revised English Bible, the New International Reader's Version, the Contemporary English Version, God's Word, the Good News Bible, the New Century Version, the New Jerusalem Bible, and the New American Bible.

Are there problems with gender inclusive language?

Some critics believe too many uses of such terms as "persons" and "people" (instead of "men") within a relatively short space can cause the translation to lose elegance very quickly.

Also, changing singular references to "he" or "him" into the third person "they" or "them" can obscure God's personal dealings with individuals. For example, Jesus' endearing promise "I will come in…and eat with *him*" is changed to "I will come in…and eat with *them*," a phrase that clearly loses the personal connection of Christ with individual believers (see Revelation 3:20). Readers might wrongly conclude that such verses are talking about a group of believers (such as the church) instead of an individual believer.

Also, gender-inclusive translations can obscure well-loved phrases deeply entrenched in the minds of Bible believers. An example would be Jesus' intention to make His disciples "fishers of men," an endearing phrase that many love.

Moreover, patriarchy was part and parcel of the biblical culture. To obscure it by removing a great deal of male-oriented language could lead people astray regarding this aspect of the Bible.

We might also note that no one has made any new historical or archeological discoveries that warrant people changing the text of the Bible. Translators ought to render the Bible as literally as possible, and then—via hermeneutics—readers can interpret such literal renderings to include women, as intended by the biblical authors.

Do gender inclusive translations change the Word of God?

Some scholars think so. They point out that throughout the Old Testament we find the phrase "Thus *says* the Lord," uttered by the prophets. God informed Moses that He would send another prophet like Moses: "I will put *my words* in his mouth, and he shall speak to them all that I command him. And whoever will not listen to *my words* that he shall speak in my name, I myself will require it of him" (Deuteronomy 18:18-19; see also Numbers 22:38; Jeremiah 1:9; 14:14; 23:16-22; 29:31-32; Ezekiel 2:7; 13:1-16).

Likewise, throughout the Bible, God often speaks His specific words "by" (or "through") the prophets (1 Kings 14:18; 16:12, 34; 2 Kings 9:36; 14:25; Jeremiah 37:2; Zechariah 7:7,12). For this reason, ignoring a prophet's words amounted to ignoring God's words (Deuteronomy 18:19; 1 Samuel 10:8; 13:13-14; 15:3,19,23; 1 Kings 20:35-36). These words therefore have divine authority (2 Timothy 3:16) and are not subject to change by human translators.

What is your best advice on Bible translations?

Own several translations and compare them with each other as you read from the biblical text. Good formal equivalence (literal) translations include the English Standard Version and the New American Standard Bible. A good "dynamic equivalence" (easier) translation is the New Living Translation. A good mid-range translation is the Holman Christian Standard Bible. Comparing two or three Bible translations will help you see the original meaning of the text quite nicely.

What about the King James Version? How can we respond to those who say it's the only legitimate Bible?

The King James Version we universally accept today is not an exact copy of the edition released in 1611. The Bible that circulates today as the "Authorized" King James Version is actually the fourth revision of 1769.

A simple way to verify this is by reading John 3:7 in today's King James Version. The spelling of the individual words in this sentence is entirely different from that of the original 1611 version. I must also point out that the punctuation, capitalization, and use of italics have changed as each respective edition came out. So, I must ask, *which* King James Version is inspired?

Moreover, if the King James Version is the only legitimate Bible, then what was God's inspired Word prior to 1611? It is highly revealing that some of the translators of the King James Version continued to use earlier English versions long after the publication of the King James Version. They even approvingly quoted from one of these Bibles—the Geneva Bible—in the original preface to the King James Version.

Also relevant to this discussion is the question of whether English is the *only* language that has God's inspired Word. What about people living in France or Spain or Russia?

Finally, it is a historical fact that the 1611 King James Version included the Apocrypha. Yet few if any who claim exclusive inspiration for the King James Version's English text would accept the Apocrypha as God's Word.

I say all this not to malign the King James Version. I say this only to stress the point that it is not the only legitimate version.

5
Interpretation of Scripture: Sense and Nonsense

Is dependence upon the Holy Spirit necessary in order to rightly interpret Scripture?

Yes. This is absolutely foundational. Scripture tells us that we are to rely on the Holy Spirit's illumination to gain insights into the meaning and application of Scripture (John 16:12-15; 1 Corinthians 2:9-11). The Holy Spirit, as the "Spirit of truth" (John 16:13), guides us so "that we might understand the things freely given us by God" (1 Corinthians 2:12). This is logical: Full comprehension of the Word of God is impossible without prayerful dependence on the Spirit of God, for He who inspired the Word (2 Peter 1:21) is also its supreme interpreter.

Why, then, do Spirit-filled Christians have different interpretations regarding what specific Bible verses mean?

That's a great question! In answering it, you might liken the Holy Spirit to a radio station that is transmitting a perfect signal. Even though that radio signal is transmitted perfectly, all kinds of different quality radio receivers are out there. Some have good reception, and some have poor reception. Some have good antennae, and others have broken antennae. Some have good batteries, and others are low on energy. This is the point: Different radio receivers have varying degrees of success in receiving that perfect signal.

Christians are much the same way. The Holy Spirit's "signal" (that is, His illumination) is always perfect. But because of varying circumstances—perhaps sin, or not walking in the Spirit, or being overly concerned about the affairs of the world, or being blinded by Satan—Christians have varying degrees of success in receiving the Spirit's illumination.

One caricature people often have of Christians is that we interpret the Bible with wooden literalism. How can we respond to this claim?

Evangelicals do not hold to a "wooden literalism"—the kind that interprets biblical figures of speech literally. The biblical context itself should govern whether we take something literally or symbolically. For example, Jesus tells obviously figurative parables to communicate spiritual truth.

A literal approach to Scripture recognizes that the Bible contains a variety of literary genres, each of which have certain peculiar characteristics that must be identified in order to interpret the text properly. Biblical genres include the historical (for example, Acts), the dramatic epic (Job), poetry (Psalms), wise sayings (Proverbs), and apocalyptic writings (Revelation). An incorrect genre judgment will lead one far astray in interpreting Scripture.

Even though the Bible contains a variety of literary genres and many figures of speech, the biblical authors most often employed literal statements to convey their ideas. And where they use a literal means to express their ideas, the Bible expositor must employ a corresponding means to explain these ideas—namely, a literal approach. Such an approach gives to each word in the text the same basic meaning it would have in normal, ordinary, customary usage—whether employed in writing, speaking, or thinking. Without such a method, communication between God and humankind is impossible.

What is the difference between exegesis and eisegesis?

Exegesis refers to drawing the meaning *out* of the text of Scripture, while eisegesis refers to superimposing a meaning *onto* the text. By using eisegesis instead of exegesis, a Marxist interpreter could, for example, so skew the meaning of the U.S. Constitution that it comes out reading like a communistic document. Cultists have done the same type of thing with Holy Scripture. They so skew the meaning of the biblical text that it comes out saying something entirely different than what was intended by the author.

Instead of superimposing a meaning onto the biblical text, the objective interpreter seeks to discover the author's intended meaning (the only *true* meaning), which cannot be altered. Meaning is *determined* by the author. It is *discovered* by readers.

What do you mean when you say that "Scripture interprets Scripture"?

Every word in the Bible is part of a verse, and every verse is part of a paragraph, and every paragraph is part of a book, and every book is part of the whole of Scripture. No verse of Scripture can be divorced from the verses around it.

Interpreting Scripture involves an immediate context and a broader context. The immediate context of a verse is the paragraph (or paragraphs) of the biblical book in question and should always be consulted when interpreting verses.

The broader context is the whole of Scripture. The entire Holy Scripture is the context and guide for understanding the particular passages of Scripture. We must keep in mind that the interpretation of a specific passage must not contradict the total teaching of Scripture on a point. Individual verses do not exist as isolated fragments, but as parts of a whole. The exposition of these verses, therefore, must exhibit them in right relation to the whole and to each other. *Scripture interprets Scripture.* If we would understand the parts, our wisest course is to get to know the whole.

The Westminster Confession affirms, "The infallible rule of interpretation of Scripture is the Scripture itself; therefore, when there is a question about the true and full sense of any Scripture, it must be searched and known by other places that speak more clearly."[1]

How important is biblical history and culture in rightly understanding the biblical text?

Critically important. As Bible scholar Gordon Lewis put it, "When we claim Biblical authority for an idea, we must be prepared to show from the grammar, the history, the culture and the context that the writer in fact taught that idea. Otherwise the Bible is not used but abused."[2] The interpreter of Scripture must step out of his Western mind-set and into a first-century Jewish mind-set, seeking to understand such things as Jewish marriage rites, burial rites, family practices, farm practices, business practices, the monetary system, methods of warfare, slavery, the treatment of captives, and religious practices. Armed with such detailed information, interpreting the Bible correctly becomes a much easier task.

What is the distinction between "descriptive" and the "prescriptive" verses as we seek to rightly interpret Scripture?

When you come across a particular part of the Bible, ask this key question: Is this passage merely *descriptive*, or is it *prescriptive*? In other words, is the passage merely *describing* something that took place in biblical times, or is it *prescribing* something that Christians should be doing for all time?

The passage concerning the tongues of fire that initially fell on those who were baptized on the Day of Pentecost (Acts 2:3-4) might illustrate this principle. Scholars believe this is descriptive, not prescriptive. We should not expect this to happen today.

Do you have any tips on how to interpret the Old Testament?

Yes. Always interpret the Old Testament in view of the greater light of the New Testament. Theologian Benjamin Warfield offers a helpful way of looking at it:

> The Old Testament may be likened to a chamber richly furnished but dimly lighted; the introduction of light [from the New Testament]

brings into it nothing which was not in it before; but it brings out into clearer view much of what is in it but was only dimly or even not at all perceived before.[3]

Can you give an example of how to interpret the Old Testament according to the greater light of the New Testament?

Christ's activities in Old Testament times provide a good example. In Isaiah 6:1-5 we are told that Isaiah witnessed the incredible glory of God. The greater light of the New Testament, however, tells us that Isaiah actually saw Jesus' glory (John 12:41).

Likewise, in the Exodus account we are told that God Almighty sustained His people in the wilderness sojourn. But the greater light of the New Testament tells us that Christ was most definitely involved in sustaining His people in the wilderness (1 Corinthians 10:1-4).

So, by approaching the Old Testament according to the greater light of the New Testament, we see things in the Old Testament we wouldn't otherwise see.

Are the sayings in the book of Proverbs to be taken as promises from God?

No. The book of Proverbs is a "wisdom book," and contains maxims of moral wisdom. The verbal root of the word *proverb* literally means "to be like" or "to be compared with." A proverb, then, is a form of communicating truth by using comparisons or figures of speech. The proverbs, in a memorable way, crystallize the writers' experiences and observations about life, and they provide principles that are generally (not always) true. The reward of "chewing on" these maxims is, of course, wisdom. But these maxims were never intended as Bible promises.

To illustrate, a verse often misconstrued as a promise is Proverbs 22:6: "Train up a child in the way he should go; even when he is old he will not depart from it." Some parents have claimed this verse as a promise, and have done everything they could to bring their children up rightly. But in some cases, the children have ended up departing from

Christianity and going astray. The parents of these children become disillusioned, and wonder what they did wrong.

The truth is that Proverbs 22:6 was never intended as a promise. Like other "wisdom sayings" in Proverbs, this verse contains a principle that is generally true. But a general principle always involves at least some exceptions to the rule. After all, God Himself is the most perfect parent ever, but His children, Adam and Eve, certainly went astray.

Was Jesus in Matthew 13 supporting the idea that we should seek a hidden, secondary meaning in Scripture passages?

By no means! In Matthew 13, Jesus is portrayed as being in front of a mixed multitude comprised of both believers and unbelievers. He did not attempt to separate the believers from the unbelievers and then instruct only the believers. Rather, He constructed His teaching so that believers would come to understand what He said, but unbelievers *would not*—and He did this by using parables.

After teaching one such parable, the disciples asked Jesus, "Why do you speak to them in parables?" (Matthew 13:10). Jesus answered: "To you [believers] it has been given to know the secrets of the kingdom of heaven, but to them [unbelievers] it has not been given" (verse 11).

The Greek word for *secret* in this passage simply means "mystery." A mystery in the biblical sense is a truth that cannot be discerned simply by human investigation but requires special revelation from God. Generally, this word refers to a truth that was unknown to people living in Old Testament times but is now revealed to humankind by God (Matthew 13:17; Colossians 1:26). In Matthew 13, Jesus provides information to believers about the kingdom of heaven that has never been revealed before.

Why did Jesus engineer His parabolic teaching so that believers could understand His teaching but unbelievers could not (Matthew 13)?

The disciples, having responded favorably to Jesus' teaching and having placed their faith in Him, already knew much truth about the

Messiah. Careful reflection on Jesus' parables would enlighten them even further.

Hardened unbelievers, however, who had willfully and persistently refused Jesus' previous teachings, were prevented from understanding the parables. Jesus was apparently following an injunction He provided earlier in the Sermon on the Mount: "Do not give dogs what is holy, and do not throw your pearls before pigs" (Matthew 7:6). Yet there is grace even here. For it is possible that Jesus may have prevented unbelievers from understanding the parables because He did not want to add more responsibility to them by imparting new truth for which they would be held responsible.

One should not miss the fact that the parables of the Sower (Matthew 13:3-9) and the Weeds (13:24-30) show that Jesus wanted His parables to be clear to those who were receptive. Jesus Himself provided the interpretation of these parables for His disciples. He did this not only so there would be no uncertainty as to their meaning but also to guide believers as to the proper method to use in interpreting the other parables. The fact that Christ did not interpret His subsequent parables shows that He fully expected believers to understand what He taught by following the methodology He illustrated for them.

Does the Bible teach "sola scriptura"?

Yes indeed. The Bible teaches that *Scripture alone* is the supreme and infallible authority for the church and the individual believer. This is not to say that creeds and tradition are unimportant, but the Bible alone is our final authority. Creeds and tradition are manmade.

Jesus said, "Scripture cannot be broken" (John 10:35). He said, "Truly, I say to you, until heaven and earth pass away, not an iota, not a dot, will pass from the Law until all is accomplished" (Matthew 5:18). He also said, "It is easier for heaven and earth to pass away than for one dot of the Law to become void" (Luke 16:17).

Jesus used Scripture as the final court of appeal in every matter under dispute. He told the Pharisees, "[You make] void the word of

God by your tradition that you have handed down" (Mark 7:13). To the Sadducees He said, "You are wrong, because you know neither the Scriptures nor the power of God" (Matthew 22:29). To the devil, Jesus consistently responded, "It is written..." (Matthew 4:4-10). So, following Jesus' lead, the Scriptures alone are our supreme and final authority.

Part 2

Questions About the
Old and New Testaments

Common Questions About the Old Testament
Common Questions About the New Testament

6
Common Questions About the Old Testament

Is there any merit to the so-called "gap theory" regarding God's work of creation (Genesis 1:1-2)?

The gap theory teaches that there was an original creation (Genesis 1:1) and that as a result of Lucifer's rebellion and fall, the earth became chaos. The picture of formlessness, emptiness, and darkness in Genesis 1:2 is allegedly a picture of divine judgment, for God could not have originally created the earth this way. Millions of years are said to have taken place between verses 1 and 2.

The gap theory has a number of problems. For one thing, the grammar of Genesis 1:1-2 does not allow for a gap. Verse 1 is an independent clause, and verse 2 is composed of three circumstantial clauses (explaining the condition of or circumstances on the earth when God began to create). There is no break between verses 1 and 2. Grammatically, then, the gap theory just doesn't fit.

The gap theory also depends on the idea that the initial formlessness of the universe is an indication of evil or judgment. However, the contexts of Job 26:7 and Isaiah 45:18 (cross-references to the Genesis creation account) do not support this idea. Gap theorists also draw an artificial distinction between the Hebrew verbs *bara'* (which they define as "create out of nothing"—Genesis 1:1) and *'asah* (which they define as "refashion"—Genesis 1:7,16,25). A careful study of these two verbs reveals that they are used *interchangeably*—the word *'asah* does not mean "refashion." Because of these and other factors, I do not give much credence to the gap theory.

Were the days mentioned in the creation account literal 24-hour days (Genesis 1:3–2:3)?

Some theologians believe the days in the creation account were simply revelatory days—that is, they were days during which God *revealed* the creation scene to Moses. (Exodus 20:11, however, clearly contradicts this view.) Other theologians believe each day in the creation account represents an age. Justification for this view is found in Joel 2:31, which portrays a day as a long period of time. Others believe the days in Genesis are literal solar days, but they say each day was separated by a huge time gap. This allegedly accounts for the apparent long geological ages that science has discovered.

Finally, some theologians believe the days of Genesis are literal solar days with no time gap between them. This is my view.

In support of this latter view, the Genesis account makes reference to evening and morning, indicating that literal days are meant (Genesis 1:5). Further, we read that God created the sun to rule the day and the moon to rule the night, thus indicating solar days (verse 16). Solar days also seem to be implied in Exodus 20:11 where we are told that "in six days the LORD made heaven and the earth, the sea, and all that is in them, but he rested on the seventh day."

Moreover, Hebrew scholars tell us that whenever a number is used with the Hebrew word for day (*yom*), it always refers to a literal solar day (no exceptions). Since God is said to have created the universe in *six* days, literal solar days must be meant.

Genesis 2:17 indicates that Adam and Eve would die the day they ate of the forbidden fruit. But they didn't die, did they?

Actually, they did die. They didn't die that day *physically*, but they did die *spiritually*.

The word "death" carries the idea of separation. Physical death involves the separation of the soul or spirit from the body. Spiritual death involves the separation of the human being from God. When Adam and Eve partook of the forbidden fruit, they were immediately separated from God in a spiritual sense. (Their consequent action of trying to hide from God in the Garden of Eden indicates their awareness of this spiritual separation.) The moment of their sin, they became "dead in...trespasses and sins" (Ephesians 2:1). Their separation and isolation from God eventually led to their physical deaths.

Why was Abel's offering accepted by God when Cain's was rejected (Genesis 4:3-5)?

I think the answer to this question is found in the attitude that each displayed in regard to their respective offerings. The biblical text says that Abel gave not only the firstborn of his flock but even "the best" (Genesis 4:4 NLT). By contrast, we read that Cain brought "an offering of the fruit of the ground" (verse 3). One gets the feeling that Cain routinely gathered some fruit and offered it to the Lord to fulfill his obligation.

Abel's faith was apparently another factor. In Hebrews 11:4 we read, "By faith Abel offered to God a more acceptable sacrifice than Cain, through which he was commended as righteous, God commending him by accepting his gifts. And through his faith, though he died, he still speaks." In contrast to Abel's faith and righteousness, Cain was apparently characterized by unbelief and unrighteousness.

Where did Cain get his wife (Genesis 4:17)?

Genesis 4:17 says, "Cain knew his wife, and she conceived and bore Enoch." Who was his wife? It is implied in the biblical text that Cain married one of his sisters. Several facts lead us to this conclusion.

First, it is clear that Adam and Eve had a number of children. Genesis 5:4 says, "The days of Adam after he fathered Seth were 800 years; and he had other sons and daughters." Since Adam and Eve were the first man and woman, and since God had commanded them (and their descendants) to be fruitful and multiply (Genesis 1:28), it seems reasonable to conclude that Cain married one of his many sisters. It is also possible that he married a niece or even a grandniece.

One must keep in mind that in the early years of the human race no genetic defects had yet developed as a result of the fall of man. By the time of Abraham, God had not yet declared this kind of marriage to be contrary to His will (see Genesis 20:12). Laws governing incest apparently did not become enacted until the time of Moses (Leviticus 18:7-17; 20:11-12,14,17,20-21). Therefore, there was no prohibition regarding marrying a sister (or a niece or grandniece) in the days of Cain.

Is it true that people in the early centuries following the creation lived incredibly long lives (Genesis 5)?

Yes indeed. In Genesis 5 we read that "all the days that Adam lived were 930 years," "all the days of Seth were 912 years," "all the days of Enosh were 905 years," and so on.

Nothing in the context of Genesis 5 indicates that this chapter is to be taken less than literally. As to why they lived so long, many commentators have suggested that a water canopy surrounded the earth prior to the flood, serving to protect the inhabitants of the earth from harmful radiation in outer space. Others suggest that prior to the flood, people were primarily vegetarians, and not meat-eaters (see Genesis 9:3), and perhaps this too contributed to the longer lives.

All this points to the truth of Psalm 139:14: Human beings are "fearfully and wonderfully made."

Are the "sons of God" mentioned in Genesis 6:2 evil angels?

This is a much-debated issue. A common view is that some evil angels cohabited with human women. Supporting this position, the Septuagint manuscripts (that is, manuscripts of an early Greek translation of the Hebrew Old Testament) have the phrase "angels of God" instead of "sons of God." This reveals that some of the early Jews understood this phrase to be referring to angels. Also, the Hebrew phrase for "sons of God" (or, more literally, "sons of Elohim") is a phrase that always refers to angels when used elsewhere in the Old Testament (see Job 1:6; 2:1; 38:7).

The "evil angel" interpretation of Genesis 6 may give us a clue as to why some angels are presently bound in prison and others are not (2 Peter 2:4). Some people argue that if the holy angels can appear as human beings and even participate in eating meals and doing good deeds (Genesis 18; Hebrews 13:2), is it not possible that at one time some fallen angels took on a human appearance and engaged in evil deeds?

If the "sons of God" in Genesis 6:2 were not evil angels, then who could they have been?

Many interpreters believe that some fallen angels possessed human men who then cohabited with "the daughters of man." This view has the merit of providing a good explanation of how angels, who are bodiless (Hebrews 1:14) and genderless beings (Matthew 22:30), could cohabit with humans.

Another common interpretation is that the phrase "sons of God" refers to the godly line of Seth (the Redeemer's line—Genesis 4:26) that intermingled with the godless line of Cain. Gleason Archer suggests, "Instead of remaining true to God and loyal to their spiritual heritage, they allowed themselves to be enticed by the beauty of ungodly women who were 'daughters of men'—that is, of the tradition and example of Cain."[1] In support of this view is the fact that human beings are sometimes called "sons" (Isaiah 43:6).

It is best not to be dogmatic on Genesis 6:2.

Was the flood of Genesis 6–8 a universal flood or a local flood?

I believe the flood was universal. The waters climbed so high on the earth that "all the high mountains under the whole heaven were covered" (Genesis 7:19). They rose so greatly on the earth that they "prevailed above the mountains, covering them fifteen cubits deep" (verse 20). (Fifteen cubits is more than twenty feet.) The flood lasted some 377 days (nearly 54 weeks), indicating more than just local flooding. The Bible also says that every living thing that moved on the earth perished, thus indicating the universality of the flood (verses 21-23).

Further, the universal view best explains the fact that there is a worldwide distribution of diluvia deposits. A universal flood would also explain the sudden death of many woolly mammoths frozen in Alaskan and Siberian ice. Investigation shows that these animals died suddenly by choking or drowning and not by freezing.[2]

Finally, many universal flood legends (more than 270) were written by people of various religions and cultural backgrounds all over the world. These people attribute the descent of all races to Noah.[3]

Why did God command Abraham to sacrifice his son as a burnt offering (Genesis 22:2)?

The context of Genesis 22 is quite clear that, ultimately, God never intended for this command to be executed. God restrained Abraham's hand just in the nick of time: "Do not lay your hand on the boy or do anything to him, for now I know that you fear God, seeing you have not withheld your son, your only son, from me" (Genesis 22:12). Scholars agree that God was only testing Abraham's faith. The test served to show that Abraham loved God more than he loved his own son.

Why was the punitive measure of an "eye for eye" required in biblical times (Exodus 21:23-25)?

Exodus 21:23-25 informs us that in bringing injury to another person, the punitive response was to be "life for life, eye for eye, tooth for tooth, hand for hand, foot for foot, burn for burn, wound for wound, [and] stripe for stripe." While this may seem like it gives license to render brutality to others, it was actually intended to *limit* brutality in society. Prior to the enforcement of this law, people had a tendency to go to extremes. Instead of an eye for an eye, people took a life for an eye. Instead of life for life, people took the life of an entire family for a person's lost life. Therefore, this law served to minimize one's response to personal injury.

Why did God order the extermination of whole peoples (Deuteronomy 20:16-18)?

It is true that God commanded His people, the Israelites, to exterminate whole peoples—the Canaanites being a primary example (Deuteronomy 20:16-18). God's command was issued not because God is cruel and vindictive, but because the Canaanites were so horrible, so evil, so oppressive, and so cancerous to society that—like a human cancer—the only option was complete removal. These were people who were burning their children in honor of their false gods, engaging in sex with animals, and all sorts of other loathsome practices (Leviticus 18:1-24; compare 18:21 with 20:3). They were unrepentant in all these activities. Human society itself would have been poisoned without the utter removal of the cancerous Canaanites. God would have been showing utter disregard for the righteous if He had not acted to stop this gangrenous nation from taking over all society.

One must keep in mind that the Canaanites had had plenty of time to repent. The biblical pattern is that when nations repent, God withholds judgment (Jeremiah 18:7-8). The case of Nineveh clearly illustrates this principle for us. God had prophesied judgment, but Nineveh repented, and God withheld that judgment (see Jonah 3). Notably, God often shows mercy where repentance is evident (Exodus 32:14; Amos 7:3).

The Canaanites were not acting blindly. They had heard of the God of the Israelites, and knew what was expected of them, but they defied Him and continued in their sinful ways, making themselves ripe for judgment.

What are we to make of Joshua 10:12-14, which speaks of Joshua bidding the sun to stand still?

Scholars have two primary suggestions as to how to interpret this passage. Some commentators believe God may have just slowed down or stopped the normal rotation of the earth so that Joshua's forces were able to complete their victory over the Amorites. Others suggest that God prolonged the daylight by some sort of unusual refraction of the sun's rays. This would have given Joshua and his men more daylight hours but not necessarily more hours in the day.

Personally, I think God stopped the earth's rotation on its axis. Such a miracle poses no problem for the Almighty God of the universe. Performing a mighty miracle (stopping the earth's rotation) is no more difficult for Him than performing a minor miracle (withering a fig tree).

It is highly revealing that the Amorites worshipped the sun and the moon as deities. Apparently, then, the true God brought about the defeat of the Amorites through the agency of their own supposed deities. This showed the utter futility of their belief in false gods.

Did Jephthah sacrifice his daughter to God (Judges 11:30-31)?

Scholars have dealt with this difficult passage in several different ways. One view is that Jephthah actually did offer his own daughter as a burnt sacrifice to the Lord. If this is the case, this does not in any way mean that God endorsed what Jephthah did. God had earlier revealed that human sacrifice was absolutely forbidden (Leviticus 18:21; 20:2-5; Deuteronomy 12:31; 18:10).

We must keep in mind that simply because something is recounted in the Bible does not mean that God agrees with it. God certainly doesn't agree with the words or actions of Satan, but the Bible nevertheless accurately reports on his words and actions. In the present case, the author of Judges may have just provided an objective account of the event without passing judgment.

One must also remember that the book of Judges deals with a period in human history when everyone was doing what was right in his or her own eyes. Judges 21:25 says, "In those days there was no king in Israel. Everyone did what was right in his own eyes." It is very possible that Jephthah was simply doing what was right in his own eyes, thereby victimizing his own daughter and going against God's will in the process.

Another way to interpret this passage is that Jephthah consecrated his daughter for service at the tabernacle for the rest of her life, devoting her to celibacy. As the apostle Paul said in Romans 12:1, people can be offered to God as "a living sacrifice."

If his daughter was indeed offered as a living sacrifice, this necessarily would involve a life of perpetual virginity, which was a tremendous sacrifice in the Jewish context of the day. She would not be able to bring up children to continue her father's lineage.

This may explain why his daughter responded by saying, "Let this thing be done for me: leave me alone two months, that I may go up and down on the mountains *and weep for my virginity*, I and my companions" (Judges 11:37).

What actually happened at Endor? Was the prophet Samuel actually summoned from the dead by a witch (1 Samuel 28:3-25)?

Scholars have suggested several explanations. Some believe the witch worked a miracle by demonic powers and actually brought Samuel back from the dead. In support of this view, certain passages seem to indicate that demons have the power to perform lying signs and wonders (2 Corinthians 11:14; 2 Thessalonians 2:9-10; Revelation 16:14). This view is unlikely, however, since Scripture also reveals that death is final (Hebrews 9:27), the dead cannot return (2 Samuel 12:23; Luke 16:24-31), and Satan cannot usurp or overpower God's authority over life and death (Job 1:12).

A second view is that the witch did not really bring up Samuel from the dead, but a demonic spirit simply impersonated the prophet. Those who hold to this view say that certain verses indicate that demons can deceive people who try to contact the dead (Leviticus 19:31; Deuteronomy 18:11; 1 Chronicles 10:13). This view is unlikely, however, because the passage seems to say that Samuel did in fact return from the dead, and that he provided a prophecy that actually came to pass.

A third view is that God sovereignly and miraculously allowed Samuel's spirit to appear in order to rebuke Saul for his sin. Samuel's spirit did not appear as a result of the woman's powers (for indeed, no human has this power). Rather, it happened only because God sovereignly brought it about. Samuel's apparent return from the dead supports this view (1 Samuel 28:14), and this caused the witch to shriek with fear (see verse 12). The witch's cry of astonishment indicates that this appearance of Samuel was not the result of her usual tricks.

Why did Solomon have so many wives (1 Kings 11:1-3)?

History reveals that Solomon was very aggressive in his foreign policy. In ancient days, a lesser king would customarily give his daughter in marriage to the greater king (in this case, Solomon) to seal a treaty. Every time a new treaty was sealed, Solomon ended up with yet another wife. These wives were considered tokens of friendship and "sealed" the relationship between the two kings. It may be that Solomon was not even personally acquainted with some of these wives, even though he was married to them.

By doing this, Solomon was utterly disobeying God. His obsession with power and wealth overshadowed his spiritual life, causing him to fall into apostasy and to worship some of the false gods of the women whom he married.

Moreover, Solomon was going against God's revealed will regarding monogamy. From the very beginning God created one woman for one man (see Genesis 1:27; 2:21-24). Deuteronomy 17:17 explicitly instructs that the king "shall not acquire many wives for himself." So Solomon sinned in two ways: (1) He engaged in polygamy, and (2) he violated God's commandment against marrying pagans, ultimately leading to his own apostasy.

In one verse we are told that Satan incited David to take a census of Israel (1 Chronicles 21:1). In another verse we are told that the Lord incited David to take this census (2 Samuel 24:1). Which account are we to believe?

We should believe *both* accounts. These are not *contradictory* accounts—they are *complementary*. They reflect different aspects of a larger truth. Taken together, we can construct a fuller picture—a composite account—of what happened.

Satan was the actual instrument used to incite David to number Israel (1 Chronicles 21:1), but God permitted Satan to do this. In the Hebrew mind-set, whatever God *permits*, God *commits*. By allowing this census taking, God is viewed as having brought about the act Himself (2 Samuel 24:1). The Hebrews were not too concerned about "first causes" and "secondary causes." Satan did what he did because he wanted to destroy David and the people of God. But God's purpose was to simply humble David and teach him and his people a valuable spiritual lesson.

Is it true that "where there is no vision [for the future], the people perish" (Proverbs 29:18 KJV)?

This verse has been grossly misunderstood by many Christians. They often twist it to say that unless we have long-range plans and a well-thought-out strategy, we will perish. But such an idea is completely foreign to the text.

The New International Version correctly renders this verse, "Where there is no revelation, the people cast off restraint; but blessed is he who keeps the law." This verse simply means that when God's Word is suppressed or silenced, people lose restraint and become ungovernable. Instead of doing God's will, they allow their own baser appetites to take over, and they indulge in all kinds of sinful activities.

We find this illustrated in the book of Exodus. Moses had left the Israelites alone for a mere 40 days when he was on Mount Sinai receiving God's law. During that time, the people lost all restraint and ended up making an idol in the form of a golden calf (Exodus 32:1-25).

Does Isaiah 53 teach that physical healing is guaranteed in the atonement?

No. It is important to note that the Hebrew word for healing (*rapha'*) can refer not only to physical healing but also spiritual healing. The context of Isaiah 53:5 indicates that spiritual healing is in view. In verse 5 we are clearly told, "He was wounded for our *transgressions*; he was crushed for our *iniquities*...with his stripes we are healed." Because "transgressions" and "iniquities" set the context, spiritual healing from the misery of human sin is in view.

Further, numerous verses in Scripture substantiate the view that physical healing in mortal life is not guaranteed in the atonement and that it is not always God's will to heal. The apostle Paul couldn't heal Timothy's stomach problem (1 Timothy 5:23), nor could he heal Trophimus at Miletus (2 Timothy 4:20) or Epaphroditus (Philippians 2:25-27). Paul spoke of "a bodily ailment" he had (Galatians 4:13-15). He also suffered a thorn in the flesh, which God allowed him to retain (2 Corinthians 12:7-9). God certainly allowed Job to go through a time of physical suffering (Job 1–2). None of these passages indicate that the sicknesses they describe were caused by sin or unbelief. Nor did Paul or any of the others act as if they thought the atonement guaranteed their healing. They accepted their situations and trusted in God's grace for sustenance. On one occasion Jesus indicated that sickness could be for the glory of God (John 11:4).

Finally, numerous verses in Scripture reveal that our physical bodies are continuously running down and suffering various ailments. Paul says that our present bodies are *perishable* and *weak* (1 Corinthians 15:42-44) and that "our outer nature is wasting away" (2 Corinthians 4:16). Death and disease will be a part of the human condition until that time when we receive resurrection bodies that are immune to such frailties (1 Corinthians 15:51-55).

7
Common Questions About the New Testament

Why would God give special revelation concerning Christ's birth to astrologers (Matthew 2:1-2)?

Astrologers of the occult seek to gain paranormal knowledge based on the movement and position of the stars. The magi were *not* involved in this type of thing. They were not seers and sorcerers of the occult in the sense that today's astrologers often are. These men were basically experts in the study of the stars. We might loosely equate them today to specialists in astronomy. Tradition tells us that three magi visited Christ, and they are said to be kings. But we do not know this for certain.

Matthew 20:29-34 says Jesus healed two blind men as He left Jericho. Mark 10:46-52 and Luke 18:35-43 say Jesus healed one man as He entered Jericho. How can we reconcile this apparent contradiction?

There are several possible explanations. One is that the healing took place as Jesus was leaving *old* Jericho and was nearing *new* Jericho (two Jerichos existed in those days). If Jesus were at a place between the two Jerichos, then, depending on one's perspective, He could be viewed as "leaving" or "entering" either Jericho. Now, apparently two blind men were in need of healing, but Bartimaeus was the more aggressive of the two, and therefore two Gospel accounts (Mark and Luke) mention only him. If the blind men were healed between the two Jerichos, this would clear up the apparent contradiction between the Gospel accounts.

Another possible explanation is that the blind men pleaded with Jesus as He entered (either the old or new) Jericho, but they didn't receive their actual healings until Jesus was leaving Jericho. It's also possible that Jesus healed one blind man as He was entering Jericho and healed two other blind men as he was leaving Jericho. Clearly, there are a number of ways of reconciling the Gospel accounts.

Did Judas die by hanging or by falling onto some rocks (Matthew 27:5; Acts 1:18)?

Matthew 27:5 tells us that Judas died by hanging himself. Acts 1:18 tells us that Judas fell onto some rocks and his body burst open. Is there a contradiction here?

No. Both accounts are true. Apparently Judas first hanged himself. Then, at some point, the rope either broke or loosened so that his body slipped from it and fell to the rocks below and burst open. (Some have suggested that Judas didn't tie the noose very well.) Neither account alone is complete. Both accounts taken together give us a full picture of what happened to Judas.

Does Jesus advocate hating one's mother, father, spouse, and children for His sake (Luke 14:26)?

In Luke 14:26 Jesus said, "If anyone comes to me and does not hate his own father and mother and wife and children and brothers and sisters, yes, and even his own life, he cannot be my disciple." In the Hebrew mind-set, to "hate" means to "love less." Jesus is simply communicating that our supreme love must be for Him alone. Everything else (and everyone else) must take second place.

Jesus said something similar in Matthew 10:37: "Whoever loves father or mother more than me is not worthy of me, and whoever loves son or daughter more than me is not worthy of me." We may *seem* to hate our lesser loves when we compare them to our love for Christ.

Who are the "other sheep" mentioned in John 10:16?

The context indicates that the "other sheep" mentioned in John 10:16 are *Gentile* believers as opposed to *Jewish* believers. As a backdrop, the Jews in the Gospels were called "the lost sheep of the house of Israel" (Matthew 10:6; 15:24), and those Jews who followed Christ were called His "sheep" (John 10).

Jesus often referred to His Jewish disciples as sheep in His flock. For example, when Jesus was giving the twelve disciples instructions for their future service, He said, "Behold, I am sending you out as sheep in the midst of wolves, so be wise as serpents and innocent as doves" (Matthew 10:16). Later, Jesus told the disciples that His crucifixion would cause them to scatter: "You will all fall away because of me this night. For it is written, 'I will strike the shepherd, and the sheep of the flock will be scattered'" (Matthew 26:31).

Now, when Jesus said, "I have other sheep that are not of this fold," He was clearly referring to non-Jewish, Gentile believers. The Gentile believers, along with the Jewish believers, "will be one flock" with "one shepherd" (John 10:16). This is in perfect accord with Ephesians 2:11-22, where we are told that in Christ, Jews and Gentiles are reconciled in *one Spirit.* Galatians 3:28 tells us that "there is neither Jew nor Greek, there is neither slave nor free, there is neither male nor female, for *you are all one in Christ Jesus.*" Likewise, Colossians 3:11 tells us that "there is not Greek and Jew, circumcised and uncircumcised, barbarian, Scythian, slave, free; but Christ is all, and in all."

Did Jesus teach that human beings are actual gods in John 10:34?

No. In John 10:34 Jesus said to some Jewish critics, "Is it not written in your Law, 'I said, you are gods'?" This verse does not teach that human beings are actual gods. Rather, it must be understood in light of Psalm 82, which Jesus was quoting.

In Psalm 82 we find God's judgment against the evil Israelite judges. The judges were called "gods" because they pronounced life and death judgments against people.[1] But they became corrupt and unjust in their dealings.

In verses 6-7, Asaph says of them, "I said, 'You are gods, sons of the Most High, all of you; nevertheless, like men you shall die, and fall like any prince.'" Asaph is clearly speaking in irony. He is saying in effect, "I have called you 'gods,' but in fact you will die like the men that you really are." When Jesus alluded to this psalm in John 10, He was saying that what the Israelite judges were called in irony and in judgment, *He is in reality.*

What did Jesus mean when He said we would do greater miracles than He did (John 14:12)?

In John 14:12 Jesus affirmed, "Truly, truly, I say to you, whoever believes in me will also do the works that I do; and greater works than these will he do, because I am going to the Father." Does this mean you and I can do more incredible miracles than Jesus did while He was on the earth? *No way!*

In this verse Jesus is simply saying that His many followers would do things greater *in extent* (all over the world) and greater *in effect* (multitudes being touched by the power of God). Jesus was referring to the whole scope of the impact of God's people and the church on the entire world throughout all history. In other words, Jesus was speaking *quantitatively,* not *qualitatively.*

Did early Christians practice communism (Acts 2:44-45)?

In Acts 2:44-45 we read, "All who believed were together and had all things in common. And they were selling their possessions and belongings and distributing the proceeds to all, as any had need."

There are several reasons to believe that this passage does not teach an abiding form of Christian communism or socialism. First, these passages are not *prescriptive*—they are simply *descriptive.* That is, our passage merely *describes* what these early Christians did. It does not *prescribe* what should take place in every subsequent generation. Nowhere does our passage make this practice out to be normative.

Second, so far as the text indicates, the system was only temporary, not a permanent arrangement. These early Christians apparently stayed together in Jerusalem, since that is where the Holy Spirit had descended and the first great turning to Christ had occurred. The necessities of living together away from home occasioned this sort of common arrangement.

Third, the communal arrangement was voluntary. The text does not indicate at all that this was a compulsory arrangement. It was apparently simply a temporary and voluntary convenience for the furtherance of the gospel in those early and crucial days of the Christian church.

Fourth, the selling of property and giving of money was only partial. The text implies that they sold only extra land and other possessions, not that they sold their only place of residence. After all, they all eventually left Jerusalem, to which they had come for the feast of Pentecost (Acts 2:1), and they went back to their homes, which were scattered all over the world (see verses 5-13).

In what way was Jesus "made...to be sin" (2 Corinthians 5:21)?

In 2 Corinthians 5:21 we read, "For our sake he made him to be sin who knew no sin, so that in him we might become the righteousness of God." Regarding Jesus being "made...to be sin," Jesus was always without sin *actually*, but He was made to be sin for us *judicially*. By His death on the cross, He paid the penalty for our sins, canceling the debt of sin against us. So, while Jesus never committed a sin *personally*, He was made to be sin for us *substitutionally*.

One must also keep in mind the Old Testament backdrop of the concept of substitution. The sacrificial victim had to be "without blemish" (see Leviticus 4:3,23,32). A hand would be laid on the unblemished sacrificial animal as a way of symbolizing a transfer of guilt (Leviticus 4:4,24,33). Note that the sacrificial animal did not thereby actually *become* sinful by nature. Rather, sin was *imputed* to the animal, and the animal acted as a sacrificial substitute. In like manner, Christ the Lamb of God was utterly unblemished (1 Peter 1:19), but our sin was *imputed* to Him, and He was our sacrificial substitute on the cross of Calvary.

Does 2 Corinthians 8:9 teach that financial prosperity is guaranteed in the atonement?

No. Second Corinthians 8:9 says, "You know the grace of our Lord Jesus Christ, that though he was rich, yet for your sake he became poor, so that you by his poverty might become rich." If Paul really intended to say that *financial* prosperity is provided for in the atonement, he was offering the Corinthians something that he himself did not possess at the time. Indeed, in 1 Corinthians 4:11 Paul informed these same individuals that he had "hunger and thirst," and was "poorly dressed and buffeted and homeless." He also exhorted the Corinthians to be imitators of his life and teaching (1 Corinthians 4:16).

In 2 Corinthians 8:9 it seems clear that Paul was speaking about spiritual prosperity, not financial prosperity. This fits both the immediate context in 2 Corinthians and the broader context of Paul's other writings. If the atonement provided financial prosperity, why did Paul inform the Philippian Christians that he had learned to be content *even when going hungry* (Philippians 4:11-12)? One would think he would have instead claimed the prosperity promised in the atonement to meet his every need.

What does Scripture mean when it says an elder of the church must be "the husband of one wife" (1 Timothy 3:12)?

This verse has been debated by Christians since the first century. There are four basic suggestions as to what it means: Some commentators believe that the elder must be married only once. No remarriage is allowed, even if the wife dies. Others think the elder must be married to one wife *at a time* (that is, no polygamy is allowed). Another view is that a single person cannot be an elder in the church. Finally, some commentators believe that the elder must be faithful to his wife (that is, he must be a "one-woman man"). I believe this is probably the correct view.

Does Revelation 7:4 teach that there will be only 144,000 "anointed" believers who go to heaven, with all other believers being assigned to live forever on a paradise earth?

No. This is a false teaching of the Watchtower Society (the Jehovah's Witnesses).[2]

Drawing a dichotomy between those with a heavenly destiny and those with an earthly destiny has absolutely no warrant in Scripture. All who believe in Christ are "heirs" of the eternal kingdom (Galatians 3:29; 4:28-31; Titus 3:7; James 2:5). The righteousness of God that leads to life in heaven is available "through faith in Jesus Christ for all who believe. *For there is no distinction*" (Romans 3:22).

Jesus Himself promised, "If anyone serves me, he must follow me; and where I am, there [that is, in heaven] will my servant be also" (John 12:26). Jesus affirmed that all believers will be together in "one flock" under "one shepherd" (John 10:16). There will not be two "flocks"—one on the earth and one in heaven. Scripture is clear: One flock, one Shepherd.

Part 3
Questions About God

The Trinity
Common Errors About God
Understanding the Holy Spirit

8
The Trinity

Was God lonely before He created the universe and the world of humankind?

No. God contains within Himself three centers of personal activity, each denoted by personal pronouns ("I," "Me"). This means that there is an incomprehensible richness in the inner life of God. During this pre-creation eternity past, the Father, Son, and Holy Spirit existed in a state of uninterrupted, completely fulfilling fellowship. The Father and the Holy Spirit enjoyed an eternal loving interaction with each other and with the Son. Recall that near the close of His three-year ministry on the earth, Jesus, in His prayer to the Father, spoke of eternity past as a matter of memory: "You loved me before the foundation of the world" (John 17:24).

Does the fact that the word *Trinity* is not in the Bible mean the doctrine is unbiblical?

No. Though the *word* is not mentioned in the Bible, the *concept* of the Trinity is clearly derived from Scripture. (I'll provide details later in the chapter.)

The Jehovah's Witnesses often say the Trinity is an unbiblical doctrine because the word is not in the Bible. Here is a good response to them: The word *Jehovah* does not appear as such in the Bible—it does not even appear in any legitimate Hebrew or Greek biblical manuscripts. The word was originally formed by Jewish scribes who joined the consonants YHWH (a biblical name of God) with the vowels from Adonai (a biblical title of God). The result was Yahowah, or Jehovah.

My point is that if you reject the doctrine of the Trinity because the word *Trinity* does not appear in the Bible, then by that same logic the doctrine of Jehovah must be considered false since this term does not appear in the Bible.

In any event, Matthew 28:19 and 2 Corinthians 13:14 are among the notable passages that establish the doctrine of the Trinity.

Does the fact that God is not a God of confusion (1 Corinthians 14:33) prove that the doctrine of the Trinity cannot be true, since this doctrine is hard to understand?

No. Simply because one is unable to fully comprehend a doctrine does not mean the doctrine is false. Human beings would need the very mind of God to understand everything about Him. Paul says, "How unsearchable are his judgments and how inscrutable his ways" (Romans 11:33). God declares, "My thoughts are not your thoughts, neither are your ways my ways, declares the LORD. For as the heavens are higher than the earth, so are my ways higher than your ways and my thoughts than your thoughts" (Isaiah 55:8-9). Paul also writes, "Now we see in a mirror dimly…Now I know in part" (1 Corinthians 13:12).

Such verses clearly point out that human reasoning has limitations. Finite minds cannot possibly understand everything there is to know about an infinite being. Creatures cannot know everything there is to know about the sovereign Creator. Just as a young child cannot understand everything his father says, so we as God's children cannot understand everything about our heavenly Father.

What, then, did the apostle Paul mean when he said, "God is not a God of confusion but of peace"? The context of 1 Corinthians makes everything clear. The Corinthian church was plagued by internal divisions and disorder, especially in regard to the exercise of spiritual gifts (1 Corinthians 1:11). God is a God of peace and not a God of confusion, so the church must seek to model itself after God and honor Him by seeking peace and avoiding disorder in its services.

How can we respond to those who claim that the doctrine of the Trinity is rooted in Babylonian and Assyrian paganism?

The Babylonians and Assyrians believed in *triads* of gods who headed up a pantheon of many other gods. But these triads constituted three separate gods (polytheism), which is utterly different from the doctrine of the Trinity, which maintains that there is *only one God* (monotheism) and three persons within the one Godhead.

Moreover, such pagan ideas predate Christianity by some 2,000 years and were geographically far removed from the part of the world where Christianity developed.[1] From a historical and geographical perspective, then, the suggestion that Christianity borrowed the Trinitarian concept from pagans is quite infeasible. Cultists who teach this idea, such as the Jehovah's Witnesses, are trying to rewrite history in order to make their doctrine denying the Trinity appear more feasible.

What are some false views of the Trinity?

There are two primary errors to avoid:

Tritheism is the view that the Godhead is composed of three utterly distinct persons in the same way that Peter, James, and John are three separate individuals. This concept views the Father, Son, and Holy Spirit as three different gods.

Modalism is the view that the Godhead is one person only and the triune aspect of His being is no more than three modes of manifestation. Broadly speaking, we might describe modalism's conception of the Trinity this way: As Father, God engages in the role of sovereign Creator. As Son, God engages in the role of Redeemer. As the Holy Spirit, God engages in the role of Sanctifier.

The fallacy of such errors will become clearer as we examine the biblical evidence for the Trinity.

What biblical evidence is there for one God?

The fact that there is only one true God is the consistent testimony of Scripture from Genesis to Revelation. It is like a thread that runs through every page of the Bible. God positively affirmed through Isaiah the prophet, "Thus says the LORD, the King of Israel and his Redeemer, the LORD of hosts: 'I am the first and I am the last; besides me there is no god'" (Isaiah 44:6). God also said, "I am God, and there is no other; I am God, and there is none like me" (46:9).

The New Testament also often emphasizes the oneness of God. In 1 Corinthians 8:4, for example, the apostle Paul asserted that "an idol has no real existence" and that "there is no God but one." James 2:19 says, "You believe that God is one; you do well. Even the demons believe—and shudder!" These and a multitude of other verses make it absolutely clear that there is one and only one God (see John 5:44; 17:3; Romans 3:29-30; 16:27; Galatians 3:20; Ephesians 4:6; 1 Timothy 2:5).

What is the biblical evidence for three persons who are called God?

On the one hand, Scripture is absolutely clear that there is only one God. Yet, in the unfolding of God's revelation to humankind, it also becomes clear that three distinct persons are called God in Scripture.

First, the Father is God. Peter refers to the saints who have been chosen "according to the foreknowledge of God the Father" (1 Peter 1:2). Second, Jesus is God. When Jesus made a post-resurrection appearance to doubting Thomas, Thomas said, "My Lord and my God" (John 20:28). Also, the Father said of the Son, "Your throne, O God, is forever and ever, the scepter of uprightness is the scepter of your kingdom" (Hebrews 1:8). Third, the Holy Spirit is God. In Acts 5:3-4, we are told that lying to the Holy Spirit is equivalent to lying to God.

Moreover, each of the three persons on different occasions is seen to possess the attributes of deity: *Omnipresence* (the quality of being present everywhere) is ascribed to the Father (John 4:19-24), the Son (Matthew 28:20), and the Holy Spirit (Psalm 139:7). Also, *omniscience* (the quality of being all-knowing) is ascribed to the Father (Psalm 139:1-2), the Son (Matthew 9:4), and the Holy Spirit (1 Corinthians 2:10). Further, *omnipotence* (the quality of being all-powerful) is ascribed to the Father (1 Peter 1:5), the Son (Matthew 28:18), and the Holy Spirit (Romans 15:19) as well.

Holiness is ascribed to each person: the Father (Revelation 15:4), the Son (Acts 3:14), and the Holy Spirit (John 16:7-14). *Eternity* is ascribed to each person: the Father (Psalm 90:2), the Son (Micah 5:2; John 1:2; Revelation 1:8,17), and the Holy Spirit (Hebrews 9:14). And each of the three is individually described as the "truth" or "true one": the Father (John 14:6-7), the Son (Revelation 3:7), and the Holy Spirit (1 John 5:6).

What is the biblical evidence for three-in-oneness in the Godhead?

In Matthew 28:19 Jesus instructs His followers, "Go therefore and make disciples of all nations, baptizing them in the name of *the* Father and of *the* Son and of *the* Holy Spirit." It is highly revealing that the word for "name" is singular in the Greek, indicating that there is one God, but there are three distinct persons within the Godhead—*the* Father, *the* Son, and *the* Holy Spirit.[2] Theologian Robert Reymond draws our attention to the importance of this verse for the doctrine of the Trinity:

> Jesus does not say, (1) "into the names [plural] of the Father and of the Son and of the Holy Spirit," or what is its virtual equivalent, (2) "into the name of the Father, and into the name of the Son, and into the name of the Holy Spirit," as if we had to deal with three separate Beings. Nor does He say, (3) "into the name of the Father, Son, and Holy Spirit" (omitting the three recurring articles), as if "the Father, Son, and Holy Ghost" might be taken as merely three designations of a single person. What He does say is this: (4) "into the name [singular] of *the* Father, and of *the* Son, and of *the* Holy Spirit," first asserting the unity of the three by combining them all within the bounds of the single Name, and then throwing into emphasis the distinctness of each by introducing them in turn with the repeated article.[3]

Very clearly, then, the Scriptures affirm that there is one God, but within the unity of the Godhead, there are three coequal and coeternal persons—the Father, the Son, and the Holy Spirit.

How can three "persons" be in one God?

Most theologians acknowledge today that the term *person* is an imperfect expression of what the Bible communicates. Some believe the word tends to distract from the unity of the Trinity. Certainly, in God there are not three separate individuals such as Peter, John, and Matthew, who have different characteristics, but only *personal self-distinctions* within the Godhead. Theologian Lewis Sperry Chafer explains this:

> In applying the term "person" to God, the word is used in a distinctive sense from its normal use in relation to human beings. Though each member of the Godhead manifests the qualities of personality, such as intellect, sensibility, and will, they do not act independently as three separate human individuals would act. Nevertheless, the personalities involved in the Trinity are expressed in such terms as "I," "Thou," "He," and the Persons of the Godhead address each other as individuals and manifest their individuality in some personal acts.[4]

So the Father, Son, and Holy Spirit are "persons" in the sense that each has the personal attributes of mind, emotions, and will, and each of the three is aware of the others, speaks to the others, and carries on a loving relationship with the others.

Do even theologians struggle to understanding the Trinity?

Yes indeed. One day while puzzling over the doctrine of the Trinity, the great theologian Augustine was walking along the beach when he observed a young boy with a bucket, running back and forth to pour water into a little hole. Augustine asked, "What are you doing?"

The boy replied, "I'm trying to put the ocean into this hole."

Augustine smiled, recognizing the utter futility of what the boy was attempting to do.

After pondering the boy's words for a few moments, however, Augustine came to a sudden realization. He realized that he had been trying to put an infinite God into his finite mind. It can't be done. We can accept God's revelation to us that He is triune in nature and that

He has infinite perfections. But with our finite minds we cannot fully understand everything about God. Our God is an awesome God.

Some verses say God the Father is the Creator; some say the Son is the Creator; and some say the Holy Spirit is the Creator. How do we reconcile these?

It is true that different passages ascribe the work of creation differently. Many Old Testament references to the creation attribute it simply to "God" or "LORD" rather than to the individual persons of the Father, Son, or Holy Spirit (Genesis 1:1; Psalm 96:5; Isaiah 37:16; 44:24). Other passages relate the creation specifically to the Father (Revelation 4:11), to the Son (John 1:3; Colossians 1:16; Hebrews 1:2), or to the Holy Spirit (Job 33:4; Psalm 104:30).

How do we put all these passages together into a coherent whole? First Corinthians 8:6 has some bearing on this issue. It describes the Father as the one "*from whom* are all things" and the Son as the one "*through whom* are all things and *through whom* we exist." Based on this, many have concluded that while the Father may be considered Creator in a broad, general sense, the Son is the actual agent or mediating *cause* of creation. Through the Son, all things came into being. Creation is viewed as being "in" the Holy Spirit in the sense that the life of creation is found in the Holy Spirit.

Should we be cautious about making absolute distinctions between the creative roles of the Father, Son, and Holy Spirit?

Such caution is wise. After all, though the Holy Spirit's role may have involved the bestowing of life, we are told elsewhere in Scripture that life is in Christ (John 1:4). Moreover, we must be careful to avoid thinking that the Son as a mediating agent ("through whom" the creation came into being) means that the Son had a lesser role than the Father. Indeed, the same Greek word for "through" (*dia*) that is used of Christ's work of creation in 1 Corinthians 8:6 is used elsewhere in Scripture of the Father's role in creation (Romans 11:36; Hebrews 2:10).

The King James Version rendering of 1 John 5:7 provides clear proof for the Trinity. However, scholars now say the words in this verse are not in the earliest Greek manuscripts. Does this mean the doctrine of the Trinity is not true?

No. Simply because this one verse has no manuscript support does not mean the doctrine of the Trinity is not true.

Numerous other passages—for example, Matthew 28:19 and 2 Corinthians 13:14—have undeniably strong manuscript support, and they establish that (1) only one true God exists, (2) three persons—Father, Son, and Holy Spirit—are God, and (3) three-in-oneness exists within the Godhead.

Regarding 1 John 5:7, it is true that this verse has no support among the early Greek manuscripts, though it is found in some Latin manuscripts. Its appearance in late Greek manuscripts is explained by the fact that Erasmus was placed under pressure by church authorities to include it in his Greek New Testament of AD 1522. (He had omitted it in his two earlier editions of 1516 and 1519 because he could not find any Greek manuscripts that contained it.) The inclusion of the verse in the Latin Bible was probably due to a scribe incorporating a marginal comment (gloss) into the text as he copied the manuscript of 1 John.

9
Common Errors About God

Is "Jehovah" God's true name?

This name is not found in the Hebrew and Greek manuscripts from which English translations of the Bible are derived. The Old Testament contains the name Yahweh—or, more literally, YHWH (the original Hebrew had only consonants).

Regarding the term "Jehovah," the ancient Jews had a superstitious dread of pronouncing the name YHWH. They felt that if they uttered this name, they might violate the third commandment, which deals with taking God's name in vain (Exodus 20:7). So, to avoid the possibility of breaking this commandment, the Jews for centuries substituted the name *Adonai* (Lord) or some other name in its place whenever they came across it in public readings of Scripture. Eventually, the fearful Hebrew scribes decided to form a new name (Jehovah) by inserting the vowels from Adonai (a-o-a) into the consonants YHWH.

Though there is no biblical justification for the term "Jehovah," it is important to recognize that scholars are not precisely clear as to the correct way to pronounce the Hebrew name YHWH. Though most modern scholars believe *Yahweh* is the correct vocalization (as I do), we can't be sure about that. Perhaps this is one reason why some legitimate translations—such as the American Standard Version of 1901 and even the King James Version (in four verses)—used the name Jehovah. Other translations use "Lord" (with small caps) to render the name Yahweh.

Does the fact that God had to rest after six days of creation mean He is not all-powerful (Genesis 2:2)?

No. God didn't have to rest in the sense that His physical energy had become depleted and He needed to recuperate. Rather, the Hebrew word for *rest* communicates the idea of "ceasing from activity." Therefore, Genesis 2:2 is simply saying that God completed His work of creation and then stopped. There was nothing further to do. The job was done.

Is it true that the God of the Old Testament is a God of judgment and wrath while the God of the New Testament is a God of love?

No. Both the Old and New Testaments point to one and the same God. And this God is a God of both love *and* judgment.

On the one hand, the Old Testament does refer to times when God judged people because the circumstances called for it. This was the case when He sent ten horrible plagues against the Egyptians (Exodus 7–11; 12:29-32). But the Old Testament also frequently refers to times when He showed love and grace. Following Adam and Eve's sin, God's promise of a coming Redeemer was an act of love and grace (Genesis 3:15). God's provision of an ark for Noah and his family was an act of love and grace (Genesis 6:9-22). God's provision of the covenants was an act of love and grace (Genesis 12:1-3; 2 Samuel 7:12-16). God's sending of the prophets to give special revelation to Israel was an act of love and grace.

In the New Testament, the love of God was continually manifested to the people through the person of Jesus Christ. In fact, we might even say that Jesus is "love incarnate." But it is also true that some of the most scathing denouncements from God—especially in regard to the Jewish leaders—came from the mouth of Jesus (see Matthew 23:27-28,33).

So, again, the God of the Old *and* New Testaments is a God of love *and* judgment.

What is modalism?

I briefly noted in the previous chapter that modalism views the Father, Son, and Holy Spirit as modes of manifestation of the one God.

More specifically, Sabellius—a third-century heretic—taught that the Father was God's mode of manifestation in the work of creation and the giving of the law. The Son was God's mode of manifestation in the incarnation and work as the Redeemer. The Holy Spirit is God's mode of manifestation in regeneration, sanctification, and the giving of grace.

This heresy is easily refuted by the fact that all three persons in the New Testament are portrayed together (Matthew 28:19; 2 Corinthians 13:14). Moreover, we read that the Father *sent* the Son (John 3:17). The Father and Son *love* each other (John 14:31). The Father *speaks* to the Son, and the Son *speaks* to the Father (John 11:41-42). The Holy Spirit *comes upon* Jesus at the baptism (Matthew 3). Jesus and the Father are viewed as having *sent* the Holy Spirit (John 15:26). Clearly these are distinct persons who interact with each other.

What is pantheism?

Pantheism is the view that *God is all* and *all is God.* The word pantheism comes from two Greek words—*pan* ("all") and *theos* ("God"). In pantheism, all reality is viewed as being infused with divinity. The god of pantheism is an impersonal, amoral "it" as opposed to the personal, moral "He" of Christianity. The distinction between the Creator and the creation is completely obliterated in this view.

How does pantheism deal with the reality of evil?

A major problem of pantheism is that it fails to adequately deal with the existence of real evil in the world. If God is the essence of *all* life forms in creation, then one must conclude that both good *and* evil stem from the same essence (God). The Bible, on the other hand, teaches that God is good and not evil. The God of the Bible is light, and "in him is no darkness at all" (1 John 1:5; see also Habakkuk 1:13; Matthew 5:48). First John 1:5 is particularly cogent in the Greek, which translates literally, "And darkness is not in him, *not in any way.*" John could not have said it more forcefully.

Jeff Amano and Norman Geisler provide an excellent example of how evil is problematic for the pantheistic view of God:

When Francis Schaeffer spoke to a group of students at Cambridge University, there was a [pantheistic] Hindu who began criticizing Christianity. Schaeffer said, "Am I not correct in saying that on the basis of your system, cruelty and noncruelty are ultimately equal, that there is no intrinsic difference between them?"

The Hindu agreed. One of the students immediately caught on to what Schaeffer was driving at. He picked up a kettle of boiling water that he was going to use to make tea and held the steaming pot over the Indian's head.

This young Hindu looked up and asked the student what he was doing.

The student said with a cold yet gentle finality, "There is no difference between cruelty and noncruelty." Thereupon the Hindu walked out into the night.[1]

Some cultists teach that in the Old Testament Jesus is "Yahweh" and the Father is "Elohim." How can we disprove this idea from the Bible?

A number of verses in the Bible demonstrate that Elohim and Yahweh are one and the same God. For example, in Genesis 27:20 Isaac's son said, "The LORD [Yahweh] your God [Elohim] granted me success." In this verse, then, we find reference to "Yahweh your Elohim" (the LORD your God).

Likewise, in Jeremiah 32:18 we find reference to the "great and mighty God [El, a singular variant of Elohim], whose name is the LORD [Yahweh] of hosts." Clearly, El (a name related to Elohim) and Yahweh are one and the same God.

Also, some clear passages in the Bible refer to Jesus individually as Elohim, thereby disproving the claim that only the Father is Elohim and Jesus is only Yahweh. In Isaiah 40:3 we read, "A voice cries: 'In the wilderness prepare the way of the LORD [Yahweh]; make straight in the desert a highway for our God [Elohim].'" This verse was written in reference to the future ministry of Christ, according to John 1:23. Within the confines of a single verse Christ is called both Yahweh *and* Elohim.

Does Genesis 1:26-27 teach that there is more than one God?

No. It is true that the word used of God in Genesis 1:26-27 is *Elohim,* and it has a plural ending (*im*). But this is actually a "plural of majesty," pointing to the majesty, dignity, and greatness of God. The plural ending gives a fuller, more majestic sense to God's name.[2]

What are we to make of the plural pronouns used of God in Genesis 1:26 and elsewhere?

In Genesis 1:26 we read, "Let *us* make man in *our* image." Do these words indicate there is more than one God?

No. Biblical grammarians tell us that the plural pronouns in the verse are a grammatical necessity. The plural pronoun "us" is required by the plural ending of Elohim: "Then God [Elohim] said, 'Let us [plural] make man in our [plural] image.'"[3] In other words, the plural pronoun "us" corresponds grammatically with the plural form of the Hebrew word Elohim. One demands the other.

Notice the words I've italicized in Genesis 1:26-27:

> Then God said, "Let us make man in *our image*, after *our likeness*. And let them have dominion over the fish of the sea and over the birds of the heavens and over the livestock and over all the earth and over every creeping thing that creeps on the earth." So God created man in *his own image*, in the *image of God* he created him; male and female he created them.

The phrases "*our* image" and "*our* likeness" in verse 26 are explained in verse 27 as "*his own* image "and "in the *image of God*." This supports the idea that even though plural pronouns are used in reference to God, only one God is meant.

Does Psalm 82:1,6 indicate that there are many gods in the universe?

No. In this passage we find God's judgment against the evil Israelite judges. These judges were, of course, intended to act righteously and be His representatives on the earth. They were to administer God's justice. They were called gods (with a little *g*) *not* because they were actual deity but because they pronounced life and death judgments over the people.[4]

These judges soon became corrupt in their dealings with men. God's charge against them was that they administered justice *unjustly*, showing favor to the wicked instead of upholding the rights of the helpless and oppressed.[5]

So, in verse 6, we find the psalmist Asaph communicating God's judgment on them. He is saying in effect, "I have called you 'gods,' but in fact you will die like the men you really are."

Does Psalm 82 give us insight on Jesus' words in John 10:34, "You are gods"?

Yes. In fact, Jesus was directly alluding to this psalm in John 10:34. He was indicating that if these finite judges were called gods with a little *g* because of the works they did among human beings (making life and death decisions over them), how much more so should Jesus be truly viewed as God because of His wondrous divine works (miracles).

Does 1 Corinthians 8:5 indicate that there are many gods in the universe?

No. First Corinthians 8:5 reads, "There may be so-called gods in heaven or on earth—as indeed there are many 'gods' and many 'lords.'" Taken alone, this verse might *seem* to teach that there are many gods. But the context of 1 Corinthians 8 is clearly monotheistic. The context is set for us in verse 4: "We know that 'an idol has no real existence,' and that 'there is no God but one.'" Then, in verse 6, we read, "For us there is one God, the Father, from whom are all things and for whom we exist, and one Lord, Jesus Christ, through whom are all things and through whom we exist."

In verse 5 Paul is not saying that there actually are many true "gods" and "lords." Rather he refers to false pagan entities who are *called* gods and lords. There is a world of difference between being *called* a god and actually *being* one. Shirley MacLaine, in her book *Out on a Limb*, said, "I am God," but that doesn't mean she *is* God. Similarly, just because Paul acknowledges that some pagan entities are "called" gods doesn't mean they actually *are* gods.

Apparently, in the context of the city of Corinth, these "gods" were the idols of Greek and Roman mythology. Paul in this verse is simply recognizing that in New Testament days many false gods were worshipped—though, in fact, such gods do not really exist. Paul, as a Hebrew of Hebrews, was monotheistic to the core and believed in only one God (1 Timothy 2:5), staying consistent with what God taught through Moses (Deuteronomy 6:4).

How can we respond to the claim that Christianity sets forth a "Father" concept of God and is therefore sexist?

God equally values both men and women. God created both men *and* women in the image of God (Genesis 1:26). Christian men and women are positionally equal before God (Galatians 3:28). The four Gospels indicate that Jesus exalted women in a very anti-woman Jewish environment (see John 4). So, Christianity cannot be said to be sexist. In fact, Jesus, the head of Christianity, vigorously fought the sexism of His day.

It is interesting to observe that while God is referred to in the Bible as "Father" (and never "Mother"), some of His actions are occasionally described in feminine terms. For example, Jesus likened Himself to a loving and saddened mother hen crying over the waywardness of her children (Matthew 23:37-39). God is also said to have given birth to Israel (Deuteronomy 32:18).

It is important to understand that God is not a gendered being as humans are. He is not of the male *sex* per se. The primary emphasis in God being called "Father" is that He is personal. Unlike the dead and impersonal idols of paganism, the true God is a personal being with whom we can relate. In fact, we can even call Him *Abba* (which loosely means "Daddy"—see Mark 14:36; Romans 8:15; Galatians 4:6). That's how intimate a relationship we can have with Him.

Does the fact that Moses spoke to God "face to face" mean that God has a physical body (Exodus 33:11)?

No. Scripture informs us that God is spirit (John 4:24). And a spirit does not have flesh and bones (Luke 24:39). So the description of Moses speaking to God "face to face" cannot be taken to mean that God actually has a physical face.

The phrase "face to face" is simply a Hebrew way of indicating "personally," "directly," or "intimately." Moses was in the direct presence of God and interacted with Him on a personal and intimate basis. The word *face,* when used of God, is an anthropomorphism—that is, it is a word used to describe God in humanlike terms.

Does the fact that Moses saw God's "back" mean God has a physical body (Exodus 33:21-23)?

No. As a backdrop, humble and meek Moses requested of God, "Please show me your glory" (Exodus 33:18). But God warned Moses, "You cannot see my face, for man shall not see me and live" (verse 20). So the Lord said to Moses, "Behold, there is a place by me where you shall stand on the rock, and while my glory passes by I will put you in a cleft of the rock, and I will cover you with my hand until I have passed by. Then I will take away my hand, and you shall see my back, but my face shall not be seen" (verses 21-23).

We know from other passages that God is spirit and He is formless (see Isaiah 31:3; John 4:24). Just as the word "hand" is an anthropomorphism, so the word "back" is an anthropomorphism.

So, what does the word "back" indicate? The Hebrew word for "back" can easily be rendered "aftereffects." Moses did not see the glory of God directly, but once it had gone past, God did allow him to view the results (or the afterglow) that His glorious presence had produced.

Does the fact that human beings are created in the image of God mean that God has a physical body like we do (Genesis 1:26-27)?

No. Genesis 1:26-27 is not referring to man being created in the *physical* image of God. Indeed, God is spirit (John 4:24), and a spirit does not have flesh and bones (Luke 24:39). God is portrayed as being invisible throughout Scripture (see John 1:18; Colossians 1:15; 1 Timothy 1:17). So whatever is meant by "image of God" must be consistent with the fact that God is an invisible spirit.

In context, being created in God's image means that human beings share, though imperfectly and finitely, in God's communicable attributes such as life, personality, truth, wisdom, love, holiness, and justice. In view of being created in God's "image," human beings have the capacity for spiritual fellowship with Him.

Does the fact that Jesus said, "Whoever has seen me has seen the Father," mean that the Father has a physical body like Jesus does (John 14:9)?

No. Remember, God is by nature spirit (John 4:24). John 14:9 simply means that Jesus is the perfect revelation of God. Jesus became a man specifically to reveal the Father to humankind: "No one has ever seen God; the only God [Jesus], who is at the Father's side, he has made him known" (1:18). That's why Jesus could say, "Whoever sees me sees him who sent me" (12:45). And that's why Jesus could affirm, "Whoever receives me receives the one who sent me" (13:20).

Jesus revealed the Father's awesome power (John 3:2), incredible wisdom (1 Corinthians 1:24), boundless love (1 John 3:16), and unfathomable grace (2 Thessalonians 1:12).

It is against this backdrop that Jesus said, "Whoever has seen me has seen the Father" in John 14:9. Jesus came as the ultimate revelation of the Father.

10
Understanding the Holy Spirit

Does the Holy Spirit's lack of a name indicate that the Spirit is not a person?

No. Spiritual beings are not always named in Scripture. For example, evil spirits are rarely named in Scripture, but rather are identified by their particular character—that is, "unclean," "wicked," and so forth (see Matthew 12:45). In the same way, by contrast, the Holy Spirit is identified by His primary character, which is holiness. To say that the Holy Spirit is not a person because a name is not ascribed to Him is simply fallacious reasoning.

Related to this issue, we must point out that the Holy Spirit is in fact related to the name of the other persons of the Trinity in Matthew 28:19: "Go therefore and make disciples of all nations, baptizing them in *the name* of the Father and of the Son and of the Holy Spirit." Just as the Father and the Son are persons, so the Holy Spirit is a person. And all three are related by the same name.

Does the fact that the Holy Spirit fills many people at the same time indicate that the Holy Spirit is not a person but is rather a force (Acts 2:4)?

No! We know this to be untrue because Ephesians 3:19 speaks of God filling all the Ephesian believers. Likewise, Ephesians 4:10 speaks of Christ filling all things, and Ephesians 1:23 speaks of Christ as the one who "fills all in all." The fact that God and Christ can fill all things does not mean that the Father and Jesus are not persons. In the same way, the fact that the Holy Spirit can "fill" numerous people does not prove that He is not a person.

What is some biblical evidence that the Holy Spirit has a mind, and is therefore a person?

The Holy Spirit's intellect is seen in 1 Corinthians 2:10 where we are told that "the Spirit searches everything" (compare with Isaiah 11:2; Ephesians 1:17). The Greek word for *search* means "to thoroughly investigate a matter." We are also told in 1 Corinthians 2:11 that the Holy Spirit "comprehends" the thoughts of God. How can the Spirit "comprehend" the thoughts of God if the Spirit does not have a mind? A force does not know things. Thought processes require the presence of a mind.

Romans 8:27 tells us that just as the Holy Spirit knows the things of God, so God the Father knows "what is the mind of the Spirit." The word translated *mind* in this verse literally means "way of thinking, mindset, aim, aspiration, striving."[1] A mere force—electricity, for example—does not have a way of thinking.

What biblical evidence is there that the Holy Spirit has emotions, and is therefore a person?

In Ephesians 4:30 we are admonished not to "grieve the Holy Spirit of God." Grief is an emotion and is not something that can be experienced by a force. Grief is something one *feels*. The Holy Spirit feels the emotion of grief when believers sin. In the context of Ephesians, such sins include lying (verse 25), anger (verse 26), stealing, laziness (verse 28), and speaking unkind words (verse 29).

What biblical evidence is there that the Holy Spirit has a will, and is therefore a person?

First Corinthians 12:11 informs us that in regard to the Holy Spirit distributing spiritual gifts to believers, He "apportions to each one individually as he wills." The phrase "he wills" translates the Greek word *bouletai,* which refers to "decisions of the will after previous deliberation."[2] The Holy Spirit makes a sovereign choice regarding what spiritual gifts each respective Christian receives. A force does not have such a will.

Do the Holy Spirit's works confirm His personality?

Yes. The Holy Spirit is seen doing many things in Scripture that only a person can do. For example, the Holy Spirit *teaches* believers (John 14:26), He *testifies* (John 15:26), He *guides* believers (Romans 8:14), He *commissions* people to service (Acts 13:4), He *issues commands* to believers (Acts 8:29), He *restrains sin* (2 Thessalonians 2:7), He *intercedes* (prays) for believers (Romans 8:26), and He *speaks* to people (John 15:26; 2 Peter 1:21).

Did the disciples receive the Holy Spirit before the day of Pentecost (John 20:21-22)?

Following His resurrection from the dead, Jesus appeared to His disciples and said to them, "'Peace be with you. As the Father has sent me, even so I am sending you.' When he had said this, he breathed on them and said to them, 'Receive the Holy Spirit'" (John 20:21-22). Does this mean that the disciples received the Holy Spirit *prior* to the day of Pentecost?

Some scholars have suggested that this was a prophetic utterance that would ultimately be fulfilled 50 days later on the day of Pentecost. However, this viewpoint doesn't seem to do justice to the sense of immediacy that is communicated in Jesus' words. I believe that in this passage we witness Jesus giving the disciples a temporary empowerment from the Holy Spirit to carry on their work of ministry until they would be fully and permanently empowered on the day of Pentecost. Since Christ had called them to a unique work, He gave them a unique empowerment for that work.

Was the prophecy of Joel 2:28-32 completely fulfilled on the day of Pentecost (Acts 2:16)?

No, I don't think so. What we see in Acts 2 is simply an example of prophetic foreshadowing. Peter, who cited Joel 2:28-32, never said this prophecy was completely fulfilled on that day. He was saying, however, that the events that occurred on Pentecost in association with the Holy Spirit were not a result of intoxication but rather were in harmony with Old Testament revelation. It is common in prophetic literature to witness foreshadowing. So the ultimate fulfillment of Joel's prophecy is yet future.

Is the baptism of the Holy Spirit the same thing as the filling of the Holy Spirit?

No. These are two separate ministries of the Holy Spirit. I believe baptism is a one-time event that takes place at the moment of conversion (1 Corinthians 12:13). If baptism did not happen at the moment of conversion, some believers wouldn't belong to the body of Christ, even though they would still be saved. I say this because it is the baptism of the Holy Spirit that joins a believer to the body of Christ.

By contrast, the filling of the Holy Spirit is not a onetime event. In fact, God desires that the filling be a continual and ongoing experience for us. In Ephesians 5:18 we are instructed, "Do not get drunk with wine, for that is debauchery, but be filled with the Spirit." The word *filled* in this verse is a present-tense imperative in the Greek.

The present tense means that it should be a perpetual, ongoing experience. The imperative means it is a command from God. Being "filled" with the Spirit is not presented as a simple option but is a divine imperative for Christians. Being "filled" with the Spirit involves being *controlled* by the Spirit. Instead of being controlled by wine and the things of this world, we are to be under the perpetual control of the Spirit.

What does the Bible say about speaking in tongues? Is this a gift I should be seeking?

The Holy Spirit is the one who bestows spiritual gifts on believers (1 Corinthians 12:11). Not every Christian has every gift. So I think Christians should be happy with whatever gift the Holy Spirit has sovereignly decided to give them.

We might glean a number of facts from Scripture about speaking in tongues:

Speaking in tongues is not the definitive evidence of the baptism of the Holy Spirit. Not all the Corinthians spoke in tongues (1 Corinthians 14:5), though all had been baptized (12:13).

The fruit of the Holy Spirit (Galatians 5:22-23) does not include speaking in tongues. Therefore, Christlikeness does not require speaking in tongues.

Most of the New Testament writers are silent on tongues. Only three books—Acts, 1 Corinthians, and Mark—mention it. (Note: Mark 16:17 is not in the two best Greek manuscripts.) Significantly, many of the other New Testament books speak a great deal about the Holy Spirit, but fail to even mention speaking in tongues.

God has given more important gifts than tongues, and believers should seek them (1 Corinthians 12:28,31).

Personally, I think people often make too big a deal out of speaking in tongues.

What is the difference between natural talents and spiritual gifts?

There are a number of key differences. Natural talents are from God, but parents transmit them to their children. Spiritual gifts come directly from God (Romans 12:3,6; 1 Corinthians 12:4). Natural talents are possessed from the moment of birth. Spiritual gifts are received when one becomes a Christian. Natural talents are generally used to benefit human beings on the natural level. Spiritual gifts bring spiritual blessing to people (1 Corinthians 12:11; Ephesians 4:11-13).

There are similarities as well. Both talents and spiritual gifts must be developed and exercised. Otherwise one will not become proficient in their use. Also, both natural talents and spiritual gifts can be used for God's glory. For example, a Christian might have the spiritual gift of teaching. He might also have the natural talent of being able to play the guitar. This person could feasibly exercise his spiritual gift of teaching by writing and performing songs that teach about God.

Is the practice of being "slain in the spirit" a biblical practice?

I don't think it is. The term is not in the Bible. In fact, neither is the experience.

I'm not saying that there are no examples in Scripture of human beings falling to their knees as they witness the incredible glory of God. This is what happened to the apostle John (Revelation 1). But this idea of being touched by a human being who is "anointed" by the Spirit and then being knocked cold is not a biblical phenomenon.

How are we to explain such experiences? It may be a psychological or emotional phenomenon. Someone may so strongly expect to be knocked cold by the Spirit thought to be present in the "anointed" preacher that when the preacher touches him or her, down he or she goes. (Sociologists have noted that this type of experience is actually common to many religions.) The powers of darkness may also be involved in this experience (see 2 Thessalonians 2:9).

Many who believe in this phenomenon like to cite certain passages in its support, such as Genesis 15:12-21, Numbers 24:4, 1 Samuel 19:20, and Matthew 17:6. But in every case they are reading their own meaning *into* the text instead of drawing the meaning *out of* the text. These passages in context offer virtually no support for the idea of being slain in the spirit.

What is the sin against the Holy Spirit (Matthew 12:31-32)?

Matthew 12:31-32 says, "Therefore I tell you, every sin and blasphemy will be forgiven people, but the blasphemy against the Spirit will not be forgiven. And whoever speaks a word against the Son of Man will be forgiven, but whoever speaks against the Holy Spirit will not be forgiven, either in this age or in the age to come."

The backdrop to this passage is that the Jews who had just witnessed a mighty miracle of Christ should have recognized that Jesus performed this miracle in the power of the Holy Spirit. After all, the Hebrew Scriptures, with which the Jews were well familiar, prophesied that when the

Messiah came He would perform many mighty miracles in the power of the Spirit (see Isaiah 35:5-6). Instead, these Jewish leaders claimed that Christ did this and other miracles in the power of the devil, the unholy spirit. This was a sin against the Holy Spirit. This shows that these Jewish leaders had hardened themselves against the things of God.

I believe that Matthew 12 describes a unique situation among the Jews, and that the actual committing of this sin requires the presence of the Messiah on the earth doing His messianic miracles. In view of this, I don't think this sin can be duplicated today exactly as described in Matthew 12.

I think it's also important to realize that a human being can repent of his or her personal sins (whatever they are) and turn to God as long as there is breath still left in his or her lungs. Until the moment of death, every human being has the opportunity to turn to God and receive the free gift of salvation (Ephesians 2:8-9).

Part 4

Questions About Jesus

11
The Humanity of Jesus

What does the name "Jesus" mean?

The angel's pronouncement that Mary's child would be called Jesus (Luke 1:31) is full of meaning. *Jesus* means "the Lord saves" or "the Lord is salvation" (or, more literally, "Yahweh saves" or "Yahweh is salvation"). This name is the counterpart of the Old Testament name "Joshua," who led Israel out of the wilderness experience into a new land and a new life. Jesus the Savior leads us out of our spiritual wilderness experience into a new sphere of existence and a new life of fellowship with God.

What is the theological significance of Matthew's genealogy of Christ (Matthew 1:1-16)?

Matthew's genealogy traces Joseph's line of descendants and deals with the passing of the legal title to the throne of David:

David ➜ Solomon ➜ Jehoikim ➜ Coniah ➜ Joseph ➜ Jesus

As Joseph's adopted son, Jesus became his legal heir so far as his inheritance was concerned. The "of whom" in the phrase "of whom Jesus was born" (Matthew 1:16) is a feminine relative pronoun, clearly indicating that Jesus was the physical child of Mary and that Joseph was not His physical father.

Matthew traced the line from Abraham and David in 39 links to Joseph. Matthew obviously did not list every individual in the genealogy. Jewish reckoning did not require every name in order to satisfy a genealogy.

Abraham and David were the recipients of the two unconditional covenants pertaining to the Messiah. Matthew's Gospel was written to Jews, so Matthew wanted to prove to Jews that Jesus was the promised Messiah. This would demand a fulfillment of the Abrahamic covenant (Genesis 12) and the Davidic covenant (2 Samuel 7). Matthew was calling attention to the fact that Jesus came to fulfill the covenants made with Israel's forefathers.

What is the theological significance of Luke's genealogy of Christ (Luke 3:23-38)?

Luke's genealogy traces Mary's lineage and carries all the way back beyond the time of Abraham to Adam and the commencement of the human race. Whereas Matthew's genealogy pointed to Jesus as the Jewish Messiah, Luke's genealogy points to Jesus as the Son of Man, a name often used of Jesus in Luke's Gospel. Whereas Matthew's genealogy was concerned with the Messiah as related to the Jews, Luke's genealogy was concerned with the Messiah as related to the entire human race.

Did Jesus, who is eternal God, become fully man?

Yes. To deny either the undiminished deity *or* the perfect humanity of Christ is to put oneself outside the pale of orthodoxy (see 1 John 4:2-3). Innumerable passages in the New Testament confirm Christ's full humanity. For example, Hebrews 2:14 tells us that "since therefore the children share in flesh and blood, he himself likewise partook of the same things, that through death he might destroy the one who has the power of death, that is, the devil." Romans 8:3 says that God sent Jesus "in the likeness of sinful flesh" to be a sin offering. The apostle Paul affirms that "in him the whole fullness of deity dwells bodily" (Colossians 2:9).

Though Jesus never surrendered any aspect of His deity in the incarnation, He experienced normal human development through infancy, childhood, adolescence, and into adulthood. According to Luke 2:40, Jesus "grew," "became strong," and was "filled with wisdom." These are things that could never be said of His divine nature. It was in His humanity that He grew, became strong, and became filled with wisdom.

Likewise, Luke 2:52 tells us that "Jesus increased in wisdom and in stature and in favor with God and man." Again, Jesus' growth in wisdom and stature is something that can only be said of His humanity.

Was Christ in His human nature different in any respect from other humans?

Christ's development as a human being was normal in every respect, with two major exceptions: Christ always did the will of God and He never sinned. As Hebrews 4:15 puts it, in Christ "we do not have a high priest who is unable to sympathize with our weaknesses, but one who in every respect has been tempted as we are, yet without sin." Christ is "holy," "innocent," and "unstained" (Hebrews 7:26). Therefore, though Christ is utterly sinless, His human nature was exactly the same as ours in every other respect.

How can we answer the claim of some critics that some events in the New Testament, such as the virgin birth, are rooted in pagan mythology?

Greek mythology taught that the Greek male gods came down to have sex with human women and gave birth to hybrid beings. This bears no resemblance to the virgin birth. When the Holy Spirit overshadowed Mary (Luke 1:35), it was specifically to produce a human nature within her womb for the *eternal* Son of God to step into, after which He was born nine months later.

Many alleged similarities between Christianity and the Greek pagan religions are either greatly exaggerated or fabricated. For example, some critics often describe pagan rituals in language they borrowed from Christianity, thereby making them *falsely appear* to be "parallel" doctrines.

Further, the chronology for such claims is all wrong. It must not be uncritically assumed that the pagan religions always influenced Christianity, for it is not only possible but probable that the influence often moved in the opposite direction. It is understandable that leaders of pagan cults that were challenged by Christianity would seek to counter the challenge by offering a pagan substitute.

Unlike mythical accounts, the New Testament accounts are based on eyewitness testimony. In 2 Peter 1:16 we read, "We did not follow cleverly devised myths when we made known to you the power and coming of our Lord Jesus Christ, but we were eyewitnesses of his majesty."

Why was the virgin birth necessary?

I can think of at least four reasons why the virgin birth was necessary: (1) By the virgin birth, God kept Jesus from possessing a sin nature from Joseph (see 2 Corinthians 5:21; 1 Peter 2:22-24; Hebrews 4:15; 7:26). (2) The Old Testament makes clear that Jesus had to be both God *and* man as the Messiah (see Isaiah 7:14; 9:6). This could only be fulfilled through the virgin birth. (3) Related to the above, Jesus is our Kinsman-Redeemer. In Old Testament times the next of kin (one related *by blood*) always functioned as the kinsman-redeemer of a family member who needed redemption from jail. Jesus became related to us *by blood* so He could function as our Kinsman-Redeemer and rescue us from sin. This required the virgin birth. (4) The virgin birth was necessary in view of the messianic prediction in Genesis 3:15. (Jesus was predicted to come from the "seed of the woman.")

What was the "star" the magi saw when Christ was born (Matthew 2:2,7,9)?

Many scholars have debated what this "star" was. I think a good argument can be made that it was a manifestation of the *Shekinah* (a Hebrew term theologians use to refer to God's presence) glory of God. Recall that this same glory had led the children of Israel through the wilderness for 40 years as a pillar of fire and a cloud (Exodus 13:21). Perhaps this "fire," manifest high in the earth's atmosphere, having the appearance of a large star from the vantage point of the earth's surface, led the magi to Christ.

The likelihood of the "star" being the Shekinah glory is supported by the fact that it would have been impossible for a single star or a confluence of stars in the stellar heavens to single out an individual dwelling in the village of Bethlehem. Only if the light of the "star" were similar to the pillar of fire that led Israel in the desert could the house be positively identified. Upon entering the house specified by the "star," the magi "saw the child with Mary his mother" (Matthew 2:11).

In what sense did Christ "make himself nothing" in the incarnation (Philippians 2:6-11)? Did He give up some or all of His divine attributes?

Christ did not give up any attributes. When He "emptied Himself" (Philippians 2:7 NASB), Jesus never *surrendered* His glory (recall the Mount of Transfiguration—Matthew 17). Rather, Jesus *veiled* His glory in order to dwell among mortal human beings.

Had Christ *not* veiled His preincarnate glory, humankind would not have been able to behold Him. It would have been the same as when the apostle John beheld the exalted Christ in His glory: "When I saw him, I fell at his feet as though dead" (Revelation 1:17).

Also, Christ could never have actually surrendered any of His attributes, for then He would have ceased to be God. But He could (and did) voluntarily choose not to use some of them on some occasions during His time on the earth in order to live among human beings and their limitations (for example, see Matthew 24:36).

During His three-year ministry, Jesus did in fact use the divine attributes of *omniscience*, knowing everything (John 2:24; 16:30); *omnipresence*, being everywhere (John 1:48); and *omnipotence*, being all-powerful (John 11). Therefore, whatever limitations Christ may have suffered when He "made himself nothing" (Philippians 2:7), He did not subtract a single divine attribute or in any sense make Himself less than God. He merely chose not to use them on some occasions.

Christ condescended by taking on the likeness (literally "form" or "appearance") of a man, and taking on the form ("very nature") of a bondservant. Christ was thus truly human. He was subject to temptation, distress, weakness, pain, sorrow, and limitation. But note that the word "likeness" suggests *similarity but difference.* "Though His humanity was genuine, He was different from all other humans in that He was sinless."[1]

How can two natures—a divine nature and a human nature—be united in the one person of Jesus Christ?

To answer this, we must first understand what a "nature" is. The word *nature*, when used of Christ's divinity, refers to all that belongs to deity, including all the attributes of deity. When used of Christ's humanity, *nature* refers to all that belongs to humanity, including all the attributes of humanity.

Though Jesus in the incarnation had both a human and a divine nature, He was only one person—as indicated by His consistent use of *I*, *Me*, and *Mine* in reference to Himself. Jesus never used the words *us*, *we*, or *ours* in reference to His human-divine person. The divine nature of Christ never carried on a verbal conversation with His human nature.

Did Jesus in the incarnation have contradictory qualities?

One of the most complex aspects of the relationship of Christ's two natures is that, while the attributes of one nature are never attributed to the other, the attributes of both natures are properly attributed to His one person. Thus Christ at the same moment in time had what seemed to be contradictory qualities.

Christ was finite and yet infinite, weak and yet omnipotent, increasing in knowledge and yet omniscient, limited to being in one place at one time and yet omnipresent. In the incarnation, the person of Christ is the partaker of the attributes of both natures, so that whatever may be affirmed of either nature—human or divine—may be affirmed of the one person.

Did Christ manifest both human and divine attributes during His three-year ministry?

Yes. Christ sometimes operated in the sphere of His humanity and in other cases in the sphere of His deity. Christ in His human nature knew hunger (Luke 4:2), weariness (John 4:6), and the need for sleep (Luke 8:23). Christ in His divine nature was omniscient (John 2:24), omnipresent (John 1:48), and omnipotent (John 11). *And all of this was experienced by the one person of Jesus Christ.*

Does Christ's human-divine union last forever?

Yes. When Christ became a man in the incarnation, He did not enter into a temporary union of the human and divine natures in one person that ended at His death and resurrection. Instead, the Scriptures make clear that Christ's human nature continues forever.

Christ's human body, which died on the cross, was transformed into a *resurrected* human body suited to His glorious existence in heaven. When Christ ascended into heaven, He ascended in His glorified human body, as witnessed by several of His disciples (Acts 1:9). When Christ returns, He will return as the "Son of Man"—a title which points to His humanity (Matthew 26:64). In the incarnation, then, Jesus permanently became the God-man.

Could Christ have sinned as a human being?

No, I don't believe so. This is known as the impeccability of Christ. The God-man, Christ, could not have sinned because in His divine nature, He does not change. He is omniscient, knowing all the consequences of sin. And He is omnipotent in His ability to resist sin. Also, Hebrews 4:15 tells us that He was tempted yet was *without* sin, and Luke 1:35 shows us that He had no sin nature like all other human beings and was perfectly holy from birth.

Also, consider this analogy between the written Word of God (the Bible) and the living Word of God (Christ): Just as the Bible has both human and divine elements and is completely without error, so Christ is fully divine and fully human and is completely without the ability to sin.

Does this mean that Christ's temptations were unreal? No. Christ was genuinely tempted, but the temptations stood no chance of luring Christ to sin. It is much like a canoe trying to attack a U.S. battleship. The attack is genuine, but it stands no chance of success.

I believe the reason Christ went through the temptation experience with the devil (Matthew 4) was not to see whether He could be made to sin, but to *prove* that He *could not* be made to sin. In fact, some theologians have suggested that Christ was the aggressor in this encounter. The devil may have hoped to avoid the encounter altogether. After 40 days in the wilderness, at the height of Christ's weakness from a human standpoint, the devil gave it his best shot in tempting Christ. The devil was unsuccessful.

12
Jesus and the Father: Equally Divine

Is Proverbs 8:22-23 referring to Jesus, and if so, does this mean Jesus is a created being?

Proverbs 8:22-23 says, "The Lord possessed me at the beginning of his work, the first of his acts of old. Ages ago I was set up, at the first, before the beginning of the earth." This passage does not refer to Jesus. Such an interpretation not only violates the context of the book of Proverbs—it also violates the whole of Scripture.

Note that the first nine chapters of Proverbs deal with wisdom personified. A personification is a rhetorical figure of speech that endows inanimate objects or abstractions with human qualities and represents them as possessing human form. In Proverbs 1–9, wisdom is figuratively endowed with human qualities.

With this in mind, it is critical to note that the text never indicates that Proverbs 8 should be taken any differently than chapters 1–7 and 9. If we take Proverbs 8:22-23 to be speaking literally about Christ, we must also assume that Christ is a woman crying in the streets (1:20-21) who lives with someone named "Prudence" (8:12).[1] Proverbs 1–9 makes no sense if one tries to read Christ into the text.

Proverbs 8:22-23 is simply speaking metaphorically of God's eternal wisdom and how it was "brought forth" (verse 24) to take part in the creation of the universe. Proverbs 8 is not saying that wisdom came into being at a point in time (for God has always had wisdom). And it certainly is not saying that Jesus is a created being. After all, the passage is not dealing with Jesus but with wisdom personified.

Does the fact that Jesus is called a "Mighty God" in Isaiah 9:6 mean He is a lesser God than "God Almighty" (the Father)?

No. Jesus is indeed called "Mighty God" in Isaiah 9:6. But in the very next chapter—Isaiah 10:21—Yahweh Himself is called "Mighty God" (using the same Hebrew phrase, *El Gibbor*). The fact that Yahweh is called "Mighty God" demonstrates that this phrase cannot refer to a lesser deity than "Almighty God" Himself. Because Jesus is also called "Mighty God," Jesus is clearly equal with God the Father.

Isaiah wasn't teaching that there are two mighty Gods in heaven, right?

Right! While both the Father (Isaiah 10:21) and Jesus (9:6) are called "Mighty God" in the book of Isaiah, there is only one God. God Himself is often quoted in Isaiah as saying, "I am the first and I am the last; besides me there is no God" (Isaiah 44:6). He also asks, "Is there a God besides me? There is no Rock; I know not any" (Isaiah 44:8). He affirms, "I am the LORD, and there is no other, besides me there is no God" (Isaiah 45:5).

The fact that both the Father and Jesus are "mighty God" should be understood within the context of the Trinity. That is, there is one God, but within the unity of the one God are three coequal and coeternal persons, the Father, the Son, and the Holy Spirit. Each of the three is equally God, but they are distinct in personhood.

Was Jesus implying that He was not good in Mark 10:17-18? Is this an argument against His deity?

In Mark 10:17-18 we read of Jesus, "As he was setting out on his journey, a man ran up and knelt before him and asked him, 'Good Teacher, what must I do to inherit eternal life?' And Jesus said to him, 'Why do you call me good? No one is good except God alone.'"

In this passage, Jesus was not claiming that He wasn't "good." Nor was He denying that He was God to the young ruler asking the question. Rather, Jesus was asking the man to examine the implications of what he was saying. In effect, Jesus said, "Do you realize what you are saying when you call Me 'good'? Are you saying I am God?" Jesus' response was not a denial of His deity but was rather a veiled claim to it.

Does the fact that Jesus said no one knows the day or hour of His return except the Father mean that He is less than God Almighty (Mark 13:32)?

No. But explaining this issue requires a little theological background. Though a bit complex, the eternal Son of God was, prior to the incarnation, *one* in person and nature (wholly divine). In the incarnation, He became *two* in nature (divine and human) while remaining *one person.*

Thus, as noted previously, Christ at the same moment in time had what seemed to be contradictory qualities. He was finite and yet infinite, weak and yet omnipotent, increasing in knowledge and yet omniscient, limited to being in one place at one time and yet omnipresent. *It was only from His humanity that Christ could say that He didn't know the day or hour of His return.* In His humanity, Jesus was not omniscient but was limited in understanding just as all human beings are. If Jesus had been speaking from the perspective of His divinity, He wouldn't have said the same thing.

How do we know Christ was omniscient?

Scripture is abundantly clear that in His divine nature, Jesus is omniscient—just as omniscient as the Father is. The apostle John said that Jesus "needed no one to bear witness about man, for he himself knew what was in man" (John 2:25). Jesus' disciples said, "Now we know that you know all things" (16:30). After the resurrection, when Jesus asked Peter for the third time if Peter loved Him, Peter responded, "Lord, you know everything; you know that I love you" (21:17).

Jesus knew just where the fish were in the water (Luke 5:4-6; John

21:6-11), and He knew just which fish contained the coin (Matthew 17:27). He knows the Father as the Father knows Him (Matthew 11:27; John 7:29; 8:55; 10:15; 17:25).

Does John 1:1 in the Greek say Jesus is God, or does it say He is merely "a god"?

This verse teaches that Jesus is God. To translate this verse as "The Word [Christ] was *a* god" is to make the worst kind of error—a denial of the deity of Christ. (This is how the Jehovah's Witnesses translate the verse.)[2]

The full deity of Christ is supported by other references in John (8:58; 10:30; 20:28). Passages in other books of the New Testament also affirm His deity (Colossians 1:15-16; 2:9; Titus 2:13; Hebrews 1:8).

Moreover, if a Greek noun does not have a definite article before it, it is not necessarily indefinite. In other words, *theos* ("God") without the definite article *ho* ("the"), as is the case in John 1:1, does not need to be translated as "a god" as the Jehovah's Witnesses have done in reference to Christ.

It is significant that *theos* without the definite article *ho* is used of Yahweh-God in the New Testament (Luke 20:38). The word *theos* in Luke 20:38 in reference to Yahweh lacks the definite article, but that does not mean He is a lesser God. The word *theos* in John 1:1 in reference to Jesus also lacks the definite article, but that does not mean that He is a lesser God either. The fact is, the presence or absence of the definite article does not alter the fundamental meaning of *theos*.

We might also note that some New Testament texts *do* use the definite article and speak of Christ as "the God" (*ho theos*). One example of this is John 20:28, where Thomas said to Jesus, "My Lord and my God." The verse reads literally from the Greek, "The Lord of me and the God [*ho theos*] of me" (see also Matthew 1:23 and Hebrews 1:8). So it does not matter whether John did or *did not* use the definite article in John 1:1—the Bible clearly teaches that Jesus *is* God, not just *a* god.

Does the fact that Jesus is called God's "only begotten Son" prove that Jesus is not God (John 3:16 KJV)?

No. The words "only begotten" do not mean that Christ was *created* (as the ancient heretic Arius taught). Rather, it means "unique" or "one of a kind." Reformed scholar Benjamin Warfield comments, "The adjective 'only begotten' conveys the idea, not of derivation and subordination, but of uniqueness and consubstantiality: Jesus is all that God is, and He alone is this."[3] Jesus is the "Son of God" in the sense that He has the same nature as the Father—a *divine* nature. Whenever Christ claimed to be the Son of God in the New Testament, His Jewish critics tried to stone Him because they correctly understood Him as claiming to be God (see John 5:18).

What did Jesus mean when He said the Father is "greater" than He (John 14:28)?

In John 14:28 Jesus said, "If you loved me, you would have rejoiced, because I am going to the Father, for the Father is greater than I." Jesus is not speaking in this verse about His nature or His essential being. Christ had earlier said "I and the Father are one" in this regard (John 10:30). Instead, He is speaking of His lowly position in the incarnation.[4] The Athanasian Creed affirms that Christ is "equal to the Father as touching his Godhood and inferior to the Father as touching his manhood."[5]

The Father was seated upon the throne of highest majesty in heaven. The brightness of His glory was uneclipsed as He was surrounded by hosts of holy beings perpetually worshipping Him with uninterrupted praise. Far different was it with His incarnate Son—despised and rejected of men, surrounded by implacable enemies, and soon to be nailed to a criminal's cross. It is from this perspective that Jesus could say that the Father is "greater" than He.

Does the fact that Jesus made reference to "my God" (John 20:17) prove that He Himself is not God?

By no means! Prior to the incarnation, Christ, the second person of the Trinity, had only a divine nature. But in the incarnation Christ took on a human nature. In the context of John 20, it would appear that it was in His humanity that Christ acknowledged the Father as "my God." Positionally speaking as a man, as a Jew, and as our high priest ("made like his brothers in every respect," Hebrews 2:17), Jesus could address the Father as "my God."

Even if Jesus were speaking from the perspective of His deity, however, His affirmation of the Father's Godhood presents no theological problem. After all, the Father conversely referred to Jesus as "O God" (Hebrews 1:8). We must understand all of this in the broader context of the Trinity.

In what sense is God the "head" of Christ (1 Corinthians 11:3)?

In 1 Corinthians 11:3 we read, "I want you to understand that the head of every man is Christ, the head of a wife is her husband, and the head of Christ is God." A close examination of this verse shows that it has nothing to do with inferiority or superiority of one person over another. Instead, it has to do with patterns of authority.

Notice that Paul says the man is the head of the woman, even though men and women are utterly equal in their essential nature. Men and women are both human and are both created in God's image (Genesis 1:26-28). Also, they are said to be "one" in Christ (Galatians 3:28). These verses, taken with 1 Corinthians 11:3, show us that *equality of being* and *authority structures* are not mutually exclusive.

In the same way, Christ and the Father are utterly equal in their divine being (Jesus said "I and the Father are one"— John 10:30). Yet, Jesus is under the Father's authority (1 Corinthians 11:3). There is thus no contradiction in affirming both an *equality of being* and *an authority structure* among the persons in the Godhead.

Does the fact that Jesus is called the "firstborn" mean He is a created being (Colossians 1:15)?

No. The word for "firstborn" in this context does not mean "first created." Rather, as Greek scholars agree, the Greek word translated as "firstborn," *prototokos*, means "first in rank, preeminent one, heir."[6] The word carries the idea of positional preeminence and supremacy. Christ is the "firstborn of creation" in the sense that He is positionally preeminent over creation and is supreme over all things.

The ancient Hebrews used their equivalent term for "firstborn" to refer to the son in the family who was in the preeminent position, regardless of whether or not that son was literally the first son born to the parents. This "firstborn" son would not only be the preeminent one in the family—he would also be the heir to a double portion of the family inheritance.

The life of David illustrates this meaning of *firstborn*. David was the youngest (*last-born*) son of Jesse. Nevertheless, Psalm 89:27 says of him, "I will make him the firstborn, the highest of the kings of the earth." Though David was the *last* one born in Jesse's family, he is called the "firstborn" because of the preeminent position God was placing him in.[7]

If Paul had meant "first created," he would not have called Christ the "firstborn" (*prototokos*) but the "first-created" (*protoktisis*)—a term that is *never* used of Christ in the New Testament.[8] Indeed, as scholar J.B. Lightfoot notes, "The fathers of the fourth century rightly called attention to the fact that the Apostle writes not *protoktisis* ['first-created'], but *prototokos* ['firstborn']."[9] Christ is preeminent over all creation!

Some say Christ is a created being because He is called "the beginning of God's creation" in Revelation 3:14. How can we respond to this idea?

The Greek word *arche*, often translated "beginning" in Revelation 3:14, has a wide range of meaning. Though *arche* can mean "beginning," the word is truly unique and also carries the important active meaning of "one who begins," "origin," "source," "creator," or "first cause." Evangelical scholars agree that this is the intended meaning of the word in Revelation 3:14.[10]

The authoritative *Greek-English Lexicon of the New Testament and Other Early Christian Literature* says the meaning of *arche* in Revelation

3:14 is "first cause."[11] Indeed, in Revelation 3:14 *arche* is used to refer to "the active beginning of the creation, the One who caused the creation, referring to Jesus Christ not as a created being, but the One who created all things (John 1:3)."[12] The English word *architect* is derived from *arche*. We might say that Jesus is the architect of all creation.

Notably, the only other two times *arche* is used in the book of Revelation, it is used of God as "the *beginning* and the end" (Revelation 21:6; 22:13).[13] Certainly the use of *arche* with God Almighty does not mean that He had a created beginning. Instead, these verses communicate the idea that God is both the *beginner* and the *consummation* of creation. He is the *first cause* of creation—He is its *final goal*.[14] The word *arche* is used in the same sense in Revelation 3:14.

Therefore, we can say that according to Revelation 3:14, Christ is the *beginner* of God's creation (see also John 1:3; Colossians 1:16; Hebrews 1:2).

Evidence for the Deity of Christ

Are the names of deity ascribed to Christ?

Yes. One very good verse to illustrate this is Isaiah 40:3, which contains a prophecy: "In the wilderness prepare the way of the LORD [Yahweh]; make straight in the desert a highway for our God [Elohim]." Mark's Gospel tells us that Isaiah's words were fulfilled in the ministry of John the Baptist preparing the way for Jesus Christ (Mark 1:2-4), relating the divine names of Yahweh and Elohim to Jesus Christ. Elsewhere in the New Testament, Jesus is also called "Lord" (Romans 10:13) and "God" (John 20:28; Titus 2:13). According to Colossians 2:9, "the whole fullness of deity dwells bodily" in Christ. Therefore, the Bible clearly ascribes divinity to Christ.

Is the divine name "I am" ascribed to Christ?

Yes. During a confrontation Jesus had with a group of hostile Jews, someone in the group said to him, "Abraham died, as did the prophets, yet you say, 'If anyone keeps my word, he will never taste death.' Are you greater than our father Abraham, who died?" (John 8:52-53).

Jesus responded, "Your father Abraham rejoiced that he would see my day. He saw it and was glad" (verse 56). The Jews mockingly replied, "You are not yet fifty years old, and have you seen Abraham?" (verse 57). Jesus then replied, "Truly, truly, I say to you, before Abraham was, I am" (verse 58).

The Jews immediately picked up stones with the intention of killing Jesus, for they recognized He was identifying Himself as Yahweh ("I

AM"). The Jews were acting on the prescribed penalty for blasphemy in Old Testament Law: death by stoning (Leviticus 24:16).

We find further evidence for Jesus' identity as the great "I AM" in the Septuagint. (The Septuagint is a Greek translation of the Hebrew Old Testament that predates Christ.) It renders the Hebrew phrase for "I AM" (God's name) in Exodus 3:14 as *ego eimi*. On a number of occasions in the Greek New Testament, Jesus used this term as a way of identifying Himself as God. For example, in John 8:24 Jesus declared, "Unless you believe that I am [*ego eimi*] he you will die in your sins." The original Greek for this verse does not have the word *he*. The verse literally reads, "Unless you believe that *I am*, you will die in your sins."

Does Christ's role as Creator of the universe constitute a proof of His deity?

Yes. As a backdrop, Yahweh affirmed in Isaiah 44:24, "I am the LORD [Yahweh], who made all things, who *alone* stretched out the heavens, who spread out the earth *by myself*." The fact that Yahweh says, "I...made all things [and] spread out the earth by myself" (Isaiah 44:24) is significant, for the New Testament affirms that Christ Himself is the Creator of "all things" (John 1:3; Colossians 1:16). This proves that Christ is God Almighty.

Does Christ's role as Savior point to His deity?

Yes. As a backdrop, in Isaiah 43:11 God asserts, "I, I am the LORD [Yahweh], and *besides me there is no savior*." This is an extremely important verse, for it indicates that (1) a claim to be Savior is, in itself, a claim to deity, and (2) only one Savior exists—God.

Against this backdrop, it is truly revealing of Christ's divine nature that the New Testament refers to Jesus as the Savior. Following the birth of Christ, an angel appeared to some neighboring shepherds and informed them of the birth of the divine Savior (Luke 2:11). Jesus is truly "our great God and Savior" (Titus 2:13).

Does Jesus have the glory of Yahweh?

No question about it. As a backdrop, in Isaiah 6:1-5 the prophet recounts his vision of Yahweh "sitting upon a throne, high and lifted up" (verse 1). The seraphim angels are portrayed as singing to one another, "Holy, holy, holy is the LORD of hosts; the whole earth is full of his glory" (verse 3). Isaiah also quotes Yahweh as saying: "I am the LORD [*Yahweh*]; that is my name; my glory I give to no other" (Isaiah 42:8).

Later, the apostle John—under the inspiration of the Holy Spirit—affirmed that Isaiah actually saw Jesus' glory (John 12:41). Yahweh's glory and Jesus' glory are equated. We also witness the glory of Jesus during His earthly ministry on the mount of transfiguration (Matthew 17:1-3) as well as following His resurrection in heaven (Revelation 1:14-16).

Will we witness Jesus' divine glory in the afterlife?

Yes indeed. As a backdrop, Yahweh in the Old Testament is described as "your everlasting light," one that would make the sun, moon, and stars obsolete (Isaiah 60:19-20). Jesus will do the same for the future eternal city in which the saints will dwell forever: "The city has no need of sun or moon to shine on it, for the glory of God gives it light, and its lamp is the Lamb" (Revelation 21:23).

How can Christ as the "crucified One" be God?

Zechariah 12:10 gives us great insight on this. In fact, in this verse Yahweh is speaking prophetically: "When they look on me, on him whom they have pierced, they shall mourn for him…" Though Yahweh is speaking, this is obviously a reference to Christ's future crucifixion. We know that "him whom they have pierced" is Jesus, for He is described this same way by the apostle John: "Every eye will see him, *even those who pierced him*" (Revelation 1:7).

Jesus died on the cross as the God-man, who was 100 percent God and 100 percent man. That's the miracle of the incarnation.

Does the fact that Christ is the giver of life indicate His deity?

It most certainly does! Psalm 119 reveals about a dozen times that it is Yahweh alone who gives and preserves life. But in the New Testament, Jesus claims this power for Himself: "As the Father raises the dead and gives them life, so also the Son gives life to whom he will" (John 5:21; see also 14:6; 1 John 5:12).

Does Jesus' title as "Son of God" point to His deity?

Absolutely! Perhaps no name or title of Christ has been so misunderstood as this one. Some have taken the term to mean that Christ came into existence at a point in time and that He is in some way inferior to the Father. Some believe that since Christ is the Son of God, He cannot possibly be God in the same sense as the Father.

Such an understanding is based on a faulty conception of what "son of" meant among the ancients. Though the term *can* refer to "offspring of," it carries the more important meaning "of the order of."[1] The phrase is often used this way in the Old Testament. For example, *sons of the prophets* meant "of the order of prophets" (1 Kings 20:35). *Sons of the singers* meant "of the order of singers" (Nehemiah 12:28). Likewise, the phrase *Son of God* means "of the order of God," and represents a claim to undiminished deity.

Ancient Semitics and Orientals used the phrase *son of* to indicate likeness or sameness of nature and equality of being.[2] Therefore, when Jesus claimed to be the Son of God, His Jewish contemporaries fully understood that He was making a claim to be God in an unqualified sense. Indeed, the Jews insisted, "We have a law, and according to that law he ought to die because he has made himself the Son of God" (John 19:7; see also 5:18). Recognizing that Jesus was identifying Himself *as* God, the Jews wanted to kill Him for committing blasphemy.

Is Christ's Sonship an eternal Sonship?

Yes. Scripture indicates that Christ's Sonship is an *eternal* Sonship (see Psalm 2:7).[3] It is one thing to say that Jesus *became* the Son of

God. It is another thing altogether to say that He was *always* the Son of God. We must recognize that if there was a time when the Son was not the Son, then—to be consistent—there was also a time when the Father was not the Father. If the first person's designation as "Father" is an eternal title, then the second person's designation as "Son" must be so regarded.

Clear evidence for Christ's eternal Sonship is found in the fact that Christ is represented as *already being* the Son of God before His birth in Bethlehem. For instance, recall Jesus' discussion with Nicodemus in John 3. Jesus said, "God so loved the world, that he *gave* his only Son, that whoever believes in him should not perish but have eternal life. For God did not *send* his Son *into* the world to condemn the world, but in order that the world might be saved through him" (John 3:16-17). That Christ—as the Son of God—was *sent into* the world implies that He was the Son of God *before* the incarnation.

Further evidence for Christ's eternal Sonship is found in the fact that Hebrews 1:2 says God created the universe *through* His "Son"— implying that Christ was the Son of God prior to the Creation. Moreover, Christ *as* the Son is explicitly said to have existed "before all things" (Colossians 1:17; compare with verses 13-14). Also, Jesus, speaking *as* the Son of God (John 8:54-56), asserts His eternal preexistence before Abraham (verse 58).

What is the significance of Jesus pronouncing people's sins forgiven?

This act shows that Christ perceived Himself as God. We see this illustrated in Mark 2, where a paralytic was lowered through a roof by his friends in order to get close to Jesus in hopes of a healing. The first thing Jesus said to the paralytic was, "My son, your sins are forgiven" (Mark 2:5).

Upon first reading, such words seem out of place. But further investigation indicates that Jesus was making an important statement. Jesus knew that all those present were aware that only God could pronounce someone's sins as being forgiven. (In Isaiah 43:25, God said, "I, I am he who blots out your transgressions for my own sake, and I will not remember your sins.") So when Jesus said "your sins are forgiven," He was clearly placing Himself in the position of God.

The scribes that were present understood Jesus' words this way, for they reasoned, "Why does this man speak like that? He is blaspheming! Who can forgive sins but God alone?" (Mark 2:7). Of course, Jesus' subsequent healing of the paralytic served to substantiate His claim to be God.

Why did Jesus always say "Truly, truly I say to you" (see John 1:51, for example) instead of "Thus says the LORD," like the Old Testament prophets did (as in Isaiah 45:1)?

Jesus always presented His teachings as ultimate and final. He never wavered in this. He unflinchingly placed His teachings above those of Moses and the prophets—and in a Jewish culture at that! He always spoke in His own authority. He never said, "Thus says the LORD," as did the prophets; He always said, "Truly, truly I say to you..." He never retracted anything He said, never guessed or spoke with uncertainty, never made revisions, never contradicted Himself, and never apologized for what He said. He even said, "Heaven and earth will pass away, but my words will not pass away" (Mark 13:31), elevating His words directly to the realm of heaven.

Jesus' teachings had a profound effect on people. His listeners always seemed to surmise that these were not the words of an ordinary man. When Jesus taught in Capernaum on the Sabbath, the people "were astonished at his teaching, for his word possessed authority" (Luke 4:32). After the Sermon on the Mount, "the crowds were astonished at his teaching, for he was teaching them as one who had authority, and not as their scribes" (Matthew 7:28-29). When some Jewish leaders asked the temple guards why they hadn't arrested Jesus when He spoke, they responded: "No one ever spoke like this man" (John 7:46).

One cannot read the Gospels long before recognizing that Jesus regarded Himself and His message as inseparable. The reason Jesus' teachings had ultimate authority was because He was (is) God. The words of Jesus were the very words of God!

Was Jesus claiming deity when He said that He and the Father "are one" (John 10:30)?

Yes, I believe so. While the Greek word for "one" (*hen*) by itself does not have to refer to more than unity of purpose, the context of John 10 is clear that much more than this is meant in terms of Jesus and the Father. How do we know this? For one thing, the Jewish leaders immediately picked up stones to put Jesus to death. They understood Jesus to be claiming to be God in an unqualified sense. Indeed, according to verse 33, the Jews said, "It is not for a good work that we are going to stone you but for blasphemy, because you, being a man, make yourself God." The penalty for blasphemy, according to Old Testament law, is death by stoning.

Jesus didn't respond by saying, "Oh, no, you've got it all wrong. I wasn't claiming to be God. I was just claiming to have a unity of purpose." Even the Jews claimed to have a unity of purpose with God. They wouldn't have tried to stone Jesus for that. They understood Jesus as He *intended* to be understood—they understood Him to be claiming deity.

Was Jesus worshipped as deity in the New Testament?

Jesus Christ was worshipped (Greek: *proskuneo*) as God many times according to the Gospel accounts. Jesus accepted worship from Thomas (John 20:28), the angels (Hebrews 1:6), some wise men (Matthew 2:11), a leper (Matthew 8:2), a ruler (Matthew 9:18), a blind man (John 9:38), an anonymous woman (Matthew 15:25), the women at the tomb (Matthew 28:9), and the disciples (Matthew 28:17). All these verses—except John 20:28, which nevertheless clearly portrays Thomas as worshipping Jesus—contain the word *proskuneo*, the same word used of worshipping the Father in the New Testament.

Did Jesus ever attempt to stop or correct people from worshipping Him?

Not once! To make my point, consider that when Paul and Barnabas were in Lystra and miraculously healed a man by God's mighty power, those in the crowd shouted, "The gods have come down to us in the likeness of men" (Acts 14:11). When Paul and Barnabas perceived that the people were preparing to worship them, "they tore their garments and rushed out into the crowd, crying out, 'Men, why are you doing these things? We also are men, of like nature with you, and we bring you good news, that you should turn from these vain things to a living God, who made the heaven and the earth and the sea and all that is in them'" (verses 14-15). As soon as they perceived what was happening, they immediately corrected the gross misconception that they were gods.

Unlike Paul and Barnabas, Jesus never sought to correct His followers when they bowed down and worshipped Him. Indeed, Jesus considered such worship perfectly appropriate. Of course, we wouldn't expect Jesus to try to correct people in worshipping Him if He truly was God in the flesh, as He claimed to be. In keeping with this, it is highly revealing that in the book of Revelation God the Father (Revelation 4:10) and Jesus Christ (5:11-14) are portrayed as receiving *the exact same worship*.

What does Jesus' acceptance of worship reveal about what He thought of Himself?

The fact that Jesus willingly received (and condoned) worship on various occasions says a lot about what He thought of Himself, for it is the consistent testimony of Scripture that *only God* can be worshipped. Exodus 34:14 tells us, "You shall worship no other god, for the LORD, whose name is Jealous, is a jealous God" (compare with Deuteronomy 6:13; Matthew 4:10). In view of this, the fact that Jesus was worshipped on numerous occasions shows His full recognition of His identity as God Almighty.

14
Christ in the Old Testament

Is there a reference to Jesus as the "Son of God" in the Old Testament?

I believe so. Proverbs 30 was authored by a man named Agur. In the first four verses of this chapter, Agur reflects on humankind's inability to comprehend the infinite God. Because of this inability, Agur abases himself and humbly acknowledges his ignorance. Agur effectively communicates the idea that reverence for God is the beginning of true wisdom.

In verse 4, Agur's reflections are couched in terms of a series of questions. He asks, "Who has ascended to heaven and come down? Who has gathered the wind in his fists? Who has wrapped up the waters in a garment? Who has established all the ends of the earth? What is his name, and what is his son's name? Surely you know!"

Many scholars concede to the likelihood of this being an Old Testament reference to the first and second persons of the Trinity, the eternal Father and the eternal Son of God.[1] And it is highly significant that this portion of Scripture is not predictive prophecy speaking about a *future* Son of God. Rather, it speaks of the Father and the Son of God in *present-tense terms* during *Old Testament times*, exercising sovereign control over the world.

What is the case for Melchizedek being a preincarnate appearance of Christ in the Old Testament?

Those who argue that Melchizedek was a preincarnate appearance of Christ usually cite Hebrews 7:3 in support of this view: "He is without father or mother or genealogy, having neither beginning of days nor end of life, but resembling the Son of God he continues a priest forever." No human being, it is argued, can be without father or mother, without genealogy, or without beginning of days or end of life. Melchizedek was also a king and a priest, like Christ. So, they say, Melchizedek must have been an appearance of the preincarnate Christ.

What is the case against Melchizedek being a preincarnate appearance of Christ in the Old Testament?

Melchizedek is described in Scripture as *resembling* the Son of God, not as actually *being* the Son of God (Hebrews 7:3). It seems best to view Melchizedek as an actual historical person—a mere human being—who was a "type" of Christ. A type is someone (or something) that prophetically foreshadows someone (or something) else.

The reason some Old Testament persons or things foreshadow someone or something in the New Testament is that God planned it that way. In the revelatory process, God in His sovereignty so arranged the outworking of history that certain individuals, things, events, ceremonies, and institutions foreshadowed Christ in His person or ministry. This, I believe, is the case with Melchizedek.

The affirmation in Hebrews 7:3 that Melchizedek had no father or mother may be taken to mean that the Old Testament has *no record* of these events. In order to bring out this typical character of Melchizedek, the biblical record—under God's sovereignty—may have purposely omitted all mention of his birth, parentage, or ancestors.

In what way was Melchizedek a type of Christ? Melchizedek's name is made up of two words meaning "king" and "righteous." Melchizedek was also a priest. Thus, Melchizedek foreshadows Christ as a righteous king/priest. Melchizedek was also the king of "Salem" (which means peace). This points forward to Christ as the King of peace.

What is a "theophany"?

The word "theophany" comes from two Greek words: *theos* ("God") and *phaino* ("to appear"). We might define a theophany as an appearance or manifestation of God, usually in visible, bodily form. I believe that theophanies in the Old Testament were actually preincarnate appearances of Christ as the "Angel of the LORD." Accordingly, I prefer the term *Christophany* (appearance of Christ).

Is the "Angel of the Lord" identified as being Yahweh, thus distinct from all other angels?

Yes. The "Angel of the LORD" (or "Angel of Yahweh") makes very definite claims to deity. A well-known example is found in the account of Moses and the burning bush: "Moses was keeping the flock of his father-in-law, Jethro, the priest of Midian, and he led his flock to the west side of the wilderness and came to Horeb, the mountain of God. And the angel of the LORD appeared to him in a flame of fire out of the midst of a bush. He looked, and behold, the bush was burning, yet it was not consumed" (Exodus 3:1-2).

Notice how the "Angel" then identified himself to Moses: "I am the God of your father, the God of Abraham, the God of Isaac, and the God of Jacob." Upon hearing the Angel's identity, "Moses hid his face, for he was afraid to look at God" (Exodus 3:6). Clearly this "Angel" was a manifestation of God.

Is the Angel of the Lord—though identified as Yahweh—also distinct from another person called Yahweh?

Yes. Though the Angel of Yahweh was recognized as being Yahweh (God), He is also recognized as being *distinct* from another person called Yahweh. In Zechariah 1:12, for example, we find the Angel of Yahweh interceding to another person called Yahweh on behalf of the people of Jerusalem and Judah: "The angel of the LORD [Yahweh] said, 'O LORD [Yahweh] of hosts, how long will you have no mercy on Jerusalem and the cities of Judah, against which you have been angry these seventy years?'"

What we have here, I believe, is *one* person of the Trinity (the second person—the preincarnate Christ as the Angel of Yahweh) interceding before *another* person of the Trinity (the first person—God the Father).

As a result of this intercession, the Father reaffirmed His intentions to bless and prosper the chosen people.

Note that the New Testament pattern is that the second person of the Trinity, Jesus, consistently intercedes with the first person, the Father (see John 17; Hebrews 7:25; 1 John 2:1). This pattern is never reversed in Scripture. (That is, we never see the Father offering intercessory prayer to Jesus.)

Some might be tempted to argue that since the Angel of Yahweh is portrayed as interceding to or calling upon Yahweh, He must be less than deity. However, the Angel's intercessory prayer to Yahweh on behalf of Judah is no more a disproof of His absolute deity than the intercessory prayer of Christ to the Father in John 17 is a disproof of His deity (see also Hebrews 7:25).

Should we therefore interpret the "Angel of the Lord" against a Trinitarian backdrop?

Most certainly! After all, how can one person who is clearly identified as God (the Angel of Yahweh) address *another* person who is just as clearly God (Yahweh)? Since there is *only one God* (Isaiah 44:6,8; 46:9), the answer must lie in the personal distinctions of the Trinity. More specifically, the answer lies in recognizing the Angel of Yahweh as the second person of the Trinity, Jesus Christ.

Are we to therefore conclude that Jesus is the visible manifestation of God in both Testaments?

This is a valid theological conclusion. While Christ is the visible God of the New Testament, the Father and the Holy Spirit characteristically do not manifest themselves visibly. Paul tells us that God the Father is invisible (Colossians 1:15; 1 Timothy 1:17) and "dwells in unapproachable light, whom no one has ever seen or can see" (1 Timothy 6:16). John's Gospel likewise tells us that "no one has ever seen God [the Father]; the only God [Jesus Christ], who is at the Father's side, he has made him known" (John 1:18). John 5:37 similarly tells us that no one has ever seen God the Father's form.

Scripture also portrays the Holy Spirit as being invisible to the human eye. In the Upper Room Discourse, for example, Jesus referred to "the Spirit of truth, whom the world cannot receive, because it neither sees him nor knows him. You know him, for he dwells with you and will be in you" (John 14:17). The invisible Holy Spirit is known by believers *because He indwells them.*

The above facts about the Father and the Holy Spirit point to Christ as being the one who visibly appeared in Old Testament times as the Angel of Yahweh. This would seem to be the only interpretation that does full justice to the above Scripture passages.

Did Yahweh send the Angel of Yahweh into the world?

Yes. Just as Christ was sent by the Father in the New Testament (John 3:17), so the Angel of Yahweh was sent by Yahweh in the Old Testament (Judges 13:8-9). The divine pattern in Scripture is that the Father is the *Sender* and the Son is the *Sent One.*

Of course, this implies no superiority of the Father or inferiority of the Son. This is simply the eternal relationship of the first and second persons of the Trinity. That the Angel and Jesus were both sent by the Father—one in the Old Testament, the other in the New—lends support to the idea that they are one and the same person.

Do the particular ministries of the Angel of Yahweh point to His identity as the preincarnate Christ?

Yes indeed. The divine Angel and Christ engaged in amazingly similar ministries. Besides interceding for the people of God (Zechariah 1:12-13; 3:1-2; John 17; Romans 8:34; Hebrews 7:25), both the Angel and Christ were involved in *revealing truth* (Daniel 4:13,17,23; 8:16; 9:21-22; John 1:1,14,18), *commissioning individuals for service* (Exodus 3:7-10; Judges 6:11-23; 13; Matthew 4:18-20; 28:19-20; Acts 26:14-18), *delivering those enslaved* (Exodus 3; Galatians 1:4; 1 Thessalonians 1:10; 2 Timothy 4:18; Hebrews 2:14-15), *comforting the downcast* (Genesis 16:7-13; Matthew 14:14; 15:32-39), *protecting God's servants*

(Psalm 34:7; Daniel 3:15-30; 6:16-23; Matthew 8:24-26), and *acting as judge* (1 Chronicles 21:14-15; John 5:22; Acts 10:42).

Such parallel ministries point to the common identity of the Angel and Jesus Christ.

Does the Angel of Yahweh appear in the New Testament?

No. And may I say that in view of the extremely active role played by the Angel of Yahweh throughout Old Testament history, His sudden disappearance after the incarnation would be strange indeed unless He was a preincarnate manifestation of Jesus Christ. There is no other way to explain the Angel's complete inactivity among human beings in New Testament times unless He is recognized as *continuing* His activity as *God incarnate*—that is, as Jesus Christ.

Some sharp readers may be thinking, *What about the references (albeit few) in the New Testament to an "angel of the Lord"?* Theologian Norman Geisler explains it this way:

> *An* angel of the Lord (Gabriel) appeared to Joseph (Matthew 1:20); *an* angel of the Lord spoke to Philip (Acts 8:26); and *an* angel of the Lord released Peter (Acts 12:7), but not *the* Angel of the Lord. Further, the New Testament "angel of the Lord," unlike "*the* Angel of the Lord" in the Old Testament, did not permit worship of himself (cf. Revelation 22:8-9), but "*the* Angel of the Lord" in the Old Testament demanded worship (cf. Exodus 3:5; Joshua 5:15).[2]

It is exceedingly important to distinguish between *an* angel of the Lord in the New Testament (a created angel) and *the* Angel of the Lord in the Old Testament (the preincarnate Christ). The reader must be cautious not to get confused on this point.

In what sense can Christ be called "Angel" ("Angel of Yahweh")?

If we are correct in saying that appearances of the Angel of Yahweh in Old Testament times were actually preincarnate appearances of Christ, then it is critical that we anchor in our minds the precise sense in which He can properly be called an angel. In accordance with its Hebrew root, the word *angel* was used of Christ in the sense of "Messenger," "One who is sent," or "Envoy."[3] This usage of the word indicates that Christ was acting on behalf of the Father. Christ, as the Angel of Yahweh, was a divine *Intermediary* between God the Father and man.

15
The Resurrection of Christ

How important an issue is the resurrection?

Very important! The apostle Paul said, "If Christ has not been raised, then our preaching is in vain and your faith is in vain" (1 Corinthians 15:14). If the resurrection did not really happen, the apostles were false witnesses, our faith is futile, we're still lost in our sins, the dead in Christ have perished, and we're the most pitiful people on the face of the earth—to say nothing of the fact that there's no hope for any of us beyond the grave. Clearly, this is a transcendentally important issue.

How did Jesus initially reveal His resurrection to His followers?

Jesus first attested to His resurrection by appearing to Mary, who then told the disciples the glorious news. That evening, the disciples had gathered in a room with the doors shut for fear of the Jews (John 20:19). This fear was well founded, for after Jesus had been arrested, Annas the high priest specifically asked Jesus about the disciples (18:19). Jesus had also previously warned the disciples in the upper room: "If they persecuted me, they will also persecute you" (15:20). These facts no doubt lingered in their minds after Jesus was brutally crucified.

Their gloom soon turned to joy. The risen Christ appeared in their midst and said to them, "Peace be with you!" (John 20:19). This phrase was a common Hebrew greeting (1 Samuel 25:6). But on this occasion Jesus' words had added significance. After their conduct on Good Friday (they all scattered like cowards after Jesus' arrest), the disciples may well have expected a rebuke from Jesus. Instead, He displayed compassion by pronouncing peace upon them.

Jesus immediately showed the disciples His hands and His side (John 20:20). The risen Lord wanted them to see that it was truly He. The wounds showed that He did not have another body but the *same* body. He was dead, but now He is alive forevermore.

How did Jesus continue to prove His resurrection to His followers?

Acts 1:3 tells us that Jesus "presented himself alive after his suffering by many proofs, appearing to them during forty days and speaking about the kingdom of God." Put another way, Jesus appeared to *too many people* over *too many days* on *too many different occasions* for His resurrection to be dismissed and explained away.

What can we say to those who claim the disciples just made up Jesus' resurrection?

It is impossible to believe that these followers—predominantly Jewish and therefore aware of God's stern commandments against lying and bearing false witness—would collectively make up such a lie. It is also impossible to fathom that these followers would then suffer and *give up their own lives* in defense of their claim of Jesus' resurrection.

Moreover, Paul said the resurrected Christ appeared to more than 500 people at a single time, *most of whom were still alive* (1 Corinthians 15:6). If Paul (or any of Christ's followers) had misrepresented the facts, wouldn't one of these 500 have come forward to dispute such claims?

The truth is, something amazing happened that converted the disciples from cowards to bulwarks of the faith—and that *something* could only have been the resurrection of Christ from the dead.

Are there any early written records of Jesus' resurrection?

Yes. The apostle Paul in 1 Corinthians 15:1-4 speaks of Christ's resurrection as part of a confession that had been handed down for years. First Corinthians was written around AD 55, a mere 20 years after Christ's resurrection. But many biblical scholars believe the confession in 1 Corinthians 15:1-4 was formulated within a few years of Jesus' death and resurrection. *Early history is reliable history!*

Does 1 Corinthians 15:44-50 indicate that Jesus resurrected in a spiritual body?

It is true that the resurrection body is called a "spiritual body" in 1 Corinthians 15:44. However, the primary meaning of "*spiritual* body" here is not an immaterial body but a supernatural, spirit-dominated body. The Greek phrase *soma pneumatikon* (translated "spiritual body" in this verse) refers to a body *directed by* the spirit, as opposed to one under the dominion of the flesh.

The Greek word for "body" (*soma*), when used of a person, always means *physical body* in the New Testament. There are no exceptions to this. Greek scholar Robert Gundry, in his authoritative book *Soma in Biblical Theology,* speaks of "Paul's exceptionless use of *soma* for a physical body."[1] Therefore, all references to Jesus' resurrection "body" (*soma*) in the New Testament must be taken to mean a resurrected *physical* body. This supports the view that the phrase "spiritual body [*soma*]" in 1 Corinthians 15:44 refers to a spirit-dominated and supernatural *physical* body.

The context in 1 Corinthians 15 indicates that Paul intended the meaning of "supernatural" in verses 40-50. I say this because the contrasts in verses 40-50—"earthly" versus "heavenly," "perishable" versus "imperishable," "weak" versus "powerful," and "mortal" versus "immortal"—show that the translation "supernatural" as a contrast to "natural" fits Paul's line of argumentation much better than the word *spiritual.*

Does 1 Peter 3:18 indicate that Jesus experienced a spiritual resurrection from the dead?

This verse says, "Christ also suffered once for sins, the righteous for the unrighteous, that he might bring us to God, being put to death in the flesh but made alive in the spirit."

This verse does not refer to a spiritual resurrection of Christ. Instead, it refers to Christ's physical resurrection by the Holy Spirit. God did not raise Jesus *as* a spirit but raised Him *by* His Spirit. This is in keeping with Romans 1:4, which tells us that Jesus "was declared to be the Son of God in power *according to the Spirit of holiness* by his resurrection from the dead, Jesus Christ our Lord."

Of course, this is not to deny that the Father and Son were involved in the resurrection as well. God the Father is often said to have raised Christ from the dead (Acts 2:32; 13:30; Romans 6:4; Ephesians 1:19-20). But without diminishing the Father's key role in the resurrection, it is just as clear from Scripture that Jesus raised Himself from the dead (John 10:17-18). Therefore, it is clear that *each* of the three persons in the Trinity—the Father, the Son, *and* the Holy Spirit—were involved in Christ's resurrection.

What scriptural considerations support the idea that Jesus resurrected physically?

The resurrected Christ Himself said, "See my hands and my feet, that it is I myself. Touch me, and see. For a spirit does not have flesh and bones as you see that I have" (Luke 24:39). Notice three things here: The resurrected Christ indicates in this verse that He is not a spirit, He points out that His resurrection body is made up of flesh and bones, and His physical hands and feet represent physical proof of the materiality of His resurrection from the dead.

In John 2:19 Jesus promised, "Destroy this temple, and in three days I will raise it up." Jesus was speaking about the temple of His physical body.

The resurrected Christ ate physical food. And He did this as a means of proving that He had a real physical body (for example, see Luke 24:42-43). It would have been deception on Jesus' part to have offered His ability to eat physical food as a proof of His bodily resurrection if He had not been resurrected in a physical body.

The physical body of the resurrected Christ was touched and handled by different people—including Mary (John 20:17) and some women (Matthew 28:9). He also challenged the disciples to physically touch Him so they could rest assured that His body was material in nature (Luke 24:39).

The body that is "sown" in death is the *very same body* that is raised in life (1 Corinthians 15:35-44).

If Jesus' resurrection body was physical in nature, how could He get into closed rooms, apparently by materialization (John 20:19)?

In John 20:19 we read, "On the evening of that day, the first day of the week, the doors being locked where the disciples were for fear of the Jews, Jesus came and stood among them and said to them, 'Peace be with you.'"

Jesus' resurrection body was *material* (see Luke 24:39). The fact that He could get into a room with a closed door does not prove He had to dematerialize in order to do it. One must keep in mind that if He had chosen to do so, Jesus could have performed this same miracle before His death in His pre-resurrection material body. As the Son of God, His miraculous powers were just as great before the resurrection. Prior to His resurrection Jesus performed miracles with His physical body that transcended natural laws, such as walking on water (John 6:16-20). But this miracle did not prove that His pre-resurrection body was immaterial or even that it could dematerialize. Otherwise, Peter's pre-resurrection walk on water would mean his body dematerialized for a moment and then quickly rematerialized (Matthew 14:29).

Scripture indicates that the resurrection body, although physical, is by its very nature a supernatural body (1 Corinthians 15:44). So it should be expected that it can do supernatural things, such as appearing in a room with closed doors.

Is there any legitimacy to Hugh Schonfield's "Passover Plot" theory?

None whatsoever. Schonfield argued that Jesus conspired with Joseph of Arimathea, Lazarus, and an anonymous young man to convince His disciples that He was the Messiah. He allegedly manipulated events to make it appear that He was the fulfillment of numerous prophecies. Regarding the resurrection, Jesus allegedly took some drugs, feigned death, and revived later. Unfortunately, the crucifixion wounds ultimately proved fatal, and He died. The plotters then stole and disposed of Jesus' body, and the appearances of Christ were simply a case of mistaken identity.[2]

This theory is full of holes. First, Christ was of the highest moral character in the way He lived His life and in His teachings. It breaches all credulity to say that Jesus was deceitful and sought to fool people into believing He was the Messiah. Moreover, many prophecies were fulfilled in the person of Jesus that He couldn't have conspired to fulfill, such as His birthplace (Micah 5:2), being born of a virgin (Isaiah 7:14), and the identity of His forerunner, John the Baptist (Malachi 3:1).

It is also highly unlikely that the plotters could have stolen Jesus' dead body in order to dispose of it. The tomb had a huge stone (weighing several tons) blocking it, it had a seal of the Roman government, and it was guarded by Roman guards trained in the art of defense and killing.

The idea that the appearances of Christ were simply a case of mistaken identity is ridiculous. Jesus appeared to *too many people* (including 500 at a single time—1 Corinthians 15:6), on *too many occasions* (12 times), over *too long a time* (40 days) for this to be the case.

How can we respond to the so-called "swoon theory" of the resurrection?

This theory suggests that Jesus didn't really die on the cross. He was nailed to the cross and suffered from loss of blood and went into shock. But He didn't die. He merely fainted (or swooned) from exhaustion. The disciples mistook Him for dead and buried Him alive in a tomb. They were easily fooled, living in the first century as they did.

Suddenly, the cold tomb woke Jesus from His state of shock. And when Jesus emerged from the tomb and was seen by the disciples, they knew He must have resurrected from the dead.

This theory is highly imaginative, but it is impossible to believe. Consider the facts: Jesus went through six trials and was beaten beyond description. He was so weak that He couldn't even carry the wooden cross bar. Huge spikes were driven through His wrists and feet. A Roman soldier thrust a spear into His side so that blood and water came out. Four Roman executioners (who had many years of experience in their line of work) goofed and mistakenly pronounced Jesus dead. More than 100 pounds of gummy spices were applied to Jesus' body, and during this process, no one saw Jesus breathing. A large stone weighing several tons was rolled against the tomb, Roman guards were placed there, and a seal was wrapped across the entrance.

So for this theory to work, Jesus would have had to wake up in the cool tomb, split off the garments, push the several-ton stone away, fight off the armed Roman guards with His bare hands, and appear to the disciples.

Therefore, this theory is nothing more than a desperate attempt— a veritable grasping at straws—by critics to explain away Christ's resurrection.

How can we respond to those who try to explain away Christ's resurrection by saying the women and the disciples went to the wrong tomb?

To believe in this theory, we'd have to conclude that the women went to the wrong tomb, that Peter and John ran to the wrong tomb, that the Jews then went to the wrong tomb, followed by the Jewish Sanhedrin and the Romans, who also went to the wrong tomb. We'd also have to say that Joseph of Arimathea, the *owner* of the tomb, went to the wrong tomb. We'd have to say that even the angel from heaven appeared at the wrong tomb.

Such a view is unreasonable, and is unworthy of serious consideration.

How could Jesus have remained in the tomb "three days and three nights" if He was crucified on Friday and rose on Sunday?

The Gospel accounts are clear that Jesus was crucified and buried on Friday, sometime before sundown. (Sundown was considered the beginning of the next day for the Jews.) This means Jesus was in the grave for part of Friday, the entire Sabbath (Saturday), and part of Sunday. In other words, He was in the tomb for two full nights, one full day, and part of two days.

How do we reconcile this with Jesus' words in Matthew 12:40? "Just as Jonah was three days and three nights in the belly of the great fish, so will the Son of Man be three days and three nights in the heart of the earth." This is not hard to explain. In the Jewish mind-set, any *part* of a day was reckoned as a *complete* day. The Babylonian Talmud (a set of Jewish commentaries) tells us that "the portion of a day is as the whole of it." So even though Jesus was really in the tomb for part of Friday, all of Saturday, and part of Sunday, in Jewish reckoning He was in the tomb for "three days and three nights."

16
Errors About Christ

Some claim Jesus was Michael the archangel in the Old Testament. Is this view correct?

No. In Daniel 10:13 Michael is specifically called "*one* of the chief princes." The fact that Michael is "one of" the chief princes indicates that he is *one among a group* of chief princes. The passage does not tell us how large that group is, but the fact that Michael is one among equals proves that he is not unique. By contrast, the Greek word used to describe Jesus in John 3:16 (God's "*only begotten*" son, as the KJV renders it) is *monogenes*—meaning "unique" or "one of a kind." He is not a "chief prince" but is rather the unique "King of kings and Lord of lords" (Revelation 19:16).

Moreover, in Hebrews 1:5 we are told that no angel can ever be called God's son: "To which of the angels did God ever say, 'You are my Son, today I have begotten you'?" Since Jesus *is* the Son of God, and since no angel can ever be called God's son, then Jesus cannot possibly be the archangel Michael.

Further, we are explicitly told in Hebrews 2:5 that the world *is not* (and *will not be*) in subjection to an angel. This being so, Christ cannot be Michael since He is said to be the ruler of God's kingdom over and over again in Scripture (Genesis 49:10; 2 Samuel 7:16; Psalm 2:6; Daniel 7:13-14; Matthew 2:1-2; 9:35; Luke 1:32-33; Revelation 19:16).

Finally, notice that the archangel Michael does not have the authority to rebuke Satan (Jude 9). By contrast, Jesus rebuked the devil on a number of occasions (for example, Matthew 17:18 and Mark 9:25).

Since Michael *could not* rebuke the devil in his own authority and Jesus *could* (and *did*) rebuke the devil in His own authority, Michael and Jesus cannot be the same person.

Was Jesus the spirit-brother of Lucifer, as Mormons claim?[1]

No. Though we could cite many passages that refute this hideous doctrine, we will limit our attention to Colossians 1:16, where we are specifically told that the entire angelic realm—including the angel Lucifer—was personally created by Jesus Christ: "By him all things were created, in heaven and on earth, visible and invisible, whether thrones or dominions or rulers or authorities—all things were created through him and for him."

It is highly revealing that Paul says that Christ created "thrones," "dominions," "rulers," and "authorities." In the rabbinical (Jewish) thought of the first century, these words were used to describe different orders of angels (Romans 8:38; Ephesians 1:21; 3:10; 6:12; Colossians 2:10,15; Titus 3:1).

We know from Scripture that Lucifer is a created angelic being— a "cherub" (Ezekiel 28:13-19; see also Isaiah 14:12-15). Since Lucifer was an angel, and since Christ created all the angels, it is very clear that Christ is not a "spirit-brother" of Lucifer. Christ is not of the created realm. He is the Creator. Lucifer and Christ are of two entirely different classes—the *created* and the *Creator.* Sometime after he was created, Lucifer rebelled against the Creator and became Satan.

New Agers say that a human Jesus became the Christ as an adult.[2] How can we respond to this?

Jesus did not "become" the Christ as an adult. Rather, he was the one and only Christ from the very beginning. When the angel announced the birth of Jesus to the shepherds, he identified Jesus this way: "Unto you is born this day in the city of David a Savior, who is Christ the Lord" (Luke 2:11). Simeon, who was filled with the Holy Spirit, recognized the babe Jesus as Christ, in fulfillment of God's promise to him that "he would not see death before he had seen the Lord's Christ" (Luke 2:26). Clearly Jesus didn't just become the Christ as an adult.

The Greek word for Christ (*Christos*) means "anointed one" and is a direct parallel to the Hebrew word for Messiah. In other words, "Messiah" and "Christ" are interchangeable words referring to the same person. Recall that Andrew went to his brother Simon and said to him, "We have found *the Messiah* (which means *Christ*)" (John 1:41). More than a hundred messianic prophecies in the Old Testament point to a *single Messiah* or Christ—Jesus Christ.

On two different occasions in the New Testament, Jesus made His identity *as* the Christ the primary issue of faith (Matthew 16:13-20 and John 11:25-27). Significantly, when Jesus was acknowledged as the Christ, He did not say to people, "You, too, have the Christ within." Instead He warned that others would come falsely claiming to be the Christ (Matthew 24:4-5,23-24).

Did Jesus go to India during His childhood years and study under Indian gurus, as New Agers claim?[3]

No. Notice that Jesus was well known in His community as a long-standing carpenter (Mark 6:3) and as a carpenter's son (Matthew 13:55). (It was customary among the Jews for fathers to teach their sons a trade during their childhood years. Jesus' father, Joseph, taught Him the trade of carpentry.) That Jesus was well known in the community as a carpenter indicates He had lived there during the preceding years, and not in India.

People who lived in and around Nazareth displayed obvious familiarity with Jesus as if they had had regular contact with Him for a prolonged time. We read that at the beginning of His three-year ministry, Jesus "came to Nazareth, *where he had been brought up.* And as was his custom, he went to the synagogue on the Sabbath day, and he stood up to read" (Luke 4:16). After He finished reading, "all spoke well of him and marveled at the gracious words that were coming from his mouth. And they said, 'Is not this Joseph's son?'" (Luke 4:22). This clearly implies that those in the synagogue recognized Jesus as a local resident. This, of course, is not surprising since He had been "brought up" in the community.

Other people seemed offended that Jesus was attracting so much attention. These seemed to be treating Him with a contempt born of familiarity (see Matthew 13:54-57). It is as if they were thinking, *We've known Jesus since He was a child, and now He's standing before us claiming to be the Messiah. What nerve and audacity He has!* They wouldn't have responded this way if they hadn't had regular contact with Him for a prolonged time.

Among those who became angriest at Jesus were the Jewish leaders. They accused Him of many offenses, including breaking the Sabbath (Matthew 12:1-14), blasphemy (John 8:58-59; 10:31-33), and doing miracles in Satan's power (Matthew 12:24). But they *never* accused Him of teaching or practicing anything learned in the East. If the Jewish leaders *could* have accused Jesus of this, they certainly *would* have.

Did Jesus ever get married?

Dan Brown, in *The Da Vinci Code*, claimed Jesus was married to Mary Magdalene. One can reportedly find historical "proof" in the late-dated Gospel of Philip, which (allegedly) speaks of Jesus kissing Mary on the mouth.

Contrary to such an idea, the New Testament never mentions Jesus getting married. Moreover, it is noteworthy that in 1 Corinthians 9:5, Paul defends his right to get married if he so chose, because other apostles had gotten married. If Jesus had been married, surely the apostle Paul would have cited Jesus' marriage as the number-one precedent.

Scripture reveals that Jesus' marriage is *yet future*. In fact, He will one day marry the "bride of Christ," which is the church (Revelation 19:7-9).

As for the Gospel of Philip, the document says "Jesus kissed her often on the..."—and then the manuscript is broken at that point. Dan Brown assumes the missing word must be "mouth," but it could just as easily be "head," "cheek," or even "hand." Nothing in the context demands that Jesus kissed Mary on the mouth. Certainly this so-called "Gospel" nowhere states that Jesus was married. And of great significance is the fact that this document dates to about AD 275, hundreds of years *after* the time of Christ and the canonical gospels (Matthew, Mark, Luke, and John). It can hardly be considered a reliable source of information about Jesus.

How can we respond to those who say that Jesus was just a good moral teacher?

No mere "example" or "moral teacher" would ever claim that the destiny of the world lay in His hands, or that people would spend eternity in heaven or hell depending on whether they believed in Him (John 6:26-40). The only "example" this would provide would be one of lunacy. And for Jesus to convince people that He was God (John 8:58) and the Savior of the lost (Luke 19:10) when He really wasn't would be the ultimate immorality. So to say that Jesus was *just* a good moral teacher *and nothing more* makes virtually no sense.

How can we respond to cults who teach that Jesus is the Father and the Holy Spirit?

Scripture is clear that the Father, Son, and Holy Spirit are distinct persons. Scripture tells us that the Father *sent* the Son (John 3:16-17), the Father and Son *love* each other (John 5:20), and the Father and Son *speak* to each other (John 11:41-42). Moreover, the Father *knows* the Son and the Son *knows* the Father (John 10:15), and Jesus is our *advocate with* the Father (1 John 2:1).

Further, it is clear that Jesus is not the Holy Spirit, for the Holy Spirit *descended* upon Jesus at His baptism (Luke 3:22). The Holy Spirit is said to be *another* comforter (John 14:16). Jesus *sent* the Holy Spirit (John 15:26). And the Holy Spirit seeks to *glorify* Jesus (John 16:13-14).

In view of these facts, it is impossible to argue that Jesus is the Father and the Holy Spirit. (See the chapter on the Trinity for more on how the Father, Son, and Holy Spirit relate to each other.)

Does the fact that Jesus is called "Everlasting Father" in Isaiah 9:6 mean that Jesus is the Father?

No. The Father is considered by Jesus as someone other than Himself more than 200 times in the New Testament. And more than 50 times in the New Testament the Father and Son are seen to be distinct within the same verse (for example, Romans 15:6; 2 Corinthians 1:3; Galatians 1:2-3; Philippians 2:10-11; 1 John 2:1; 2 John 3).

If the Father and the Son are distinct, then in what sense can Jesus be called "Everlasting Father" (Isaiah 9:6)? This phrase is better translated *Father of eternity,* and carries the meaning "possessor of eternity." *Father of eternity* is here used "in accordance with a custom usual in Hebrew and in Arabic, where he who possesses a thing is called the father of it. Thus, *the father of strength* means strong; *the father of knowledge,* intelligent; *the father of glory,* glorious."[4] According to this common usage, the meaning of *Father of eternity* in Isaiah 9:6 is "eternal." Christ as the "Father of eternity" is an eternal being.[5]

The Targum—a simplified paraphrase of the Old Testament Scriptures utilized by the ancient Jews—rendered Isaiah 9:6, "His name has been called from of old, Wonderful Counselor, Mighty God, *He who lives forever…*"[6] Clearly, the ancient Jews considered the phrase *Father of eternity* as indicating the eternality of the Messiah.

Does John 10:30 teach that Jesus and the Father are the same person?

No. In John 10:30 Jesus affirmed, "I and the Father are one" (John 10:30). This verse does not mean that Jesus and the Father are one and the same person. We know this to be true because in the phrase "I and the Father are one" is a first person plural—"we are" (*esmen* in the Greek). The verse literally reads from the Greek, "I and the Father *we are* one." If Jesus intended to say that He and the Father were one *person,* He certainly would not have used the first person plural, which clearly implies *two* persons.

Moreover, the Greek word for "one" (*hen*) in this verse refers *not* to personal unity (that is, the idea that the Father and Son are one person) but to unity of essence or nature (that is, that the Father and Son have the same divine nature). This is evident in the fact that the form of the word in the Greek is neuter, not masculine. Further, the verses that immediately precede *and* follow John 10:30 distinguish Jesus from the Father (John 10:25,29,36,38).

Does John 14:7-11 prove that Jesus is God the Father, as some cultists claim?

No. In this extended passage Jesus said, "If you had known me, you would have known my Father also...Whoever has seen me has seen the Father...Do you not believe that I am in the Father and the Father is in me?...Believe me that I am in the Father and the Father is in me..." (John 14:7,9-11). These verses prove only that the Father and the Son are one in *being,* not that they are one *person.*

Notice that in the preceding verse (John 14:6), Jesus clearly distinguishes Himself from the Father when He says, "No one comes *to* the Father except *through* me." The words "to" and "through" would not make any sense if Jesus and the Father were one and the same person. They only make sense if the Father and Jesus are distinct persons, with Jesus being the Mediator between the Father and humankind.

Further, when Jesus said, "Whoever has seen me has seen the Father" (John 14:9), He wasn't saying He *was* the Father. Rather, Jesus is the perfect revelation of the Father (1:18). Jesus, the *second* person of the Trinity, is the perfect revelation of the Father, the *first* person of the Trinity.

Does 2 Corinthians 3:17 prove that Jesus is the Holy Spirit, as some cultists claim?

No. In 2 Corinthians 3:17 we read, "Now the Lord is the Spirit, and where the Spirit of the Lord is, there is freedom." Many expositors view this verse as saying that the Holy Spirit is "Lord" not in the sense of being Jesus but in the sense of being Yahweh (the Lord

God). We know the verse is not saying that Jesus is the Holy Spirit, for just earlier in 2 Corinthians 3 the apostle Paul clearly distinguishes between Jesus and the Holy Spirit (see verses 3-6). Further, as noted previously, the whole of Scripture indicates that Jesus is not the Holy Spirit (see John 14:16; 15:26; 16:7,13-14).

Part 5

Questions About Humanity

The Origins of Humankind
Humans Related to God
The Human Fall into Sin

17
The Origins of Humankind

Do scientists believe our universe had a beginning?

Scientists today by and large agree that the universe had a beginning. They may disagree as to *how* that beginning happened, but they largely agree *that* there was a beginning.

A *beginning* implies the existence of a *Beginner*—a Creator. As Scripture says, "Every house is built by someone, but the builder of all things is God" (Hebrews 3:4).

Is there evidence that an Intelligent Designer was involved in the creation of the universe?

By observing the world and universe around us, it becomes apparent that a Designer was indeed involved. Everything is just perfect for life on the earth—*so* perfect and *so* "fine-timed" that it gives every indication that it came from the hands of an Intelligent Designer (God). The earth's size, composition, distance from the sun, rotational period, and many other factors are all just right for life. The chances of even one planet having all of these factors converge by accident are almost nonexistent.

In keeping with this, the genetic code of all biological life on the earth gives evidence of intelligent design. In fact, the information contained in genetic code is far more complex than that found in computer software. The complex design implies the existence of a Designer (God). (For more information on this, see chapter 34, "Apologetics and Intelligent Design Theory.")

Does the fossil evidence support or contradict evolution?

Billions of fossils have been discovered virtually all over the world. Dinosaur graveyards are scattered all around, located in such places as the Rockies, South Africa, Central Asia, and Belgium. Fossils of marine invertebrates are found almost everywhere. Fossils of ocean fish, mollusk shells, and even a whale have been discovered on various mountains.

With this abundance of evidence, one would expect that if evolutionary theory were true, the fossil record would show a step-by-step progression from simple life forms to increasingly complex life forms. However, the fossil record actually shows that species throughout geologic history have remained remarkably stable (not changing) for exceedingly long periods of time, and that there was a sudden explosion of life forms during the Cambrian Age (the first period of the Paleozoic Era).

So astonishing is the explosion of life forms during the Cambrian period that some refer to it as "biology's big bang." Many of the animal types that appear in the Cambrian era continue to the present day.

An objective consideration of the Cambrian explosion reveals that there is no evolutionary descent of life forms, and no slow modifications taking place in life forms as a result of natural selection. The truth is that the prevailing characteristic of fossil species is *stasis*—that is, there is an absence of change in the fossils.

Creationists therefore believe the fossil evidence is more in line with their view than with evolutionary theory. The intermediate fossils certainly show no transition of one species into another—for example, a transition of a "primitive primate relative" into a human being—as one would expect if evolution were true.

Are dinosaurs mentioned in the Bible?

There is a good possibility. For example, Job 40:15 tells us, "Behold, Behemoth, which I made as I made you; he eats grass like an ox." While some have claimed that the behemoth must be either an elephant or a hippopotamus, verse 17 tells us that "his tail" is "stiff like a cedar." (Neither the elephant nor the hippopotamus has such a giant tail.) Many have thus concluded that this sounds more like a dinosaur. It may be that the behemoth is a brontosaurus or a similar plant-eating dinosaur.

Also, Job 41:1 asks, "Can you draw out Leviathan with a fishhook or press down his tongue with a cord?" Many believe that the Leviathan might be a marine dinosaur, or at least a very large crocodile. After all, it is far too large to capture with a fishhook. So it must be a giant sea creature of some sort.

Is evolution's dependence on ongoing positive mutations feasible?

No. Science proves that the great majority of mutations are, in fact, detrimental to the organism. Indeed, scientists have found that more than 99 percent are harmful, destructive, and disadvantageous to the organism, as one textbook indicates:

> Experiments have conclusively shown that most mutations are harmful (about 99.9%), and some are even deadly. Mutations seem to result from "accidents" which occur in the genes, and the chance that such an accident could be helpful rather than harmful is very small indeed. Two-headed snakes and albino squirrels are considered to be genetic disasters instead of the beginnings of new and more advanced creatures.[1]

Most mutations cause deterioration and breakdown in the organism. Such changes tend to make the organism less well suited for its environment, thereby threatening its very survival. It does not take a rocket scientist to know that if most mutations are destructive to an organism, then any series of multiple mutations will, on average, have a much-increased chance of harming that organism. This fact greatly undermines evolutionary theory.

How do positive mutations relate to the information in DNA?

The impossibility of positive mutations bringing about new species is proven in the fact that this would require tremendous amounts of new information being added to the DNA (which carries genetic information). But numerous studies and experiments have demonstrated that not only do mutations fail to produce new information—they actually delete information and thus bring harm to the organism. Mutations generally involve some kind of copying error in the DNA, kind of like typing mistakes, and therefore are incapable of increasing information.

It thus becomes absurd to think that, over a long period of time, enough information was added to cause a single-celled organism to eventually evolve into a complex human being with a brain, eyes, ears, nose, heart, kidneys, liver, and all the other complex organs. It is inconceivable how any of the above individual complex organs could develop through mutations, and the idea that these multiple complex organs evolved in a single species so as to function synergistically with each other as an interrelated whole through positive mutations is beyond all comprehension.

Does the second law of thermodynamics contradict evolution?

Yes indeed. The second law of thermodynamics says that in an isolated system (a system that neither loses nor gains energy from outside of itself, like our universe), the natural course of things is to degenerate. The universe is running down, not evolving upward.

Although the total amount of energy remains constant and unchanged, it always has the tendency to become less available for usable work as time goes on. The second law basically means that the universe is getting increasingly disorderly. All we have to do is nothing, and everything deteriorates, collapses, breaks down, and wears out, all by itself.

Based on the second law of thermodynamics, we must conclude that our universe is headed toward an ultimate "heat death" in which there will be no more energy conversions. The amount of usable energy will eventually deplete. Our universe is decaying. It is eroding. It is moving from order to disorder. The universe—and everything in the universe, including our sun, our bodies, the machines we build, my car—is running down.

Does the second law of thermodynamics indicate that the universe had a beginning?

Yes indeed. If the second law of thermodynamics is true, then the universe must not be eternal. Therefore, the universe must have had a beginning. If the universe is running down and nature's processes are proceeding *in just one direction* (decay and disorder), the inescapable inference is that everything had a beginning. If you compare the universe to a clock, there had to be a time when the clock was fully wound up.

Do evolutionists make false claims about having observed evolution in progress?

Many evolutionists have falsely claimed that the scientific evidence suggests that evolution is true. These individuals generally appeal to the fact that mutations *within* a species are a proven scientific fact (microevolution). But it requires an incredible leap of logic to say that the existence of mutations *within* species proves the possibility of mutations or transformations into *entirely new* species (macroevolution).

Studies in DNA and genetics indicate that sufficient genetic potential exists to produce a wide range of variety within a particular species, but one species cannot transform into another. For example, variations have occurred within the "dog kind," but we never witness the dog evolving into another species, even during times of severe environmental pressure. Some variations have occurred within the "cat kind," but we never witness the cat evolving into another species, even during times of severe environmental pressure.

Is theistic evolution a biblical concept?

No, I don't think so. Theistic evolution involves the notion that God initially began creation and then used evolution to produce the various life forms in our universe. God allegedly entered into the process of time to modify what was developing. Those who hold to this view generally attempt to reconcile the findings of science with the Bible.

The doctrine of theistic evolution has many serious problems. For one thing, it must make a complete allegory out of Genesis 1:1–2:4, for which there is no warrant. Certainly the suggestion that humanity is derived from a nonhuman ancestor (a common view among theistic evolutionists) cannot be reconciled with the explicit statement of man's creation in Genesis 2:7. Man did not evolve but instead was created from the dust of the ground. Further, if Adam was not a real historical person, then the analogy between Christ and Adam in Romans 5:12-21 utterly breaks down.

Certainly Christ believed in a literal creation of Adam and Eve (Matthew 19:4; Mark 10:6). (Christ Himself was their Creator—John 1:3; Colossians 1:16; Hebrews 1:2,10.) If His words cannot be trusted in these particulars, how can anyone be sure His words can be trusted in other matters?

Is man composed of two aspects (body and soul/spirit) or three aspects (body, soul, and spirit)?

This has been a much-debated issue. The dichotomist view is that man is composed of two parts—material (body) and immaterial (soul/spirit). In this view, "soul" and "spirit" are seen as essentially the same. Man's entire immaterial part is called "soul" in 1 Peter 2:11 and "spirit" in James 2:26. Therefore, they must be interchangeable.

Trichotomists see the soul and spirit as separate substantive entities. Man is viewed as consisting of three realities—body, soul, *and* spirit. Trichotomists generally say that the body involves world-consciousness, the soul involves self-consciousness, and the spirit involves God-consciousness. Support for this view is found in Hebrews 4:12 and 1 Thessalonians 5:23.

Perhaps a few distinctions would be helpful. If we are talking about mere *substance,* then we must conclude that man has only a material and an immaterial aspect. However, if we are talking about *function,* then we may say that within the sphere of man's immaterial aspect there are a number of functions—including that of soul and spirit.[2] Other components of man's immaterial nature include the heart (Hebrews 4:12; Matthew 22:37), the conscience (1 Peter 2:19; Hebrews 10:22), and the mind (Romans 12:2).

What does the Bible say about the equality of the races?

God created *all* races of man. All human beings are completely equal—equal in terms of their creation (Genesis 1:28), the sin problem (Romans 3:23), God's love for them (John 3:16), and God's provision of salvation for them (Matthew 28:19).

The apostle Paul affirmed, "He made from one man every nation of mankind to live on all the face of the earth, having determined allotted periods and the boundaries of their dwelling place" (Acts 17:26). Moreover, Revelation 5:9 tells us that God's redeemed will be from "every tribe and language and people and nation." There is therefore no place for racial discrimination, for all humans are equal in God's sight.

What does the Bible say about male-female equality?

Jesus had a very high view of women. In a Jewish culture where women were discouraged from studying the law, Jesus taught women right alongside men as equals (Matthew 14:21; 15:38). And when He taught, He often used women's activities to illustrate the character of the kingdom of God, such as baking bread (Luke 13:20), grinding corn (Luke 17:35), and sweeping the house to find a lost coin (Luke 15:8-10).

Some Jewish rabbis taught that a man should not speak to a woman in a public place, but Jesus not only spoke to a woman (who, incidentally, was a Samaritan) but also drank from her cup in a public place (John 4:1-30). The first person He appeared to after rising from the dead was Mary and not the male disciples (John 20). Clearly, Jesus had a very high view of women.

Galatians 3:28 tells us that there is neither male nor female in Jesus Christ. First Peter 3:7 says men and women are fellow heirs of grace. Ephesians 5:21 speaks of mutual submission between man and wife. In John 7:53–8:11 Jesus wouldn't permit the double standard of the woman being taken in adultery and letting the man go free. In Luke 10:39 Jesus let a woman sit at His feet, which was a place reserved for the male disciples. Verses such as these show that in God's eyes men and women are spiritually equal.

Nevertheless, Scripture also speaks of male leadership in the family and in the church (Ephesians 5:22; 1 Corinthians 11:3; 14:34; 1 Timothy 2:11). God is a God of order.

18
Humans Related to God

How can man's free will be reconciled with God's sovereignty?

Scripture portrays God as being absolutely sovereign (Acts 15:8; Ephesians 1:11; Psalm 135:6). Scripture also portrays man as having a free will (Genesis 3:1-7). It is certainly inscrutable to man's finite understanding how both divine sovereignty and human free will can both be true, but both doctrines are taught in Scripture. In fact, both of these are often seen side by side in the span of a single verse.

For example, in Acts 2:23 we read, "This Jesus, delivered up according to the definite plan and foreknowledge of God, you crucified and killed by the hands of lawless men." Here we see *divine sovereignty* ("according to the definite plan and foreknowledge of God") and *human free will* ("you crucified and killed by the hands of lawless men").

We also see both doctrines in Acts 13:48: "When the Gentiles heard this, they began rejoicing and glorifying the word of the Lord, and as many as were appointed to eternal life believed." God's *sovereignty* is clear ("as many as were appointed to eternal life") as is *man's free will* (they "believed").

It has been suggested that divine sovereignty and human free will are like parallel railroad tracks that are often found side by side in Scripture, and the tracks never come together on this side of eternity. When we enter glory, we will no doubt come to a fuller understanding of these biblical doctrines. Now we see as in a mirror darkly. Then we shall see clearly (1 Corinthians 13:12).

What is the distinction between God's sovereignty and naturalistic determinism?

Determinism says that all events (including human actions) occur by necessity, being caused by previous events. There is a perpetual outworking of cause-and-effect relationships. No deity need be involved.

In God's sovereignty, God is in control of causes *and* effects, moving all things toward a purposeful end. He is in control of primary and secondary causes, and moves all things according to His will.

How do the major theological "camps" handle the issue of God's "predeterminism" as related to the doctrine of salvation?

According to extreme Calvinism, *predetermination is in spite of foreknowledge*. In this view, God operates with such unapproachable sovereignty that His choices are made with no consideration of the choices made by human beings. God sovereignly saves whomever He wishes to save. Arminians say a big problem with this view is that it essentially involves a denial of free choice on the part of human beings.

According to Arminianism, *God's predetermination is based on His foreknowledge*. In this view, God in His omniscience knows in advance what choices every human being will make, including whether they will accept or reject salvation. On the basis of this foreknowledge, God elects to salvation those whom He foreknows will accept Christ. The problem with this view is that the Bible doesn't *only* indicate that God knows things in advance. It also indicates that God *actually determines* what will happen (Isaiah 14:24; 46:10; Proverbs 16:9; 19:21; 21:1).

According to moderate Calvinism, *God's predetermination is in accord with His foreknowledge*. According to this view, God's election is based neither on His foreknowledge (Arminianism) nor in spite of His foreknowledge (extreme Calvinism). Instead, it is *"according to* the foreknowledge of God" (1 Peter 1:2). In this view, there is no chronological or logical priority of election and foreknowledge. All aspects of God's eternal purpose are equally timeless (and simultaneous). Both divine sovereignty and human freedom are fully operational in this system.

If it is true that God is sovereign in all things, then why should we pray?

It is true that God is sovereign over all things (Ephesians 1:18-23). But we must recognize that God has sovereignly ordained not only the "ends" but also the "means" to those "ends." In other words, God has sovereignly ordained not only to bring certain things about—He has also ordained to accomplish certain things as a result of the individual prayers of His people. So we should most definitely pray for specific needs (see Philippians 4:6). We must never forget the scriptural teaching that we do not have because we do not ask God (James 4:2).

What kinds of things ought to be included in our daily prayers?

Prayer has a number of components. In prayer we ought always to give thanks to God for everything we have (Ephesians 5:20; Colossians 3:15). We should "enter his gates with thanksgiving" (Psalm 100:4; see also Psalm 95:2).

Like David, praise for God should always be on our lips (Psalm 34:1; 103:1-5,20-22). We should "continually offer up a sacrifice of praise to God" (Hebrews 13:15). Like the psalmist, we should bow down in worship before the Lord our Maker (Psalm 95:6; Revelation 14:7), and do so with "reverence and awe" (Hebrews 12:28). We should worship Him alone (Exodus 20:3-5; Deuteronomy 5:7).

Confession in prayer is wise, for "whoever conceals his transgressions will not prosper, but he who confesses and forsakes them will obtain mercy" (Proverbs 28:13; see also 1 John 1:9).

In the Lord's Prayer, we are exhorted to pray for our daily needs (Matthew 6:11). The apostle Paul wrote, "Do not be anxious about anything, but in everything by prayer and supplication with thanksgiving *let your requests be made known to God*" (Philippians 4:6).

How can prayer be beneficial to my life?

God promises that He answers the prayers of His people. Prayer can bring enlightenment regarding God's purposes for us (Ephesians 1:18-19), and it can help us understand God's will (Colossians 1:9-12). It also increases our love for other people (1 Thessalonians 3:10-13) and can bring about encouragement and strength as we face the difficulties of daily living (2 Thessalonians 2:16-17).

In addition to keeping us from harm and pain (1 Chronicles 4:10), prayer can deliver us from our troubles (Psalm 34:15-22). It can also keep us from succumbing to lies and falsehood (Proverbs 30:7-9).

Prayer not only can bring about our daily food (Matthew 6:11), it also helps us to live righteously (1 Thessalonians 5:23). Prayer can bring about healing (James 5:14-15).

Prayer can be beneficial in many more ways!

What guidance does Scripture provide regarding getting our prayers answered?

Scripture provides a number of principles for effective praying. One principle is that all our prayers are subject to the sovereign will of God. First John 5:14 instructs us, "This is the confidence that we have toward him, that if we ask anything according to his will he hears us." Prayer should not be an occasional practice but rather a continual practice. We are instructed in 1 Thessalonians 5:17 to "pray without ceasing." Further, we must recognize that sin is a hindrance to prayer being answered. Psalm 66:18 says, "If I had cherished iniquity in my heart, the Lord would not have listened." Living righteously, on the other hand, is a great benefit to prayer being answered. Proverbs 15:29 says, "The LORD is far from the wicked, but he hears the prayer of the righteous."

A good model prayer is the Lord's Prayer, found in Matthew 6:9-13. In this one prayer we find praise (verse 9), personal requests (verses 11-13), and an affirmation of God's will (verse 10).

We must also be persistent. The tenses in the Greek of Matthew 7:7-8 communicate the idea, "*Keep on asking* and it will be given; *keep on seeking* and you will find; *keep on knocking* and the door will be opened." Don't give up. Pray in faith. As Mark 11:22-24 puts it, we need to place our faith in God and believe that we have received what we have asked for. If what we have asked for is within God's will, we will receive it.

Finally, pray in Jesus' name (John 14:13-14). Jesus is the "bridge" between humanity and God the Father. We have the wonderful privilege of going to the Father and praying in the name of His dear Son.

If your prayer seems unanswered, keep trusting God no matter what. He has a reason for the delay. You can count on it.

Does God hear the prayers of non-Christians?

On the one hand, God is omniscient (Psalm 139:1-5). Therefore, He is aware in every way of the utterances of human beings the world over. Nothing escapes His attention. The real question is this: Does God personally *respond* to the prayers of non-Christians?

I think sometimes He does. For example, God certainly hears the prayer of a sinner who is praying to receive Christ as Savior by faith. I also think that in the process leading up to that person's conversion, God may answer some prayers along the way to show that person that he or she is dealing with the one true God. In other words, God may answer such prayers as a way of confirming that He is real and He is there.

Having said that, it is only Christians—those in the family of God—who can go before God and call Him "Abba" (loosely meaning *daddy*—Galatians 4:6) and claim the many promises God makes to those in His family (2 Peter 1:4).

How can God say He loves Jacob but hates Esau (Romans 9:13)?

The word "hate" should not be taken to mean that God had the human emotional sense of disgust, disdain, and a desire for revenge against Esau. God did not have a negative psychological emotion that burned against Esau. Rather the word should be understood as the Hebrew idiom it is—a word that means "to love less" (see Genesis 29:30-33). We might loosely paraphrase Romans 9:13, "In comparison to my great love for Jacob, my feeling for Esau, whom I 'love less,' may *seem* like hatred, even though I don't really emotionally hate him."

It seems cruel that God hardened Pharaoh's heart (Exodus 4:21). Is that fair?

Ten times in the text of Scripture it is said that the Pharaoh hardened *his own* heart (Exodus 7:13-14,22; 8:15,19,32; 9:7,34-35; 13:15), and ten times that God hardened Pharaoh's heart (4:21; 7:3; 9:12; 10:1,20,27; 11:10; 14:4,8,17). The Pharaoh hardened his own heart seven times *before* God first hardened it, though the prediction that God would do it preceded all.

It is evident that God hardens on the same grounds as showing mercy. If men will accept mercy, He will give it to them. If they will not, thus hardening themselves, He is only just and righteous in judging them. Mercy is the effect of a right attitude, and hardening is the effect of stubbornness or a wrong attitude toward God.

It is like the clay and the wax in the sun. The same sunshine hardens one and softens the other. The responsibility is with the materials, not with the sun. Scholars have suggested that the danger of resisting God is that He will eventually give us over to our own choices (see Romans 1:24-28).

Even so, it must be pointed out that God has always exercised His sovereign right of choice (Exodus 9:6-13). And we sinners can hardly call Him to task for it. The Maker has an indisputable right to do as He pleases with what He makes (verses 14-21).

Some Scriptures say that God does not change His mind (1 Samuel 15:29). Other Scriptures seem to portray God changing His mind (see verse 11). What are we to make of this?

On the one hand, God is unchanging in His essence or nature (Malachi 3:6) and is unchanging in His eternal purposes (see Ephesians 1). But this does not mean that God is some kind of Robot Automaton who cannot interact with His creatures and respond to them.

God promised to judge the Ninevites but then withheld judgment after the entire city repented (see the book of Jonah). Many people fail to realize that God has what you might call a built-in repentance clause to His promises of judgment. This clause is found in Jeremiah 18:7-10:

> If at any time I declare concerning a nation or a kingdom, that I
> will pluck up and break down and destroy it, and if that nation,

concerning which I have spoken, turns from its evil, I will relent of the disaster that I intended to do to it. And if at any time I declare concerning a nation or a kingdom that I will build and plant it, and if it does evil in my sight, not listening to my voice, then I will relent of the good that I had intended to do to it.

God changes His policy toward humans when He beholds a change in their actions. When God sees repentance, He responds with mercy and grace.

Does God always heal when Christians ask for it?

No. Sometimes God may have something He wants to teach a believer by allowing him or her to go through a time of sickness. God allowed Epaphroditus (Philippians 2:25-27), Trophimus (2 Timothy 4:20), Timothy (1 Timothy 5:23), Job (Job 1–2), and Paul (2 Corinthians 12:9) to suffer through periods of sickness. He does the same with us.

While the healing of our bodies in our mortal state is not guaranteed in the atonement, ultimate healing (in terms of our resurrection bodies) *is* guaranteed in the atonement. Our resurrection bodies will never get sick, grow old, or die (see 1 Corinthians 15:50). That's something to look forward to.

Today when Christians get sick, they should certainly pray for healing (see James 5:15). Also, contrary to the claims of certain televangelists, we should not be hesitant about going to the doctor. God can work a healing directly, or He can work a healing through the instrumentality of a doctor. God never portrays doctors in a negative light. Luke was a doctor. And Jesus Himself said, "Those who are well have no need of a physician, but those who are sick" (Matthew 9:12).

If we remain sick, we must continue to trust in God and rely on His grace, as did the apostle Paul (2 Corinthians 12:9). Our attitude should be that whether we are healthy or sick, we will always rest in God's sufficiency (Philippians 4:13).

Should Christians who are hurting in their relationship with God or struggling with a behavioral problem seek help from pastoral counseling, or is it better to join a recovery group?

I believe the pastor of the local church should be the primary counselor for the Christian. This is not to say that a biblically oriented recovery group is never warranted. Sometimes it may be. But why not make the pastor—who interprets life's problems through the lens of Scripture—the primary source of biblical counseling?

Such biblical counseling should include *an emphasis on the importance of becoming biblically literate.* Biblical doctrine enables us to develop a realistic worldview, without which we are doomed to ineffectual living (Romans 12:3; 2 Timothy 4:3-4). Doctrine can protect us from false beliefs that can lead to destructive behavior (1 Timothy 4:1-6; 2 Timothy 2:17-19; Titus 1:11).

Biblical counseling should also include *an emphasis on what the Bible says about the nature of man.* This includes his soul (1 Peter 2:11), his spirit (Romans 8:16), his heart (Hebrews 4:12), his conscience (1 Peter 2:19), and his mind (Romans 12:2).

A pastor should try to give the struggling Christian *a thorough understanding of man's sin nature.* Too often, "recovery" experts speak of getting rid of mere "character defects." The truth is, the whole "old" self is defective and depraved (2 Corinthians 4:4; Ephesians 4:18; Romans 1:18–3:20).

He should also perhaps emphasize *the threefold enemy of the Christian.* This enemy includes (1) *the world* (including the things of the world, which are expressions of "the desires of the flesh and the desires of the eyes and pride in possessions," 1 John 2:16), (2) *the flesh* (the sinful nature that is bent on sexual immorality, impurity, discord, jealousy, fits of rage, selfish ambition, dissensions, factions and envy, and drunkenness, Galatians 5:20-21), and (3) *the devil*, who seeks to tempt us (1 Corinthians 7:5), deceive us (2 Corinthians 11:14), afflict us (2 Corinthians 12:7), and hinder us (1 Thessalonians 2:18).

The pastor should also emphasize *dependence upon the Holy Spirit.* Scripture tells us that self-control is the fruit of the Holy Spirit (Galatians 5:22-23). As we habitually depend upon the Spirit (verse 25), such fruit will inevitably grow in our lives.

The counseling should also include *an emphasis on the sufficiency of God's grace.* God's grace enables us to cope with difficulties that can be overwhelming when approached through human strength alone (2 Corinthians 12:9-10).

And finally, there should be *an emphasis on faith.* Without faith in God it is impossible to effectively deal with behavioral problems and live victorious Christian lives (see 1 Thessalonians 5:8).

Once the counselee has recovered, he or she can serve as a shining example to others of the truth of Paul's inspiring affirmation: "I can do all things through him who strengthens me" (Philippians 4:13).

19
The Human Fall into Sin

What is "original sin"?

When Adam and Eve sinned, it didn't just affect them in an isolated way. It affected the entire human race. In fact, ever since then, every human being born into the world has been born in a state of sin.

The apostle Paul said that "sin came into the world through one man, and death through sin, and so death spread to all men because all sinned" (Romans 5:12). Indeed, "by the one man's disobedience the many were made sinners" (Romans 5:19; see also 1 Corinthians 15:21-22).

In Psalm 51:5 David said, "Behold, I was brought forth in iniquity, and in sin did my mother conceive me." According to this verse human beings are born into the world in a state of sin. The sin nature is passed on *from conception*. This is why Ephesians 2:3 says we are "by nature children of wrath." Every one of us is born into this world with a sin nature.

Was death the result of sin?

Yes. Scripture connects sin and death directly (Romans 5:12). One causes the other. Death came into the universe as a result of sin (Genesis 2:17).

This means that death is not natural. It is an unnatural intruder. God intended human beings *to live*. Death is therefore something foreign and hostile to human life. Death has arisen because of our rebellion against God. It is a form of God's judgment.

But there is grace even in death. For death, as a judgment against sin, serves to prevent us from living forever in a state of sin. When Adam and Eve sinned in the Garden of Eden (Genesis 2:17; 3:6), God assigned an angel to guard the Tree of Life. This was to protect against Adam and Eve eating from the Tree of Life while they were yet in a body of sin. How horrible it would be to live eternally in such a state.

By death, then, God saw to it that man's existence in a state of sin had definite limits. And by sending a Savior into the world—the Lord Jesus Christ—God made provision for taking care of the sin problem (John 3:17). Those who believe in Him will live eternally at His side, the sin problem having been banished forever.

Does the Bible make a distinction between mortal sins and venial sins?

Some people distinguish between *mortal sins* (deadly sins) and *venial sins* (lesser sins). The problem with such a view is that if a person grows up thinking that most of his sins have been venial sins, he may view himself as an essentially good person. He may not see himself as being in dire need of a Savior.

The Bible makes no such distinction between mortal sins and venial sins. It is true that some sins are worse than others (Proverbs 6:16-19), but never does Scripture say that only certain kinds of sin lead to spiritual death. *All* sin leads to spiritual death, not just one category of sins (Romans 3:23).

The truth is, *every single sin* a person commits is a mortal sin in the sense that it brings about spiritual death and separates us from God. Scripture reveals that even the smallest sin makes us legally guilty before God and warrants the death penalty (Romans 6:23).

It is sobering to realize that Scripture says every one of us is unrighteous before God. Romans 3:10-12 tells us, "'None is righteous, no, not one; no one understands; no one seeks for God. All have turned aside; together they have become worthless; no one does good, not even one." If words mean anything, we're all in dire trouble and need a Savior!

Does God punish children for their parents' sins (Numbers 14:18)?

I don't think so. The primary verse of dispute is Numbers 14:18, where we read, "The LORD is slow to anger and abounding in steadfast love, forgiving iniquity and transgression, but he will by no means clear the guilty, visiting the iniquity of the fathers on the children, to the third and the fourth generation."

I believe it is the consistent teaching of Scripture that God punishes people for *their own* sins. In Deuteronomy 24:16 we read, "Fathers shall not be put to death because of their children, nor shall children be put to death because of their fathers. Each one shall be put to death for his own sin." Moreover, in Ezekiel 18:14-20 we read that children will not die for the sins of their fathers.

So, how are we to interpret Numbers 14:18? I think this verse is referring to the fact that parents pass on to their children sinful patterns of behavior. A parental environment of alcoholism may produce a child who ends up drinking. A parental environment of yelling may produce a child who verbally abuses others. A parental environment where the father looks at pornography may produce a son who does likewise.

There are all kinds of examples of this type of thing in Scripture. Ahaziah "did what was evil in the sight of the LORD and walked in the way of his father and in the way of his mother" (1 Kings 22:52). "His mother was his counselor in doing wickedly" (2 Chronicles 22:3). Similarly, in Jeremiah 9:14 we read of those who "have stubbornly followed their own hearts and have gone after the Baals, as their fathers taught them." So, again, Numbers 14:18 is likely dealing with sinful patterns of behavior being passed on from one generation to the next.

Is it possible for the Christian to attain sinless perfection in this life?

No. A number of scriptural facts rule this out as a possibility. To begin, 1 John 1:8 tells us, "If we say we have no sin, we deceive ourselves, and the truth is not in us." Since this epistle was written to Christians

(1 John 2:12-14,19; 3:1; 5:13), it seems clear that Christians in mortal life should never make the claim to have attained perfection.

Second, this view does not take adequate account of the fact that each of us is born into the world with a sinful nature that stays with us until we die (Ephesians 2:3). The presence of the sin nature would seem to make any form of perfectionism impossible.

Third, the great saints of the Bible seemed to all recognize their own intrinsic sinfulness (Isaiah 6:5; Daniel 9:4-19; Ephesians 3:8). If anyone could have attained perfection, certainly Isaiah, Daniel, and the apostle Paul would have been contenders. But none of them succeeded. Why? Because they still had the sin nature in them that erupted in their lives from time to time.

So, for us to claim to be able to attain sinless perfection is, in the words of one theologian, *a perfect error.*

How can we respond to New Agers who say that Jesus taught that man's basic problem is ignorance of his divinity?

The biblical Jesus taught that human beings have a grave sin problem that is altogether beyond their means to solve. He taught that human beings are by nature evil (Matthew 12:34; Luke 11:13) and are capable of great wickedness (Mark 7:20-23; Luke 11:42-52). Moreover, Jesus said that humans are utterly lost (Luke 15:10), need to repent before a holy God (Mark 1:15), and need to be born again (John 3:3,5,7).

Jesus often spoke of human sin with metaphors that illustrate the havoc sin can wreak in one's life. He described human sin as a blindness (Matthew 15:14; 23:16-26), sickness (Matthew 9:12), being enslaved in bondage (John 8:34), and living in darkness (John 3:19-21; 8:12; 12:35-46). Moreover, Jesus taught that this is a universal condition and that all people are guilty before God.

Jesus also taught that not only external acts render a person guilty of sin—inner thoughts do this as well (Matthew 5:28). He taught that from within the human heart come "evil thoughts, sexual immorality, theft, murder, adultery, coveting, wickedness, deceit, sensuality, envy, slander, pride, foolishness." Jesus affirmed that "all these evil things come from within, and they defile a person" (Mark 7:21-23). Moreover, Jesus affirmed that God is fully aware of every person's sins—both external acts and inner thoughts. Nothing escapes His notice (Matthew 10:26; 22:18; Luke 6:8; John 4:17-19). Humans are quite obviously *not* divine!

What is the "sin that leads to death" mentioned in 1 John 5:16-17?

The "sin that leads to death" in 1 John 5:16-17 has been the cause of much concern among many believers. Some believe it refers to the spiritual death of unbelievers. Others believe that it refers to the physical death of believers as a result of committing either (1) a particular identifiable sin that is seen as the sin that leads to death or (2) a sin (*any* sin) that is persistently committed in an unrepentant attitude.

I personally believe the sin that leads to death might be viewed as a permanent separation of the believer into the *kosmos* (the fallen world system) which subsequently ends up killing him. There is a close relationship in John's writings between sin, death, and the *kosmos* ("the world"). A believer's relationship to the sin that leads to death is directly proportional to his relationship to the *kosmos*, for the *kosmos* (the evil world) is a death system. To become a part of this system *and remain entrenched there* is subsequently to come within the grips of death.

So, the sin for which death is a rapid consequence is *permanently retrogressing* into the *kosmos* death system. Other individual sins—whether related to lust of the flesh, the lust of the eyes, or the pride of life—can be committed that will not likely end in death. But in light of the fact that these lesser sins are a part of the *kosmos* system, it is possible that one such sin—if unrepented of and persisted in—could ultimately lead one to commit the greater sin of total separation into the *kosmos* death system. In such a condition, the *kosmos* ends up killing the believer. The death system yields its fruit—death.

Part 6

Questions About Salvation

The Gospel That Saves
The Security of the Christian's Salvation
God's Part and Man's Part
The Role of Baptism
Christians as Witnesses
All About the Church

20
The Gospel That Saves

Are the heathen really lost?

Yes. I must emphasize that if the heathen are not really lost, then many of the teachings of Christ become absurd. For example, John 3:16—"God so loved the world, that he gave his only Son, that whoever believes in him should not perish but have eternal life"—becomes meaningless.

If the heathen are not lost, Christ's post-resurrection and pre-ascension commands to His disciples are a mockery. In Luke 24:47 Christ commanded that "repentance and forgiveness of sins should be proclaimed in his name to all nations, beginning from Jerusalem." Similarly, in Matthew 28:19 He said, "Go therefore and make disciples of all nations, baptizing them in the name of the Father and of the Son and of the Holy Spirit." These verses might well be stricken from the Scriptures if human beings without Christ are not lost.

If the heathen are not really lost, then the Lord's words were meaningless when He said to His disciples, "As the Father has sent me, even so I am sending you" (John 20:21). Why did the Father send Him? Jesus Himself explained that "the Son of Man came to seek and to save the lost" (Luke 19:10).

If the heathen do not need Christ and His salvation, then neither do we. Conversely, if we need Him, *so do they.* The Scriptures become a bundle of contradictions, the Savior becomes a false teacher, and the Christian message becomes "much ado about nothing" if the heathen are not lost.

Scripture makes it very plain: "There is salvation in no one else, for there is no other name under heaven given among men by which we must be saved" (Acts 4:12). The Bible says, "There is one God, and there is one mediator between God and men, the man Christ Jesus" (1 Timothy 2:5).

Is it possible that the heathen can become saved through other religions?

Not a chance! Other religions do not lead to God. The one sin for which God judged the people of Israel more severely than any other was that of participating in heathen religions. Again and again the Bible implies and states that God hates, despises, and utterly rejects anything associated with heathen religions and practices. Those who follow such idolatry are not regarded as groping their way to God but rather as having turned their backs on Him, following the ways of darkness. Jesus is the *only* way of salvation (John 14:6; Acts 4:12; 1 Timothy 2:5).

Has God given a witness to the heathen by putting His law in their hearts?

I believe so. Scripture reveals that God has given a certain amount of "light" to every single person in the world. Paul speaks of this law written on human hearts in Romans 2:15. Every person has some sense of God's "oughts" and "ought nots" in his or her heart:

> [Everyone] has some conception of the difference between right and wrong; he approves of honesty; he responds to love and kindness; he resents it if someone steals his goods or tries to injure him. In other words, he has a conscience which passes judgment on his behavior and the behavior of others, something the Bible calls a law written on his heart.[1]

Has God given a witness to the heathen in the universe around us?

Yes. In beholding the world and the universe, it is evident that someone made the world and the universe (Psalm 19:1-6). Since the creation of the world, God's invisible qualities—His eternal power and divine nature—have been clearly seen and understood from that which He created (Romans 1:20).

We know from other Scripture verses that God is an invisible spirit (John 4:24). The physical eye cannot see Him. But His existence is nevertheless reflected in what He has made—the creation. The *creation,* which is visible, reveals the existence of the *Creator,* who is invisible.

Because all human beings can see the revelation of God in creation, all people—regardless of whether they've heard about Christ or have read the Bible—are held accountable before God. *All are without excuse.* Their rightful condemnation, as objects of God's wrath, is justified because their choice to ignore the revelation of God in creation is indefensible (see Psalm 19:1-6; Romans 1:20).

What if the heathen respond positively to the "light" of their conscience or God's witness of Himself in the creation?

The Scriptures clearly indicate that those who respond to the limited light around them (such as God's witness of Himself in the universe) will receive further, more specific "light." This is illustrated in the life of Cornelius. This Gentile was obedient to the limited amount of "light" he had received—that is, he had been obedient to Old Testament revelation (Acts 10:2). But he didn't have enough "light" to believe in Jesus Christ as the Savior. So God sent Peter to Cornelius's house to explain the gospel, after which time Cornelius believed in Jesus and was saved (Acts 10:44-48).

In view of the above, we must not allow God's name to be impugned by those who imply that God is unfair if He judges those who have never heard the gospel. As we have seen, God has given a witness of Himself to *all* humanity. Moreover, God desires all to be saved (1 Timothy 2:4) and doesn't want anyone to perish (2 Peter 3:9). He certainly takes no pleasure in the death of the unsaved (Ezekiel 18:23).

Let us remember that God is a *fair* Judge. "God will not do wickedly, and the Almighty will not pervert justice" (Job 34:12). "Shall not the Judge of all the earth do what is just?" (Genesis 18:25).

What is universalism?

Universalism states that sooner or later all people will be saved. This position holds that the concepts of hell and punishment are inconsistent with a loving God.

The older form of universalism, originating in the second century, taught that salvation would come after a temporary period of punishment. The more recent form of universalism declares that all human beings are now saved, though all do not realize it. Therefore, the job of the preacher and the missionary is to tell people they are already saved.

Do those who teach universalism appeal to Scripture?

Yes. Bible verses are typically twisted out of context in support of universalism. Such passages, interpreted properly, do not support universalism.

For instance, John 12:32 says that Christ's work on the cross makes possible the salvation of both Jews and Gentiles. Notice, however, that in the same passage, the Lord warned of judgment of those who reject Christ (verse 48). Philippians 2:10-11 assures us that someday all people will acknowledge that Jesus is Lord, but not necessarily as Savior. (Even those in hell will have to acknowledge Christ's Lordship.) And 1 Timothy 2:4 expresses God's desire that all be saved, but it does not promise that all *will* be. This divine desire is only realized in those who exercise faith in Christ (Acts 16:31).

How do we know some people will be unsaved in the end?

The Scriptures consistently categorize people into one of two classes (saved/unsaved, or believers/unbelievers), and they portray the final destiny of every person as being one of two realities (heaven or hell). For example, in Matthew 13:49 Jesus said, "So it will be at the close of the age. The angels will come out and separate the evil from the righteous." Two classes are mentioned—unbelievers and believers, spoken of as "the evil" and "the righteous."

In Matthew 25:32 we read of the judgment that follows Jesus' second coming: "Before him will be gathered all the nations, and he will separate people one from another as a shepherd separates the sheep from the goats." Here believers and unbelievers are differentiated by the terms "sheep" and "goats." The sheep will enter into God's kingdom (verse 34) and inherit eternal life, but the goats go into eternal punishment (verse 46).

Clearly, then, the Scriptures speak of two categories of people (the saved and the unsaved) and two possible destinies (heaven for the saved, hell for the unsaved). Each respective person ends up in one of these places based upon whether or not he or she placed saving faith in Christ during his or her time on the earth (Acts 16:31).

What is the gospel?

Perhaps the best single definition of the gospel in Scripture is found in 1 Corinthians 15:3-4, where the apostle Paul affirmed, "I delivered to you as of first importance what I also received: that Christ died for our sins in accordance with the Scriptures, that he was buried, that he was raised on the third day in accordance with the Scriptures."

The gospel, according to this passage, has four components: (1) Man is a sinner, (2) Christ is the Savior, (3) Christ died as man's substitute, and (4) Christ rose from the dead.

This is the gospel Paul and the other apostles preached. It is the gospel we too must preach.

Do people have to plead for mercy in order to be saved?

No. This is a misconception about the gospel. In truth, this idea is never found in Scripture. Salvation comes by faith in Christ alone (John 3:16; Acts 16:31) and is based upon God's grace (Ephesians 2:8-9). God provides pardon for anyone who believes. No one has to plead for it.

Must we successfully follow Christ's example in order to be saved?

No, though some have indeed taught this idea. *The Imitation of Christ* by Thomas à Kempis has been interpreted by some to teach that we become Christians by living as Christ did and obeying His teachings, seeking to behave as He behaved.

From a scriptural perspective, we simply do not have it in us to live as Christ lived. We are fallen human beings (Romans 3:23). Like the apostle Paul, we tend to do the things we know we shouldn't do, and we don't do the things we know we should do (Romans 7:15-17). Only the Holy Spirit working in us can imitate Christ in our lives (Galatians 5:16-23).

Is prayer a requirement to be saved?

No. Some have taught that one must pray the "prayer of repentance" to be saved. The scriptural perspective is that even though prayer may be a vehicle for the expression of one's faith, it is the faith that brings about salvation (John 3:16-17; Acts 16:31), not the prayer through which that faith is communicated. In fact, one can bypass prayer altogether by simply exercising faith in one's heart, and one becomes saved at that moment.

We must always remember that salvation is a free gift that we receive by faith in Christ (Ephesians 2:8-9). This is the glorious message of the gospel.

Does Psalm 19:1 tell us the gospel of Jesus Christ can be found in the stars (or the zodiac)?

I don't think so. That's not to deny that the stars can witness to God (Psalm 19:1). But you'll never find the gospel there. While people all over the world can understand something of God's power and glory by observing the stellar universe (Romans 1:20), they need an objectively communicated gospel to be saved. As I've indicated earlier, 1 Corinthians 15:3-4 tells us this gospel has four components: (1) Man is a sinner, (2) Christ is the Savior, (3) Christ died as man's substitute, and (4) Christ rose from the dead.

The stars cannot communicate this information.

Related to this, it's important to note that there is no uniform zodiac constellation. Some claim there are 24 zodiac signs, while others count eight, ten, or fourteen. This makes it impossible to interpret the stars in a uniform way.

Moreover, there is no uniform message behind the stars. The star-formed zodiac signs can be assigned whatever meaning the interpreter subjectively decides upon. The purported messages behind the signs are completely arbitrary.

What is the theological doctrine known as justification?

Humankind's dilemma of "falling short" pointed to the need for a solution—and that solution is found in justification (Romans 3:24). The word *justification* is a legal term and involves being "declared righteous" or "acquitted."

Negatively, the word means that one is once-and-for-all pronounced *not guilty* before God. Positively, the word means that man is once-and-for-all pronounced *righteous.* The very righteousness of Christ is imputed to the believer's life. From the moment that we place faith in Christ, God sees us through the lens of Christ's righteousness.

Though the Jews had previously tried to earn a right standing with God by works, Paul indicated that God's declaration of righteousness (justification) is given "by his grace as a gift" (Romans 3:24). The word grace literally means "unmerited favor." It is because of God's unmerited favor that human beings can freely be "declared righteous" before God. And this declaration occurs the moment a person exercises faith in Christ.

What is the difference between the Roman Catholic view of justification and the Protestant view?

Justification in the Roman Catholic view involves a transformation whereby the individual actually *becomes* righteous. It is viewed as a process by which God gradually perfects us. This process is furthered by good works and participation in the sacraments.[2]

By contrast, Protestants view justification as a singular and instantaneous event in which God declares the believing sinner to be righteous. Justification viewed in this way is a judicial term in which God makes a legal declaration. It is not based on performance or good works. It involves God's pardoning of sinners and restoring them to a state of righteousness. This declaration of righteousness takes place the moment a person trusts in Christ for salvation (Luke 7:48-50; Acts 10:43; Romans 3:25,28,30; 8:33-34; Galatians 4:21–5:12; 1 John 1:7–2:2).

It must also be noted that evangelicals believe in justification *by faith in Christ alone.* Good works do not contribute to justification at all but are rather viewed as the result of justification. Salvation comes about through faith (Romans 4; Galatians 3:6-14). Good works, however, are a byproduct of salvation (Matthew 7:15-23). Good works should result from the changed purpose for living that salvation brings.

Does redemption have an objective basis?

Yes it does. Scripture reveals that redemption is based entirely on the death of Christ upon the cross (2 Corinthians 5:19-21). The word *redemption* literally means "ransom payment." This is a word adapted from the slave market. We were formerly enslaved to sin and Satan, but Jesus ransomed us by His death on the cross. His shed blood was the ransom payment (Romans 3:25). Salvation is thus a free gift for us, but it cost Christ everything.

Where does the word *Christian* come from?

The word *Christian* is used only three times in the New Testament—the most important of which is Acts 11:26 (see also Acts 26:28 and 1 Peter 4:16). In Acts 11:26, we are told simply and straightforwardly, "In Antioch the disciples were first called Christians." This would have been around AD 42, about a decade after Christ died on the cross and was resurrected from the dead.

What does the term mean? The answer is found in the "ian" ending—for among the ancients this ending meant "belonging to the party of." "Herodians" belonged to the party of Herod. "Caesarians" belonged to the party of Caesar. "Christians" belonged to Christ. And Christians were loyal to Christ, just as the Herodians were loyal to Herod and Caesarians were loyal to Caesar.

The significance of the name *Christian* was that these followers of Jesus were recognized as a distinct group. They were seen as distinct from Judaism and as distinct from all other religions of the ancient world. We might loosely translate the term *Christians* as "those who belong to Christ," "Christ-ones," or perhaps "Christ-people." *They are ones who follow the Christ.*

Why are Christians called "saints"?

Many people have wrongly concluded that only certain unusually holy and pure people become "saints." But Scripture indicates that all who believe in Jesus Christ are properly categorized as saints. The word literally means, "one who is set apart" (see Romans 1:7; Philippians 1:1).

A saint is not one who has, in his or her own strength and power, attained a certain level of purity. Rather, a saint is one who has believed in Jesus Christ and has accordingly been washed from the stain of sin. Because of Jesus we are clean. We are saints not because of what we can do but because of what Jesus has already done for us. He died on the cross and thereby did away with the sin problem for all who believe in Him.

Is it possible for a sinner to become saved following the moment of death?

No. I say this because of the clear teaching in Luke 16:19-31. Once the rich man had died and ended up in a place of great suffering, he had no further opportunity for redemption. Nothing could be done at that point to ease his situation at all (Luke 16:24). Hebrews 9:27 assures us that judgment follows the moment of death. Thus the words in 2 Corinthians 6:2 have a sense of urgency: "*Now* is the day of salvation." There are no opportunities beyond death's door. One must choose *for* or *against* the Christ of the Bible in this life.

What about 1 Peter 3:18-19? Does this verse indicate that the gospel can be preached to the dead, implying a second chance?

This passage says, "Christ...[was] put to death in the flesh but made alive in the spirit, in which he went and proclaimed to the spirits in prison." Many evangelical scholars believe that the "spirits in prison" are fallen angels who grievously sinned against God. These spirits may have been the fallen angels of Genesis 6:1-6 who were disobedient to God during the days of Noah (entering into sexual relations with human women).

The Greek word for "proclaimed" (*kerusso*) in 1 Peter 3:19 is not the word used for preaching the gospel. Instead, it points to a proclamation of victory. This passage may imply that the powers of darkness thought they had destroyed Jesus at the crucifixion. But in raising Him from the dead, God turned the tables on them—and Jesus Himself proclaimed their doom. If this is the correct interpretation, it is clear the verse has nothing to do with human beings having a "second chance."

Another possible interpretation is that between His death and resurrection, Jesus went to the place of the dead and proclaimed a message to the wicked contemporaries of Noah. The proclamation, however, was not a gospel message. It was a proclamation of victory.

Still another possible interpretation is that this passage portrays Christ making a proclamation *through the person of Noah* to those who are *now* spirits in prison because they rejected His message (compare with 1 Peter 1:11; 2 Peter 2:5). Therefore, it may be that the Spirit of Christ made a proclamation through Noah to the ungodly humans who, at the time of Peter's writing, were "spirits in prison" awaiting final judgment.[3]

Regardless of which of the above interpretations is correct, evangelical scholars unanimously agree that this passage does not teach that people can hear and respond to the gospel in the next life (see 2 Corinthians 6:2; Hebrews 9:27).

What about 1 Peter 4:6? Does this verse imply a second chance?

First Peter 4:6 says, "This is why the gospel was preached even to those who are dead, that though judged in the flesh the way people are, they might live in the spirit the way God does."

Evangelical scholars suggest that perhaps the best way to interpret this difficult verse is to read it as referring to those who are *now* dead but who heard the gospel *while they were yet alive.* This makes sense in view of the tenses used: The gospel *was* preached (in the past) to those who *are* dead (presently). As one scholar put it, "The preaching was a past event...The preaching was done not after these people had died, but while they were still alive."[4]

21
The Security of the Christian's Salvation

Is it true that faith in Christ alone saves a person?

Yes. Close to 200 times in the New Testament salvation is said to be by faith alone—with no works in sight. John 3:15 assures us that "whoever believes in him may have eternal life." In John 5:24 Jesus says, "Truly, truly, I say to you, whoever hears my word and believes him who sent me has eternal life. He does not come into judgment, but has passed from death to life."

Likewise, in John 11:25 Jesus says, "I am the resurrection and the life. Whoever believes in me, though he die, yet shall he live." In John 12:46 Jesus says, "I have come into the world as light, so that whoever believes in me may not remain in darkness." John 20:31 affirms that his gospel was written "so that you may believe that Jesus is the Christ, the Son of God, and that by believing you may have life in his name."

The scriptural testimony is that we are saved *by* faith but *for* works. Works are not the condition of our salvation, but a consequence of it. We are saved not *by* works, but by the *kind of faith* that produces works.

What does James 2:17,26 mean when it says that faith without works is dead?

Martin Luther said it best: James 2 is not teaching that a person is saved by works. Rather a person is "justified" (declared righteous before God) by faith alone, but *not by a faith that is alone*. In other words, genuine faith will always *result* in good works in the saved person's life.

James is writing to Jewish Christians ("to the twelve tribes"—James 1:1) who were in danger of giving nothing but lip service to Jesus. His intent, therefore, was to distinguish true faith from false faith. He shows that true faith results in works, which become visible evidences of faith's invisible presence. In other words, good works are the "vital signs" indicating that faith is alive.

Apparently some of these Jewish Christians had made a false claim of faith. James indicates that merely claiming to have faith is not enough, for genuine faith is evidenced by works. As one scholar put it, "Great claims may be made about a corpse that is supposed to have come to life, but if it does not move, if there are no vital signs, no heartbeat, no perceptible pulse, it is still dead. The false claims are silenced by the evidence."[1]

The fact is, apart from the spirit, the body is dead—it's a lifeless corpse. By analogy, apart from the evidence of good works, faith is dead. It is lifeless and nonproductive. That is what James is teaching in this passage.

What about James 2:21? Does this verse teach that Abraham was justified before God by works and not by faith?

No. In this verse James is not talking about justification *before God* but rather justification *before other human beings.* This is clear from the fact that James stressed that we should "show" (James 2:18) our faith. That is, our faith must be something that can be seen by others via our "works" (verses 18-20).

Note that James acknowledged that Abraham was justified before God by faith, not works, when he said, "Abraham believed God, and it was counted to him as righteousness" (James 2:23). When he said that Abraham was "justified by works," he was speaking of what Abraham did that could be seen by other human beings—namely, his act of obedience in offering his son Isaac on the altar (verses 21-22).

Contrary to James, who talked about justification *before other humans,* the apostle Paul spoke about justification *before God.* Paul declared, "To the one who does not work but trusts him who justifies the ungodly, his faith is counted as righteousness" (Romans 4:5). Indeed, "he saved us, not because of works done by us in righteousness, but according to his own mercy" (Titus 3:5).

We conclude that while Paul is stressing the *root* of justification (faith in God), James is stressing *the fruit* of justification (works before men). But each man acknowledges both doctrines. Paul, for example, taught that we are saved by grace through faith, but then he quickly added that good works ought to follow salvation (verse 10).

What is the "Lordship salvation" issue all about?

The issue involved in Lordship salvation is the nature of salvation and saving faith: What *is* saving faith? What does it mean to trust in Jesus as Lord and Savior?

Lordship salvation proponents say that in order to be saved, one must not only believe and acknowledge that Christ is Savior but also be willing to submit to His Lordship. In other words, there must be—at the moment one trusts in Christ for salvation—a willingness to commit one's life absolutely to the Lord, even though the actual practice of a committed life may not follow immediately or completely.

Non-Lordship proponents argue that such a pre-salvation commitment to Christ's Lordship compromises salvation by grace ("unmerited favor"). They argue that accepting Jesus as Lord does not refer to a subjective commitment to Christ's Lordship in order to become saved, but rather involves a repentance (a changing of one's mind) about one's ideas of who Christ is (Messiah-God) and exercising faith in Him. Repentance from sin is *what follows* in the Christian's daily walk with the Lord.

Martin Luther gives us a good insight on this issue. He said that "faith alone justifies, but not the faith that is alone." He said that "works are not taken into consideration when the question respects justification. But true faith will no more fail to produce them than the sun can cease to give light."

What does the Bible say about our eternal security in salvation?

I believe that once a person exercises saving faith in Jesus Christ, he or she is forever in the family of God. In 1 Corinthians 12:13 we are told that at the moment of salvation the Holy Spirit places us in the body of Christ. Once we're infused into the body of Christ, we're never excised from the body. Ephesians 1:13 and 4:30 thus indicate that at the moment of believing in Jesus Christ for salvation, we are permanently "sealed" by the Holy Spirit unto the day of redemption.

Moreover, we read in John 10:28-30 that it is the Father's purpose to keep us secure despite anything that might happen once we've trusted in Christ. Nothing can snatch us out of His hands. God's plans cannot be thwarted (Isaiah 14:24). Further, Romans 8:29-39 portrays an unbroken chain that spans from the predestination of believers to their glorification in heaven. This indicates the certainty of all believers reaching heaven.

Another fact we need to keep in mind is that Christ regularly prays for each Christian (Hebrews 7:25; see also John 17). With Jesus interceding for us, we're secure. (His prayers are always answered!)

Of course, the fact that a believer is secure in his salvation doesn't mean he is free to sin. If the Christian sins and remains in that sin, Scripture says that God will discipline him or her just as a father disciplines his children (see Hebrews 12:7-11).

Does Hebrews 6:4-6 teach that Christians can lose their salvation?

In Hebrews 6:4-6 we read the following:

> It is impossible to restore again to repentance those who have once been enlightened, who have tasted the heavenly gift, and have shared in the Holy Spirit, and have tasted the goodness of the word of God and the powers of the age to come, if they then fall away, since they are crucifying once again the Son of God to their own harm and holding him up to contempt.

Christians have different takes on this difficult verse. Those who subscribe to Arminian theology believe this passage indicates that a Christian can indeed lose his or her salvation. If this interpretation is correct, one would also have to conclude that it is impossible to be saved a second time.

Others interpret this passage as referring to people who have a "said faith" as opposed to a "real faith" in Jesus Christ. They are professed believers, but not genuine believers. It is suggested that the "falling away" mentioned in Hebrews 6 is from the knowledge of the truth, not from an actual personal possession of it.

Still others interpret this passage as a warning to Christians to move on to spiritual maturity. I subscribe to this third view. Note that the context of Hebrews 6:4-6 is set for us in verses 1-3, where the author exhorts his readers to "go on to maturity."

Maturity was an important issue for the Jews of the first century who had converted to Christ and become Christians. The Jews living in and around the Palestine area were under the authority of the high priest. The high priest had sufficient influence to cause a Jew to lose his job, have his kids kicked out of synagogue school, and much more. Many scholars believe that when some Jews became Christians in the first century, the high priest put some heavy-duty pressure (*persecution*) on them.

This caused some of the Jewish Christians to become a bit gun-shy in their Christian lives. They were not as open about their Christian faith. Perhaps they thought that if they kept quiet about their faith and withdrew from external involvement in Christian affairs (like church attendance), the high priest would lighten up on them.

The author of the book of Hebrews saw this as a retreat from spiritual maturity in Christ. He thus encouraged them to move on to maturity in Christ.

The motivation of Hebrews 6:4-6, then, is not "Shape up or you lose your salvation." Instead, it is, "Because you're already Christians and have made a commitment to Him, let's move on to maturity, even though the circumstances are difficult." This was a message those first-century Jewish converts really needed to hear.

Can a Christian have his or her name blotted out of the book of life (Revelation 3:5)?

No, I don't think so. Revelation 3:5 says, "The one who conquers will be clothed thus in white garments, and I will never blot his name out of the book of life. I will confess his name before my Father and before his angels."

Notice that the same John who wrote the book of Revelation wrote elsewhere about the absolute security of each individual believer (see John 5:24; 6:35-37,39; 10:28-29). Therefore, however one interprets Revelation 3:5, one shouldn't interpret it to mean a believer can lose his or her salvation.

Many scholars believe this verse utilizes a Hebrew literary device in which a positive truth is taught by negating its opposite. In other words, the positive truth that believers' names will *always be in* the book of life is taught by negating the opposite idea (their names will *never be blotted out*).

This seems to fit with what other verses communicate about the book of life. For example, in Luke 10:20 Jesus said to the disciples, "Do not rejoice in this, that the spirits are subject to you, but rejoice that your names are written in heaven" (Luke 10:20). In Hebrews 12:23 we read of "the assembly of the firstborn who are enrolled in heaven."

22
God's Part and Man's Part

What is the case for election being based on God's foreknowledge?

Election involves God choosing certain individuals for salvation. This is the question: Did God base this election on foreknowledge or His sovereign will?

Many believe God used His foreknowledge to look down the corridors of time to see who would respond favorably to His gospel message, and on that basis He elected certain persons to salvation. Those who favor this view say that Scripture teaches that God's salvation has appeared to all people, not merely the elect (Titus 2:11). Also, the Bible teaches that Christ died for all (1 Timothy 2:6; 4:10; Hebrews 2:9; 1 John 2:2). There are numerous exhortations in Scripture to turn to God (Isaiah 31:6; Joel 2:13; Acts 3:19), to repent (Matthew 3:2; Luke 13:3,5; Acts 2:38; 17:30), and to believe (John 6:29; Acts 16:31; 1 John 3:23).

Scripture seems to indicate that election is based on God's foreknowledge of who would respond positively to such exhortations (Romans 8:28-30; 1 Peter 1:1).

Are there theological problems with the view that election is based on God's foreknowledge?

Yes. To begin, some statements indicate that the Father *gave* certain ones to Christ (John 6:37; 17:2,6,9). Christ said, "No one can come to me unless the Father who sent me draws him" (John 6:44). Moreover, in Romans 9:10-16 God is said to have chosen Jacob rather than Esau, even before they were born and before they had done either good or bad.

We read in Acts 13:48 that "as many as were appointed to eternal life believed." Ephesians 1:5-8 and 2:8-10 represent salvation as originating in the choice of God and as being all of grace (see also Acts 5:31; 11:18; Romans 12:3; 2 Timothy 2:25). Finally, many claim that if election is not unconditional and absolute, then God's whole plan is uncertain and liable to miscarriage.

What is the case for election being based on God's sovereignty?

There are a number of arguments supporting the idea that God's election was based on His sovereign choice: Biblical statements support election by choice (Acts 13:48). The whole process of salvation is a gift of God (Romans 12:3; Ephesians 2:8-10). Certain verses speak of human beings having been given to Christ (John 6:37; 17:2), and Scripture indicates that the Father draws people to Christ (John 6:44).

There are examples in Scripture of the sovereign calling of God upon individuals, such as Paul (Galatians 1:15) and Jeremiah (Jeremiah 1:5), even before they were born. Election is necessary because of humanity's total depravity (Job 14:1; Jeremiah 13:11; Romans 3:10-20), as well as the sin nature's prevention of humanity's ability to initiate a relationship with God (Ephesians 2:1). Election is compatible with God's sovereignty (Proverbs 19:21; Jeremiah 10:23). Election is portrayed as being from all eternity (2 Timothy 1:9). It is on the basis of election by choice that the appeal to a godly life is made (Colossians 3:12; 2 Thessalonians 2:13; 1 Peter 2:9).

Are there theological problems with the view that election is based on God's sovereign choice?

Yes. Two primary arguments have been suggested against this view:

First, some advocates of this view suggest that if election is limited by God, then surely the atonement must be limited as well. However, this conclusion is clearly refuted by John 1:29, 3:16, 1 Timothy 2:6, Hebrews 2:9, and 1 John 2:2.

Second, others argue that election by choice makes God responsible for "reprobation." However, those not included in election suffer only their due reward. God does not "elect" a person to hell. Those not elected to salvation are left to their own self-destructive ways.

What facts can we all agree on regarding the doctrine of election?

Whichever view one concludes is the correct one, the following facts are agreeable to everybody: (1) God's election is ultimately loving (Ephesians 1:4-11), (2) election is an act that glorifies God (Ephesians 1:12-14), and (3) the product of election is a people who do good works (Ephesians 2:10; see also Colossians 3:12).

I've heard people describe Reformed theology with the acronym TULIP. What does this mean?

This acronym represents the five doctrinal pillars of Reformed theology. The first is *total depravity*, which does not suggest that human beings are completely devoid of any good impulses, but it does indicate that every human being is engulfed in sin to such a severe degree that he or she can do nothing to earn merit of any kind before God. The second is *unconditional election*, which means that God's choice of certain persons to salvation is not dependent upon any foreseen virtue or faith on their part. Rather, it is based on His sovereignty.

The third is *limited atonement.* This doctrine says that Christ's atoning death was only for the elect. The fourth, *irresistible grace*, is the idea that those whom God has chosen for eternal life will, as a result of God's grace, come to faith and thus to salvation. This view is also called efficacious grace. Finally, *perseverance of the saints* is the teaching that those who are genuine believers will endure in the faith to the end.

What do Arminians believe?

Arminianism is a theological movement that stemmed from the teachings of Dutch theologian Jacobus Arminius (1560–1609).

We can summarize the beliefs of Arminianism under the following five pillars: (1) God elected people to salvation who He foreknew would of their own free will believe in Christ and persevere in the faith. (2) In His atonement at the cross, Jesus provided redemption for all humankind, making all humankind savable. But Christ's atonement becomes effective only for those who believe in Jesus. (3) Human beings cannot save themselves. The Holy Spirit must effect the new birth. (4) Prevenient grace from the Holy Spirit enables the believer to respond to the gospel and cooperate with God in salvation. (5) Believers have been empowered by God to live a victorious life, but they are capable of turning from grace and losing their salvation.

Arminians obviously believe quite differently from Calvinists. For example, Calvinists believe that God elected people according to His sovereign will and not based on His foreknowledge of how humans would respond to the gospel. Calvinists believe that Christ died only for the elect. Calvinists also believe that genuine believers will endure in the faith to the end.

What is the doctrine known as "limited atonement"?

Limited atonement (a doctrine I disagree with) is the view that Christ's atoning death was *only* for the elect. Another way to say this is that Christ made no atoning provision for those who are not of the elect.

What verses are cited in support of the doctrine of limited atonement?

Some advocates of this view cite Matthew 1:21, which says, "She will bear a son, and you shall call his name Jesus, for he will save *his people* from their sins." They may also appeal to Matthew 20:28: "The Son of Man came not to be served but to serve, and to give his life as a ransom *for many*." They might point out that Jesus also said, "This is my blood of the covenant, which is poured out *for many* for the forgiveness of sins" (Matthew 26:28). They may further note that he said, "I lay down my life *for the sheep*" (John 10:15).

They also may appeal to Paul, who said to the Ephesian elders, "Pay careful attention to yourselves and to all the flock, in which the Holy

Spirit has made you overseers, to care for *the church of God*, which he obtained with his own blood" (Acts 20:28). Also, they may point to Ephesians 5:25: "Husbands, love your wives, as Christ loved *the church* and gave himself up *for her*." The writer of Hebrews is sometimes cited because he says that "Christ, having been offered once to bear the sins *of many*, will appear a second time, not to deal with sin but to save *those* who are eagerly waiting for him" (Hebrews 9:28). Others might appeal to John 15:13: "Greater love has no one than this, that someone lays down his life for *his friends*."

What are the primary arguments offered in support of limited atonement?

Some people point out that the Bible says Christ died for a specific group of people. Those for whom He suffered and died are variously called His "sheep" (John 10:11,15), His "church" (Acts 20:28; Ephesians 5:25-27), His "people" (Matthew 1:21), and the "elect" (Romans 8:32-35). Also, they suggest that because the elect were chosen before the foundation of the world (Ephesians 1), Christ could not honestly be said to have died *for all* human beings.

Some advocates of limited atonement say Christ is defeated if He died for all people and all people aren't saved. Others say that if Christ died for all people, then God would be unfair in sending people to hell for their own sins. Christ paid for the sins of the elect. Lost people pay for *their own* sins.

Also, others suggest that Christ didn't pray for everyone in His high priestly prayer in John 17. He prayed only for *His own*, so Christ must not have died for everyone. Some advocates of limited atonement have charged that unlimited atonement tends toward universalism. Therefore, unlimited atonement cannot be the correct view.

In the Middle Ages such scholars as Prosper of Aquitaine, Thomas Bradwardine, and John Staupitz taught limited atonement. It is claimed that even though John Calvin did not explicitly teach the doctrine, it seems implicit in some of his writings.

Though terms such as "all," "world," and "whosoever" are used in Scripture in reference to those for whom Christ died, these words are to be understood in terms of the elect. "All" refers to "all *of the elect*" or "all *classes of people*" (Jew and Gentile). "World" refers to the "world *of the elect*." "Whosoever" means "whosoever of the elect."

What are the scriptural arguments that prove the doctrine of unlimited atonement?

Unlimited atonement is the view that Christ died for the sins of all people in the world. Following is a sampling of supportive verses (with relevant portions italicized): In Luke 19:10 we read, "The Son of Man came to seek and to save *the lost*." The lost in this verse refers to the *collective whole* of lost humanity, not just to the lost elect. Jesus is also called the "Lamb of God, who takes away the sin *of the world*" (John 1:29). John Calvin says "world" here refers "indiscriminately to the whole human race."[1]

In John 3:16 we read, "God so loved *the world*, that he gave his only Son, that *whoever* believes in him should not perish but have eternal life." Contextually this verse alludes to Numbers 21. Moses put up a bronze serpent so that if "anyone" looked to it, he experienced physical deliverance from serpent bites (Numbers 21:9). Christ likewise says that "whoever" believes on the uplifted Son of Man shall experience spiritual deliverance.

In John 4:42 some Samaritans referred to Jesus as "the Savior *of the world*." The Samaritans were surely not thinking of the world of the elect. First Timothy 4:10 refers to "the Savior *of all people, especially of those who believe*." Apparently the Savior has done something for *all* human beings, though it is less in degree than what He has done for those who believe.[2]

Romans 5:6 says, "Christ died *for the ungodly*." It doesn't make much sense to read this as saying that Christ died for the ungodly among the elect, but rather *all* the ungodly of the earth. Also, Romans 5:18 informs us that "as one trespass led to *condemnation for all men*, so one act of righteousness leads to *justification and life for all men*." Calvin commented, "Though Christ suffered for the sins of the whole world...yet all do not receive Him."[3]

First John 2:2 says, "He is the propitiation for *our* sins, and *not for ours only* but also for the sins *of the whole world.*" It would not make sense to interpret this verse as saying, "He is the propitiation for our [*the elect's*] sins, and not for ours [*the elect's*] only but also for the sins of the whole world [*of the elect*]."

Isaiah 53:6 says, "*All we* like sheep have gone astray...and the LORD has laid on him the iniquity *of us all.*" The same "all" that went astray is the "all" for whom the Lord died. In 2 Peter 2:1, we are told that Christ even paid the price of redemption for false teachers who deny Him.

Does the doctrine of unlimited atonement fit well with the universal proclamation of the gospel?

Yes. Such a universal proclamation would make sense *only* if the doctrine of unlimited atonement were true. In Matthew 24:14 Jesus said, "This gospel of the kingdom will be proclaimed throughout the whole world as a testimony to all nations." In Matthew 28:19 Jesus said, "Go therefore and make disciples of all nations." In Acts 1:8 Jesus said, "You will be my witnesses in Jerusalem and in all Judea and Samaria, and to the end of the earth."

With such passages in mind, it is legitimate to ask, "If Christ died only for the elect, how can Scripture offer salvation to *all* persons without some sort of insincerity, artificiality, or dishonesty being involved in the process?" Is it not improper to offer salvation to everyone if in fact Christ did not die to save everyone? The fact is, those who hold to limited atonement cannot say to any sinner with true conviction, "Christ died *for you.*"

How can we put the "limited" and "unlimited" verses together so that, taken as a whole, all the verses are interpreted in a harmonious way without contradicting each other?

The two sets of passages—one seemingly in support of limited atonement, the other in support of unlimited atonement—are not irreconcilable. It is true that Scripture indicates that the benefits of

212 | THE BIG BOOK OF BIBLE ANSWERS

Christ's death belong to God's "sheep," His "people," and the like, but it would have to be shown that Christ died *only* for them in order for limited atonement to be true. No one denies that Christ died for God's "sheep" and His "people." It is only denied that Christ died *exclusively* for them.[4] Certainly if Christ died for the whole of humanity, there is no logical problem in saying that He died for a specific *part* of the whole.[5]

23

The Role of Baptism

What is the case for baptism by sprinkling?

Christians who opt for sprinkling point out that a secondary meaning of the Greek word *baptizo* is "to bring under the influence of." This fits sprinkling better than immersion.

Moreover, it is argued, baptism by sprinkling better pictures the coming of the Holy Spirit upon a person. Jesus said, "John baptized with water, but you will be baptized with the Holy Spirit not many days from now" (Acts 1:5). When this promise was fulfilled, the Holy Spirit *descended upon their heads* (2:3). Peter then said this phenomenon was a fulfillment of what Joel prophesied in the Old Testament: "I will *pour out* my Spirit on all flesh" (2:17). Based on this, some advocates of this view argue that baptism by pouring or sprinkling best symbolizes this truth.

Some people suggest that immersion would have been impossible in some of the baptisms portrayed in Scripture. They believe that in Acts 2:41, for example, it would have been impossible to immerse all 3,000 people who were baptized. The same is said to be true in regard to Acts 8:38, 10:47, and 16:33.

What is the biblical case for baptism by immersion?

The primary meaning of the Greek word *baptizo* is "to immerse." And the prepositions normally used in conjunction with *baptizo* (such as "into" and "out of" the water) clearly picture immersion and not sprinkling. The Greek language has perfectly acceptable words for "sprinkling" and "pouring," but these words are *never* used in the context of baptism in the New Testament.

It is a fact that the ancient Jews practiced baptism by immersion. So it is likely that the Jewish converts to Christianity (including the disciples, who came out of Judaism) would have followed this precedent.

Jesus Himself was baptized by immersion, after which "he went up from the water" (Matthew 3:16). Likewise, Phillip baptized the Ethiopian eunuch by immersion, for "they both went down into the water, Philip and the eunuch, and he baptized him" (Acts 8:38). John the Baptist baptized people "near Salim, because water was plentiful there" (John 3:23). Why baptize where there's lots of water unless the baptisms were by immersion?

Certainly baptism by immersion best pictures the significance of death to the old life and resurrection to the new life in Christ (Romans 6:1-4). And, despite what sprinkling advocates say, in every instance of water baptism recorded in the New Testament, immersion was practiced. Arguments that there was not enough water to accomplish immersion are weak and unconvincing. Archeologists have uncovered ancient pools all over the Jerusalem area.

Even though I believe immersion is the biblical norm of baptism, it is not an inflexible norm. God accepts the believer on the basis of his or her faith in Christ and the desire to obey Him, not on the basis of how much water covers the body at the moment of baptism.

Does Acts 2:38 teach that a person must be baptized in order to be saved?

No, I don't think so. Admittedly, this is not an easy verse to interpret. But a basic principle of Bible interpretation is that difficult verses are to be interpreted in light of the easier, clearer verses. One should never build a theology on difficult passages.

The great majority of passages dealing with salvation in the New Testament affirm that salvation is by faith alone. A good example is John 3:16-17: "God so loved the world, that he gave his only Son, that whoever believes in him should not perish but have eternal life. For

God did not send his Son into the world to condemn the world, but in order that the world might be saved through him." In view of such clear passages, how is Acts 2:38 to be interpreted?

A single word in the verse gives us the answer. The verse reads, "Peter said to them, 'Repent and be baptized every one of you in the name of Jesus Christ *for* the forgiveness of your sins, and you will receive the gift of the Holy Spirit.'"

Students of the Greek language have often pointed out that the Greek word "for" (*eis*) is a preposition that can indicate *causality* ("in order to attain") or a *result* ("because of"). When I say, "I'm taking an aspirin *for* my headache," I am using "for" in a *resultant* sense. Obviously this means I'm taking an aspirin *as a result* of my headache. I'm not taking an aspirin *in order to attain* a headache.

The sentence "I'm going to the office *for* my paycheck" uses "for" in a *causal* sense. Obviously this means I'm going to the office *in order to attain* my paycheck.

In Acts 2:38 the word "for" is apparently used in a resultant sense. The verse might be paraphrased, "Repent, and be baptized every one of you in the name of Jesus Christ *because of* (or *as a result of*) the remission of sins." The verse is not saying, "Repent, and be baptized every one of you in the name of Jesus Christ *in order to attain* the remission of sins."

Therefore, this verse, properly interpreted, indicates that water baptism *follows* the salvation experience.

Does Mark 16:16 teach that a person must be baptized in order to be saved?

This is another difficult passage. As noted previously, however, a basic principle of Bible interpretation is that difficult verses should be interpreted in light of the easier, clearer verses. Also, it is helpful to know that Mark 16:16 is not found in some of our earliest manuscripts.

Having said that, notice the latter part of the verse: "Whoever believes and is baptized will be saved, but *whoever does not believe will be condemned*" (Mark 16:16). *Unbelief* brings condemnation, not a lack of being baptized. When one rejects the gospel, refusing to believe it, that person is condemned.

Does John 3:1-5 teach that a person must be baptized in order to be saved?

Some have concluded that the reference to being "born of water" in John 3:5 means one must be baptized in water in order to be saved. But this is not what Jesus was intending to teach.

The context of John 3 clarifies Jesus' intended meaning. Being "born again" (literally, "born from above") simply refers to God's gift of eternal life to the one who believes in Christ (John 3:3; Titus 3:5). Being "born again" thus places one into God's eternal family (1 Peter 1:23) and gives the believer a new capacity and desire to please the Father (2 Corinthians 5:17).

Critical to a proper understanding of John 3:1-5 is verse 6: "That which is born of the flesh is flesh, and that which is born of the Spirit is spirit." Flesh can only reproduce itself as flesh—and flesh cannot pass muster with God (see Romans 8:8). The law of reproduction is "according to its kind" (see Genesis 1). So, likewise, the Spirit produces spirit.

In Nicodemus's case, we find a Pharisee who would have been trusting in his physical descent from Abraham for entrance into the Messiah's kingdom. The Jews believed that because they were physically related to Abraham, they were in a specially privileged position before God. Christ, however, denied such a possibility. Parents can transmit to their children only the nature that they themselves possess. Each parent's nature is sinful because of Adam's sin, so each parent transmits a sinful nature to the child. And what is sinful cannot enter the kingdom of God (John 3:5). The only way one can enter God's kingdom is to experience a spiritual rebirth, and this is precisely what Jesus is emphasizing to Nicodemus.

But this is the problem: Nicodemus did not initially comprehend Jesus' meaning. Nicodemus wrongly concluded that Jesus was speaking of something related to physical birth. He could not understand how a person could go through physical birth a second time (John 3:4). So,

Jesus picked up on Nicodemus's line of thought and sought to move the argument from physical birth to spiritual birth.

Notice how Jesus went about His explanation to Nicodemus. He first speaks about being "born of water and the Spirit" in John 3:5, and then explains what He means by this in verse 6. It would seem that "born of water" in verse 5 is parallel to "born of the flesh" in verse 6, just as "born of...the Spirit" in verse 5 is parallel to "born of the Spirit" in verse 6. Jesus' message, then, is that just as one has had a physical birth to live on the earth, so one must also have a spiritual birth in order to enter the kingdom of God. One must be "born from above." The verse thus has nothing whatsoever to do with water baptism.

Can we be sure that baptism is not necessary for salvation?

The words of the apostle Paul settle the issue: "Christ did not send me to baptize but to preach the gospel" (1 Corinthians 1:17). Paul here draws a clear distinction between baptism and the gospel. And since it is the gospel that saves (1 Corinthians 15:1-2), baptism is clearly not necessary to attain salvation.

That is not to say that baptism is unimportant. I believe that baptism should be the first act of obedience to God following a person's conversion to Christ. But even though we should obey God and get baptized, we mustn't forget that our faith in Christ, not baptism, is what saves us (Acts 16:31; John 3:16). Baptism is basically a public profession of faith. It says to the whole world, "I'm a believer in Jesus Christ and have identified my life with Him."

Are we to be baptized only "in the name of Jesus Christ" (Acts 2:38), and not in the name of the Father, the Son, and the Holy Spirit?

No, I don't think so. This idea is based on a misinterpretation of Acts 2:38: "Repent and be baptized every one of you *in the name of Jesus Christ* for the forgiveness of your sins, and you will receive the gift of the Holy Spirit."

218 | THE BIG BOOK OF BIBLE ANSWERS

As a backdrop, it is important to understand that the phrase *in the name of* in biblical times carried the meaning "by the authority of." Therefore, the phrase in Acts 2:38 cannot be interpreted to be some kind of a magic baptismal formula. The verse simply indicates that people are to be baptized *according to the authority of Jesus Christ*. The verse does not mean that the words "in the name of Jesus Christ" must be liturgically pronounced over each person being baptized.

If we were consistent in using the strict "baptism only in the name of Jesus Christ" logic, we'd have to pronounce the words "in the name of Jesus" over everything we did. For, indeed, Colossians 3:17 instructs us, "Whatever you do, in word or deed, *do everything in the name of the Lord Jesus*." Clearly the words "in the name of Jesus Christ" are not intended as a formula.

I believe that a baptism "in the name of Jesus Christ" makes good sense in the context of Acts 2, because the Jews ("men of Judea" in verse 14; "men of Israel" in verse 22), to whom Peter was preaching, had rejected Jesus as the Messiah. It is logical that Peter would call on them to repent of their rejection of Jesus the Messiah and become publicly identified with Him via baptism.

Does the reference to "baptism for the dead" in 1 Corinthians 15:29 mean that we can be baptized on behalf of our dead loved ones?

No. Scripture is abundantly clear that this life (on the earth) is the only time we have to choose either *for* or *against* Christ. Once we die, all opportunities vanish. Hebrews 9:27 tells us, "It is appointed for man to die once, and after that comes judgment."

Notice that throughout 1 Corinthians, the apostle Paul refers to the Corinthian believers and himself using first-person pronouns ("we," "I"). But when he comes to 1 Corinthians 15:29—the verse dealing with baptism for the dead—Paul switches to the third person ("they"). A plain reading of the text would seem to indicate that Paul is referring to people outside the Christian camp in Corinth. And he seems to be disassociating himself from the group practicing baptism for the dead.

Some people believe Paul is referring to a cultic practice in Corinth, a city well known for its pagan beliefs.

Whatever baptism for the dead is, Paul certainly did not encourage his hearers in any way to practice it. He merely used the case as an illustration. The Bible does not mention this baptism until Paul, and it does not mention it afterward. Christ does not mention it, nor do any of the other apostles.

The fact that there are no further opportunities for salvation following death is illustrated in Luke 16:19-31, which deals with the fate of the rich man and Lazarus. Once the rich man had died and ended up in a place of great suffering, he had no further opportunity for redemption. Nothing could be done at that point to ease his situation at all (verses 24-26). A baptism for the dead would have had no effect on his or anyone else's situation.

This highlights the importance of the words in 2 Corinthians 6:2, "Now is the day of salvation." There are no opportunities beyond death's door. One must choose *for* or *against* the Christ of the Bible in this life.

What is the case for the baptism of infants?

Proponents of the baptism of infants often argue that infant baptism is analogous to circumcision in the Old Testament, which was done to infant boys. They reason that if circumcision (the sign of the Old Testament covenant) was done on children, then there is no reason to prohibit baptism (the sign of the New Covenant) being performed on children as well.

Moreover, four times the New Testament mentions whole households being baptized (Acts 16:15,33; 18:8; 1 Corinthians 1:16). Since whole families usually include infants or small children, it is reasonable to conclude that these are examples of infant baptisms.

What is the case against the baptism of infants?

The biblical pattern is that a person gets baptized *following* his or her conversion experience. The truth is, infants are not old enough to believe, and belief in Christ is a condition for being saved (John 3:18,

36; 20:31; Acts 16:31). For this reason, we never once witness Jesus or any of the disciples baptizing an infant.

Moreover, nowhere does the text of Scripture say that any infants were baptized when household baptisms took place. This is a supposition. It seems clear that at least some of the household baptisms mentioned in the New Testament involved *all believers*. For example, we read of Crispus's household that "Crispus, the ruler of the synagogue, believed in the Lord, *together with his entire household*" (Acts 18:8). Likewise, it would seem that the household of Stephanas were all believers, for 1 Corinthians 16:15 reveals that the members of this household "have devoted themselves to the service of the saints."

Note also that not a single verse in the New Testament indicates that baptism is a sign of the New Covenant. Rather, communion is the sign of the New Covenant (1 Corinthians 11:25). Having said all this, it is certainly permissible and right for young children who have trusted in Christ to get baptized.

24
Christians as Witnesses

Is there a sense in which all of us are missionaries?

Yes indeed! A Christian leader once said, "Every heart with Christ is a missionary; every heart without Christ is a mission field." Christians can be missionaries wherever they are—whether it be abroad or in our home country. We can be missionaries in our schools, shopping centers, libraries, theaters, the workplace, and anywhere we happen to be.

Some people claim that Jesus is "one of many ways to God." As witnesses of Christ, how can we respond to this idea?

This line of thinking tries to argue that all the leaders of the world religions were pointing to the same God. This is not true, however. The reason we can say this is that the leaders of the different world religions had different (and *contradictory*) ideas about God.

Jesus taught that there is only one God and that He is triune in nature (Matthew 28:19). Muhammad taught that there is only one God, but that God cannot have a son, and there is no Trinity. Krishna in the Bhagavad Gita (a Hindu scripture) indicated he believed in a combination of polytheism (there are many gods) and pantheism (all is God). Confucius believed in many gods. Zoroaster taught that both a good god and a bad god exist. Buddha taught that the concept of God was essentially irrelevant.[1]

Obviously, these religious leaders are not pointing to the same God. If one is right, all the others are wrong. If Jesus is right (and *He is*), then all the others are wrong.

Jesus claimed that what He said took precedence over all others. He said He is humanity's *only* means of coming into a relationship with God (John 14:6). This was confirmed by those who followed Him (Acts 4:12; 1 Timothy 2:5). And Jesus warned His followers about those who would try to set forth a different Christ (Matthew 24:4-5).

Jesus is totally unique. He proved the veracity of all He said by resurrecting from the dead (Acts 17:31; Romans 1:4). None of the other leaders of the different world religions did that.

How can we go about witnessing to Jews?

I like to witness to Jews using the method suggested by Stuart Dauermann.[2] As one reads through the Bible, we find progressively detailed prophecies about the identity of the Messiah. Obviously, as the prophecies become increasingly detailed, the field of qualified "candidates" becomes increasingly narrow. The Old Testament has more than 100 messianic prophecies.

In showing a Jewish person that Jesus is the Messiah, one effective approach is to begin with very broad prophecies (such as the Messiah being born of a woman—Genesis 3:15) and then narrow the field to include increasingly specific and detailed prophecies (such as the Messiah being born of a virgin—Isaiah 7:14). You might use "circles of certainty" to graphically illustrate your points as you share these prophecies. You can use any Old Testament messianic prophecies you want during the witnessing encounter. As you move from broad prophecies to more narrow prophecies, the circles of certainty progressively narrow until they focus on only one person—Jesus Christ.

What broad and increasingly specific messianic prophecies would you suggest for my "circles of certainty" in witnessing to Jews?

Here are my favorites:

Circle 1: The Messiah's humanity. Scripture says that the Messiah had to become a human being. This circle is obviously a very large one.

The Messiah's humanity is predicted in Genesis 3:15 and fulfilled in Galatians 4:4-5. (Open your Bible and read these verses aloud while witnessing.)

Circle 2: The Messiah's Jewishness. Scripture says the Messiah had to be Jewish—that is, He had to be a descendant of Abraham, Isaac, and Jacob. This narrows the circle considerably. Of all human beings who have ever lived, only *Jewish* human beings would qualify. Read aloud from Genesis 12:1-3, where God makes a covenant with Abraham (the "father" of the Jews). You might also read aloud from Genesis 28:10-15, which shows that the promised seed was to come through the line of Abraham, Isaac, and Jacob.

Circle 3: The Messiah's tribal identity. The circle gets even narrower when it is demonstrated that the Messiah had to come from the tribe of Judah, which Genesis 49:10 demonstrates. Here Jacob is on his death-bed. Before he dies, he affirms that the scepter (of the ruling Messiah) would be from the tribe of Judah.

Circle 4: The Messiah's family. Scripture tells us that the Messiah had to be from David's family. This narrows the circle still further. The Messiah's descent from David's family is affirmed in 2 Samuel 7:16 and reaffirmed in Jeremiah 23:5-6.

Circle 5: The Messiah's birthplace. Scripture clearly prophesies that the Messiah was to be born in Bethlehem. This narrows the circle of possible candidates for the Messiah tremendously. Read aloud from Micah 5:2.

Circle 6: The Messiah's manner of life, rejection, and death. Point the Jewish person to Isaiah 53:1-9. Note from these verses that: (1) The Messiah was to be despised and rejected by His fellow Jews. (2) He would be put to death following a judicial proceeding. (3) He would be guiltless. Obviously these facts about the Messiah narrow the circle still further.

Circle 7: The Messiah's chronology. Point the Jewish person to Daniel 9:24-26. Regarding this passage, note the following facts: (1) The city of Jerusalem would be rebuilt, as would the temple. (2) The Messiah would come. (3) The Messiah would then be "cut off" (die), but not for Himself. (4) The city and the temple would then be destroyed. Note especially that the Messiah had to come and die *prior* to the destruction of the second temple, which occurred in AD 70.

Is there anyone who has fulfilled all these conditions? Is there anyone who was a human being, a Jew, from the tribe of Judah and the family of David, born in Bethlehem, despised and rejected by the Jewish people, executed as a result of a judicial proceeding, guiltless, and came and died before the destruction of the second temple in AD 70?

Yes! His name was Jesus!

How can we arouse the liberal Christian's interest in true Christianity?

Emphasize that Christianity ultimately is a relationship, not a religion. Christianity is not just a set of doctrines or creeds—a "dead orthodoxy." Rather it involves a personal relationship with the living Lord of the universe. This is the most important truth you will want to leave the liberal to ponder because this is the ingredient of true Christianity that the liberal Christian is most painfully lacking.

Liberal Christians admit that one of their goals has been to make Christianity relevant to the masses of humanity by stripping the Bible of miracles. (They think modern people cannot accept such unscientific concepts.) The paradox, however, is that for everyone to whom Christianity is "made relevant," there are thousands for whom it is made irrelevant. Indeed, the liberal version of Christianity lacks an authentic and supernatural spirituality to help people and give them hope in the midst of life's problems. You can capitalize on this deficiency by talking about how a personal relationship with Jesus provides all the strength you need to deal with life's harsh realities.

In addressing the spiritual bankruptcy of liberalism, you can also use the liberal's recognition of God's love as a launchpad to emphasize that God loved humankind *so much* that He sent Jesus into the world to die on the cross to rescue humankind from hell. Be sure to note that Jesus—love incarnate—spoke of God's wrath and the reality of hell in a more forceful way than any of His disciples ever did (see, for example, Matthew 25:46). Therefore, God's love is not incompatible with the reality of hell. Jesus affirmed that His mission of love was to provide atonement for human sin (for which there is plenty of empirical evidence in our world) by His sacrificial death on the cross (Mark 10:45; John 12:23-27).

Inform the liberal that if he or she really wants to experience the love of God, the place to begin is a living relationship with Jesus Christ. Then tell him or her about your relationship with Jesus. There is no better way to close a discussion with a liberal Christian than by giving your testimony, focusing on how your personal relationship with Jesus has changed your life forever.

Witnessing to Muslims

Should witnessing encounters with Muslims focus on its false doctrines?

I advise that you not begin your conversations with Muslims by slamming Muhammad (Islam's prophet), the Quran (Islam's sacred text), or Allah (Islam's god). That will close the Muslim's mind. You don't want to do that. Your conversation will essentially be over if you start out by saying bad things about that which the Muslim has revered his or her entire life.

Later, after you become friends with the Muslim (and he or she learns to trust and respect you), you can raise questions about these issues. But don't allow your initial encounters with the Muslim to focus on the negative aspects of their religion. It's much better to focus more attention on a positive presentation of Christianity—for example, the identity of Jesus, Jesus' work of salvation at the cross, and the gospel that saves.

How can I talk to a Muslim about Jesus?

Use the Quran as a launchpad to talk about Jesus. The Quran speaks of Jesus' virgin birth, His ability to heal people and raise them from the dead, His being the Messiah, His being an "all-righteous" one, and His eventual return to judge the earth (Quran 3:45,49; 4:158; 82:22). Use these statements from the Quran as a "starting point" for introducing the Muslim to the *biblical* view of Jesus—that He is God in human flesh who came to redeem humankind by dying on the cross.

Will Jesus' sacrifice on the cross make sense to a Muslim?

Probably not at first. He or she may question the idea that one person can die in place of another. But there's a good way to explain it. In the Quran, the story of Abraham sacrificing his son is included. (The Quran says Ishmael was the son to be sacrificed, not Isaac. Don't get bogged down in this. You can correct this minor point later.) The main point to focus on is that the Quran uses the words "ransom" and "sacrifice" to speak of the animal that was sacrificed in place of Ishmael. Use this as a launchpad to talk about Jesus' *ransom* and *sacrifice* as the Lamb of God.

How can I talk to a Muslim about the Islamic view that salvation hinges on good works?

Since Muslims believe in a works-oriented salvation,[3] share with them what the Bible says about this. Romans 3:20 tells us, "By works of the law no human being will be justified in his sight, since through the law comes knowledge of sin." In other words, the law shows us what sin is, but it can't save us. Only faith in the divine Savior (Jesus) can save us (see Galatians 3:24).

Be sure to emphasize the grace of God. Ephesians 2:8-9 tells us, "By grace you have been saved through faith. And this is not your own doing; it is the gift of God, not a result of works, so that no one may boast."

Let the Muslim know that no one (yourself included) is good enough to earn salvation. You might give your testimony to emphasize what Jesus has done for you. Talk about your absolute assurance of heaven.

Should I give the Muslim a Bible?

By all means, yes. Ask your Muslim friend or acquaintance to read the Gospel of Luke. Muslims love good stories, and Luke's Gospel has many great stories illustrating God's love for sinners (such as the parable of the lost coin and the parable of the lost sheep). Tell him or her that you'd be interested in meeting again to talk about what Luke's Gospel says about Jesus. Be sure to bathe all your subsequent witnessing encounters in prayer.

Is there any other advice you can give?

Yes. Christian men should witness to Muslim men, and Christian women should witness to Muslim women. If you have a Muslim over for dinner, don't serve pork. Make sure the women in your house are dressed modestly. Don't ask a Muslim man about his wife, for that can be considered inappropriate. Don't be offended if the Muslim doesn't like your pets (they generally view dogs as unclean farm animals). *Pray a lot!*

Witnessing to Children

Is there an "age of accountability"—that is, an age at which children become responsible before God?

Yes—though the "age" is not the same for every child. Obviously, some children mature faster than others. A verse that relates to this issue is James 4:17, where we read, "Whoever knows the right thing to do and fails to do it, for him it is sin." It would seem from this verse that when a child truly comes into a full awareness and moral understanding of "oughts" and "shoulds," he or she *at that point* has reached the age of accountability.

Is it possible to evangelize little children, or should we wait until they are older?

I think evangelist Billy Graham is right when he says that "conversion is so simple that the smallest child can be converted."[4] The great Charles Spurgeon likewise said, "Children need to be saved and *may* be saved."[5]

The apostle Paul, speaking to young Timothy, said, *"From child-hood* you have been acquainted with the sacred writings, which are able to make you wise for salvation through faith in Christ Jesus" (2 Timothy 3:15). Obviously, if Timothy had been taught the Scriptures from childhood, it's never too early to begin sharing gospel truths with our children.

Timothy's mother started his training in the Scriptures at a very early age and *continued* this training throughout his childhood. I say this because of the present tense verb in this verse ("you have been acquainted with the sacred writings"). The present tense indicates continuous, ongoing action. Timothy's mother didn't just sporadically talk to him about the Scriptures; she *regularly* spoke to him about the Scriptures.

I can think of many people who have followed Timothy's lead in becoming Christians at a very young age. Corrie ten Boom became saved at age five, revivalist Jonathan Edwards at age seven, Billy Graham at age six, and his wife Ruth at age four.[6]

The condition of salvation is simple faith in Christ (Acts 16:31). It is a fact that the most trusting people in the world are children. Children have not acquired the obstructions to faith that often come with education. No wonder, then, that the Scriptures instruct us to become like children in order to enter into the kingdom of God (Matthew 18:3). As adults, we must develop the same kind of trust that little children naturally have.

How can gospel truths be shared with children?

There is no set formula for evangelizing your child. But one helpful method is to read Bible stories to your child that illustrate being lost and getting saved. Children love to hear stories. Two of my favorite Bible stories that illustrate this truth are the parable of the lost sheep (Luke 15:4-7) and the parable of the lost coin (Luke 15:8-10).

I like to illustrate the sin problem by talking about a bow and arrow. If you aim at a target with the bow and arrow, sometimes you "miss the target." This is one of the meanings of the word "sin" in the New Testament. In our lives, we "miss the target" when we don't live as God wants us to.

How can we explain to children what Jesus did for us at the cross?

Explain that God loves us very much. But because each of us has "missed the target" in our lives, there is a wall or barrier between us and God. Our relationship with God has been broken. Jesus, by dying on the cross, took the punishment for our sins so we wouldn't have to. Jesus has thereby made it possible for us to have our relationship with God restored.

I like to talk about the "record of debt" mentioned in Colossians 2:14 as a means of illustrating this. (You might call it a "bad behavior list" when speaking to your child.) Back in ancient days, whenever someone was found guilty of a crime, the offender was put in jail and a bad behavior list was posted on the jail door. This paper listed all the crimes the offender was found guilty of. Upon release, after serving the prescribed time in jail, the offender was given the bad behavior list, and on it was stamped, "Paid in full."

Christ took the bad behavior list of each of our lives and nailed it to the cross. Jesus' sacrifice "paid in full" the price for our sins. Because of Him, the "bad behavior list" of our whole life has been tossed into the trash can. Our relationship with God is restored.

How can we explain to children that salvation is a free gift?

First read Ephesians 2:8-9 to your child using an easy-to-read translation. This verse says salvation is a gift from God. A gift cannot be earned. It is free.

You might illustrate this truth with your child's birthday. Most kids on their birthday receive one or more gifts. But as soon as they receive the gift, they don't go get their allowance so they can pay for it. You can't pay for a gift. *It's free.* All you have to do is receive it.

Similarly, you can't buy the gift of salvation. God gives it to us free. All we have to do is receive it.

We "receive" this wonderful gift by placing our faith in Jesus. Placing faith in Jesus is not a complicated thing. It involves taking Jesus at His word. Faith involves believing that Jesus was who He said He was (God). Faith also involves believing that Jesus can do what He claimed He could do—He can forgive me and make me part of His family.

What if my child has questions?

Count on the fact that your child *will* have questions. Children are naturally inquisitive. If you let them know they're allowed to ask questions about what you're saying, you can count on them to do so. Don't rush your discussion when sharing the gospel. Allow as much time as it requires. If you're not sure about the best answer, let him or her know you'll talk about the answer on another day. Then do some research.

If my child responds positively to the gospel, what next?

You can lead your child in a simple prayer. The prayer might go something like this:

> Dear Jesus:
>
> I want to have a relationship with You and get to know You.
> I know I can't save myself, because I know I'm a sinner.
> Thank You for dying on the cross for me and taking the
>   punishment for my sins.
> I believe You died for me, that You rose again, and I accept Your
>   free gift of salvation by faith.
> Thank You, Jesus.
>
> Amen.

Ask your child if he really believes what he just said to God in prayer. If he does, he is now saved. He is a Christian. Tell him that the angels in heaven are cheering right now because he became a Christian (Luke 15:10).

Following this, avail yourself of some of the excellent Christian resources designed specifically for little children (easy Bibles, books, videos, and the like). Now is the time to begin a regular regimen of building biblical principles into your child's worldview.

25
All About the Church

Does being "saved" make you a part of the universal church?

Yes. The universal church may be defined as the ever-enlarging body of born-again believers who comprise the universal Body of Christ over whom He reigns as Lord. Although the members of the church may differ in age, sex, race, wealth, social status, and ability, they are all joined together as one people (1 Corinthians 12:13). All of them share in one Spirit and worship one Lord (Ephesians 4:3-6). This body is comprised of only believers in Christ. The way you become a member in this universal body is to simply place faith in Jesus Christ. If you're a believer, *you're in*!

Is it okay for Christians not to attend a local church?

No. Hebrews 10:25 specially warns against "neglecting to meet together." The Christian life as described in Scripture is to be lived within the context of the family of God and not in isolation (see Ephesians 3:14-15; Acts 2). Moreover, it is in attending church that we become equipped for the work of ministry (Ephesians 4:12-16). Further, it is within the context of attending church that we can receive the Lord's Supper (1 Corinthians 11:23-26).

The Bible knows nothing of a "lone ranger Christian." Many logs burning together burn very brightly, but when a log falls off to the side, the embers quickly die out (see Ephesians 2:19; 1 Thessalonians 5:10-11; and 1 Peter 3:8).

Was the church existent in Old Testament times?

No. In Matthew 16:18, Jesus affirmed, "I *will* build my church" (future tense). This indicates that at the moment He spoke these words, the church was not yet existent. This is consistent with the Old Testament, for there is no reference there to the "church." The church is clearly portrayed as distinct from Israel in such passages as 1 Corinthians 10:32, Romans 9:6, and Hebrews 12:18-24.

Scripture indicates that the church was born on the day of Pentecost (see Acts 2; compare with 1:5; 11:15; 1 Corinthians 12:13). We are told in Ephesians 1:19-20 that the church is built on the foundation of Christ's resurrection, meaning that the church couldn't have existed in Old Testament times. The church is also called a "new man" in Ephesians 2:15.

Is Peter the "rock" upon which the church is built (Matthew 16:18)?

No, I don't think so. This idea is based on a faulty understanding of Matthew 16:18, where Jesus said to Peter: "I tell you, you are Peter, and on this rock I will build my church, and the gates of hell shall not prevail against it."

A number of factors in the Greek text challenge the idea that Peter is "this rock." First, the reference to Peter in this verse is in the second person ("you"), but "this rock" is in the third person (verse 18). Moreover, "Peter" (*petros*) is a masculine singular term, whereas "rock" (*petra*) is a feminine singular term. Therefore, they do not have the same referent. What is more, the same authority Jesus gave to Peter (Matthew 16:18) is later given to all the apostles (Matthew 18:18). Clearly, then, Peter is not unique.

Ephesians 2:20 affirms that the church is "built on the foundation of the apostles and prophets, Christ Jesus himself being the cornerstone." Two things are clear from this: First, *all* the apostles, not just Peter, are the foundation of the church. Second, the only one who was given a place of uniqueness or prominence was Christ, the cornerstone. Indeed,

Peter himself referred to Christ as the "cornerstone" of the church (1 Peter 2:7) and the rest of believers as "living stones" (verse 5) in the superstructure of the church.

Does the Bible teach that the Christian church today can have fallible prophets?

Some people in recent years have argued that the New Testament allows for the fallibility of prophets. This view serves to excuse fallible prophecies among modern-day Christians who claim to have the gift of prophecy.

Such individuals note that some New Testament prophets never said "Thus says the LORD" like the Old Testament prophets, and therefore this allegedly allows for the possibility of errors among New Testament prophets. Such an argument fails to recognize that not even all Old Testament prophets said "Thus says the LORD" before their pronouncements (see, for example, 2 Samuel 23:2 and Amos 7:1; 8:1). Scripture indicates that the *same* Holy Spirit that spoke through the Old Testament prophets (2 Samuel 23:2) spoke through the New Testament prophets (Acts 21:11), thus allowing for *no* error.

It is also sometimes argued that New Testament believers were urged to judge or weigh what was being offered as prophecy. This allegedly implies that a New Testament prophet could be in error (1 Corinthians 14:29).

Contrary to this view, the reason this instruction was given was to guard against *false* prophets pretending to set forth prophecies from God. The idea is that if a prophecy comes from a true prophet of God, it will be in line with what previous prophets of God have revealed (since God doesn't contradict Himself). If a prophet tries to pawn off some revelation that contradicts the previous prophets, it is clear that such a person is a *false* prophet (see Deuteronomy 13 and 18). Understood in this way, then, the weighing of prophetic statements cannot be taken to imply that New Testament prophets made mistakes.

How do we know the New Testament prophets were on the same level of infallibility as the Old Testament prophets?

I suggest four considerations: (1) New Testament prophets are portrayed in the New Testament as being in continuity with their Old Testament predecessors (see Malachi 3:5; Matthew 11:11; Revelation 22:7). (2) The New Testament prophets were placed alongside the apostles as the foundation of the church (Ephesians 2:20), and since the apostles' revelations were divinely authoritative and infallible (1 Corinthians 14:37), we theologically infer that the New Testament prophets were likewise authoritative and infallible. (3) The New Testament prophets received revelations from God (1 Corinthians 14:29), and were therefore just as infallible as Old Testament prophets who received revelations from God. (4) The New Testament prophets gave bona fide predictive prophecies (Acts 11:28; 21:11), just as the Old Testament prophets did (see Deuteronomy 18:22).

Are there apostles today?

No, not in the biblical sense. Scripture indicates that the church was built on the *foundation* of the apostles and prophets (Ephesians 2:20). Once a foundation is built, it does not need to be built again. It is built *upon.*

Biblical apostles had to be eyewitnesses of the risen Christ (Luke 1:1-4; Acts 1:21-26; 5:32; 1 Corinthians 9:1). Paul indicated he was the *last person* to behold the risen Christ and receive an apostolic commission (1 Corinthians 15:8). Moreover, the Epistles 2 Peter and Jude (among the last New Testament books written) exhort believers to avoid false doctrines by recalling the teachings of the New Testament apostles (2 Peter 1:12-15; 2:1; 3:2,14-16; Jude 3,4,17-19). Further, the book of Revelation indicates that the biblical apostles are accorded a special honor by having their names inscribed on the twelve foundations of the eternal city (Revelation 21:14).

What is the case for the ordination of women in the church?

A heavily debated issue today relates to the ordination of women. Traditionalists have long believed that only men should be ordained as elders and pastors/ministers of churches. However, a growing body of churches and denominations worldwide have broken with tradition and are now ordaining women.

Members of some of these churches claim that women can be ordained so long as they are under the authority of the (male) head pastor. Miriam the prophetess helped Moses shepherd the Israelite nation while she was in submission to Moses (Exodus 15). Also, Scripture mentions other female prophetesses (Luke 2:36-38; Acts 2:17-18; 21:9; 1 Corinthians 11:5), and if women can prophesy, they can participate in any ministry.

Jesus and the apostles used many gifted women to help care for and bring the lost to salvation, thus allowing them to participate in a pastoral role (Mark 15:41; Luke 8:2; John 4:28-29,39; Acts 18:18,26; Colossians 4:15). Priscilla (wife of Aquila) apparently carried out some pastoral functions, including helping to train Apollos (Acts 18).

There is no indication that women are excluded from having the spiritual gift of teaching (Romans 12:7; 1 Corinthians 12:28-29; Ephesians 4:12). Therefore, they can participate in ministry. Women—like men—are often recognized as "fellow workers" in ministry (Romans 16:3; Philippians 4:2), and therefore ought to be recognized in ordination.

What is the case against the ordination of women in the church?

The vast majority of churches throughout history have held that only males can be ordained as elders and pastors/ministers in churches. Arguments offered against the ordination of women include the following:

All the disciples and apostles were male, thereby establishing a pattern of male leadership (see Matthew 19:28; Revelation 21:14).

Also, from Genesis to Revelation we witness a pattern of male leadership among God's people. The appearance of a female prophetess is rare. Also, one of the biblical qualifications to be an elder or overseer is that the candidate for either office must be the husband of one wife (1 Timothy 3:2; Titus 1:6), which obviously excludes women.

While some Scripture verses indicate that women can have the gift of teaching, this is tempered by other Scripture verses that restrict the function or role of women in the church. For example, the apostle Paul said women are not permitted to teach or to have authority over men (1 Timothy 2:11-14).

Paul stated that women are to keep silent in church and are to be subordinate (1 Corinthians 14:33-36).

This remains a hotly debated issue. Too often, participants in the debate often end up generating more heat than light. Whatever one's position, Christians should agree to disagree in an agreeable way.

What is the case for worshipping on Saturday instead of Sunday?

Christians who opt for Saturday worship often appeal to the fact that God made the Sabbath at creation for *all* people (Genesis 2:2-3; Exodus 2:11).

The fourth of the Ten Commandments requires worship on the seventh day—Saturday (Exodus 20:8-11). The Ten Commandments are *unchangeable* laws, and therefore Sabbath worship is for today. It is both a day of rest and a memorial of God's work of creation.

Christ Himself observed the Sabbath (Mark 1:21), and is the Lord of the Sabbath (Mark 2:28).

The apostle Paul, during New Testament times, preached on the Sabbath (Acts 17:2). Gentiles in the New Testament worshipped on the Sabbath (Acts 13:42-44). Matthew, Mark, and Luke, writing *after* the resurrection, spoke of the Sabbath as an existing institution (Matthew 24:20; Mark 16:1; Luke 23:56).

For these and other reasons, some people argue that the day of worship should be the Sabbath, or Saturday.

When did Christians start worshipping on Sunday? And what was the main reason for the switch?

Church history reveals that by the beginning of the second century, worship on the first day (Sunday) was a nearly universal practice. The patristic writers (early church fathers) generally cited the resurrection of Christ as the primary reason for celebrating on this day.

The Epistle of Barnabas (AD 70–100) said, "Wherefore, also, we keep the eighth day [*Sunday*] with joyfulness, the day also on which Jesus rose again from the dead. And when He had manifested Himself, He ascended into the heavens."[1]

Ignatius (AD 35–107) spoke of "no longer observing the Sabbath, but living in the observance of the Lord's Day."[2]

Justin Martyr said, "Sunday is the day on which we all hold our common assembly, because," among other reasons, "Jesus Christ our Savior on the same day rose from the dead."[3]

Clement of Alexandria (AD 150–211), Tertullian (AD 155–230), and Cyprian (d. AD 258) all worshipped on Sunday.

Do those who worship on Sunday believe they are fulfilling the spirit of the Sabbath by worshipping on the Lord's Day?

Yes. And there are two primary reasons for this:

First, the primary aspects of the Sabbath—rest and worship—are fulfilled just as much on Sunday as was the case on Saturday. To the Pharisees, Jesus affirmed, "The Sabbath was made for man, not man for the Sabbath" (Mark 2:27). The point Jesus was making is that the Sabbath was not instituted to enslave people, but to benefit them. The spirit of Sabbath observance is continued in the New Testament observance of rest and worship on the first day of the week (Acts 20:7; 1 Corinthians 16:2).

Second, Colossians 2:17 tells us the Sabbath was "a shadow of the things to come, but the substance belongs to Christ." The Sabbath observance was associated with redemption in Deuteronomy 5:15 where Moses stated, "You shall remember that you were a slave in the land of Egypt, and the LORD your God brought you out from there with a mighty hand and an outstretched arm. Therefore the LORD your God commanded you to keep the Sabbath day."

The Sabbath was a shadow of the redemption that would be provided in Christ. It symbolized the rest from our works and an entrance into the rest of God provided by Christ's finished work on the cross. A transition from worshipping on the Sabbath day to the Lord's day therefore makes good sense.

What are some biblical and theological reasons for worshipping on Sunday instead of Saturday?

Although the moral principles expressed in the commandments are reaffirmed in the New Testament, the command to set Saturday apart as a day of rest and worship is the only commandment not repeated. There are very good reasons for this: New Testament believers are not under the Old Testament Law (Romans 6:14; Galatians 3:24-25; Colossians 2:16), and the Sabbath commandment is a part of that Law.

The apostle Paul indicated that one's choice to observe special days is a matter of personal conscience (Romans 14:5), and no one should cast judgment on them. Jesus was raised from the dead and appeared to some of His followers on a Sunday (Matthew 28:1). Jesus made continuing resurrection appearances on succeeding Sundays (John 20:26). John had his apocalyptic vision on a Sunday (Revelation 1:10). The descent of the Holy Spirit took place on a Sunday (Acts 2:1). The early church was given the pattern of Sunday worship, and this they continued to do regularly (Acts 20:7; 1 Corinthians 16:2).

Significantly, no rules of Sabbath observance were imposed upon Gentile believers by the Jerusalem Council—meaning that Sabbath observance was not considered to be among the requirements the Gentile believers had to concern themselves with (Acts 15:28-29). Paul indicated that a required observance of a special day as a divine obligation goes against the gospel of grace which he communicated to the Galatians (see Galatians 4:9-10).

Paul gave instructions to the Corinthian church about taking a special relief offering on the first day of every week (Sunday) for the Christians in Jerusalem (1 Corinthians 16:1-2). He likely stipulated "first day of every week" because he knew that they met for worship on that day.

It is for these and other reasons that most Christians worship on Sunday rather than on the Jewish Sabbath.

How do churches differ on the issue of what kind of music to include in worship services?

An issue that is somewhat controversial among some Christians relates to whether only traditional hymns should be used in worship services, or whether modern contemporary music is also acceptable. Some churches have opted for traditional hymns alone, others utilize only contemporary Christian songs, and others use a hybrid approach, seeking to combine the best of both worlds. Yet other churches offer its members two kinds of services each week—a traditional service and a contemporary service.

What is the case for using only traditional hymns in church services?

The lyrics in hymns are typically richer, more poetic, and generally more doctrinally oriented than contemporary songs. Many hymns were written by spiritual giants of the past, including men like Martin Luther and Charles Wesley. This rich heritage of music ought to be passed on to each new generation of Christians.

Because many churchgoers are accustomed to hymns, churches that introduce contemporary music risk losing some of the old faithful attenders. Because contemporary music is sometimes on the loud side (utilizing full bands), some people may feel the volume detracts from the worship. To some people, contemporary music is too showy—too oriented toward performance—and thus detracts from true worship of the Lord.

What is the case for using contemporary Christian music in worship services?

Because most unchurched people have never sung a hymn in their lives, it makes sense to include music in the service that they can more easily relate to. Martin Luther put Christian words to some of the popular bar songs of his day, and therefore his music was the "contemporary music" of his day. Therefore, contemporary music should be allowed in our day.

Some of today's contemporary artists are actually writing hymns, so there should be no objection to using them in worship services. Because many in church listen to Christian radio, it makes sense to include songs in the service that most people are already familiar with. Some of today's praise choruses have been specifically designed to be conducive to worship, and therefore ought to be used in church services.

What can all churches agree on, regardless of the type of music they use in church services?

Despite the divergence of opinions that exists among Christians on this matter, churches without exception can agree with the following three foundational points: (1) Worship should be a part of our church services. (2) Singing hymns and spiritual songs should be a central part of this worship. (3) The *message* conveyed by music is more important than the *mode*. Therefore, sound theology is more important than the sound by which it is expressed. Beyond this, we must simply agree to disagree in an agreeable way regarding our differences on the matter.

Personally, I opt for including both traditional hymns and contemporary music in church services.

Why do some churches refuse to use musical instruments in worship services?

As a backdrop, Christians throughout history have universally sung hymns and songs as a part of corporate worship and praise to God. Within this broad framework, however, a division has long existed within the body of Christ. Some Christians believe hymns and songs should only be sung in church without instrumental accompaniment (*a cappella* singing). Other Christians (most Christians) believe hymns and songs are to be sung with instrumental accompaniment.

Representative churches among those who believe hymns and songs should be sung *without* instrumental accompaniment are the Primitive Baptists, the Churches of Christ, and the Church of God in Christ (Mennonite). Such churches typically cite two reasons not to use musical instruments: Musical instruments are not mentioned in the New Testament in the context of church services. The use of such instruments is a sign of worldliness, and all semblances of worldliness should be avoided in church services.

What is the case for using musical instruments in church services?

Many traditional Baptist, Methodist, Presbyterian, Roman Catholic, and other mainstream denominational churches use an organ (or sometimes piano) to accompany singing. An increasing number of churches within each of these denominations now use full bands or orchestras. There is wide diversity on this issue.

Personally, I think those who refuse to use musical instruments ought to reconsider their position. Though I understand the concern, I see no rational basis for saying the use of musical instruments is a sign of worldliness. And as for the silence of the New Testament on the issue, mere *omission* does not mean *exclusion*.

The broader context of the whole of Scripture reveals quite a bit about the use of musical instruments. Because this issue is so controversial and divisive among some Christians, I've chosen to give an extended treatment to this issue.

Certainly various musical instruments were often used in producing music as a part of worship in the Jewish temple (1 Chronicles 25). It is well known that many of the Psalms were originally designed for musical accompaniment. Psalm 4 was to be accompanied "with stringed instruments" (see the superscript of Psalm 4). Psalm 5 was to be accompanied with "flutes" (see the superscript of Psalm 5). Psalm 6 was to be accompanied with stringed instruments, including an "eight-string lyre" (see the superscript of Psalm 6 in the NASB).

Scripture tells us that "David and all the house of Israel were making merry before the LORD, with songs and lyres and harps and tambourines and castanets and cymbals" (2 Samuel 6:5; see also verse 21). David affirms that "4,000 shall offer praises to the LORD with the instruments that I have made for praise" (1 Chronicles 23:5).

We are also told, "The priests stood at their posts; the Levites also, with the instruments for music to the LORD that King David had made for giving thanks to the LORD—for his steadfast love endures forever—whenever David offered praises by their ministry; opposite them the priests sounded trumpets, and all Israel stood" (2 Chronicles 7:6). The Levites were stationed "in the house of the LORD with cymbals, harps, and lyres, according to the commandment of David" (2 Chronicles 29:25).

The psalmist proclaims, "I will praise you with the lyre, O God, my God" (Psalm 43:4). He exults, "I will also praise you with the harp for your faithfulness, O my God; I will sing praises to you with the lyre, O Holy One of Israel" (Psalm 71:22).

Indeed, "Praise him with trumpet sound; praise him with lute and harp! Praise him with tambourine and dance; praise him with strings and pipe! Praise him with sounding cymbals; praise him with loud clashing cymbals!" (Psalm 150:3-5). Such instrumental music and singing continued to be common in the post-exilic period (Ezra 3:10-11; Nehemiah 12:27-47).

Many today believe that since musical instruments were used so predominantly in Old Testament worship, including in temple worship, then certainly God's people in New Testament times—many of them Jewish converts to Christianity—can follow this same pattern. *Not a single verse in the New Testament prohibits it.*

In the New Testament, the apostle Paul says Christians ought to be about the business of "addressing one another in psalms and hymns and spiritual songs, singing and making melody to the Lord with all your heart" (Ephesians 5:19). Paul further exhorts, "Let the word of Christ dwell in you richly, teaching and admonishing one another in all wisdom, singing psalms and hymns and spiritual songs, with thankfulness in your hearts to God" (Colossians 3:16; see also Matthew 26:30; Acts 16:25; James 5:13).

While musical instruments are not mentioned, they are not forbidden either. And since *omission* does not mean *exclusion*, there is no reason that musical instruments should not be used as we sing songs and hymns in praise to God.

Notice in Revelation 5:8 that when we worship God in heaven, we will still use harps. If musical instruments were used in *past* worship of God in Old Testament times and will be used in *future* worship of God in heaven, there is no good reason that such instruments should not be used in our worship of God in the *present*.

What does the New Testament teach on tithing?

I do not believe that Christians today are under the Old Testament ten-percent tithe system. In fact, we are not obligated to a percentage tithe at all. There's not a single verse in the New Testament where God specifies that believers should give ten percent of their income to the church.

Before you conclude that I don't think we should financially support the church, let me rush to say that I believe the New Testament concept is that of *grace giving*. We are to freely give as we have been freely given to. And we are to give as we are able (2 Corinthians 8:12).

For some, this will mean less than ten percent. But for others whom God has materially blessed, this will mean much more than ten percent. Let us not forget that a poor person who gives three percent of his income may actually be giving more generously than a rich person giving twenty percent of his income.

Is the starting point for having a right attitude toward tithing a giving of ourselves to the Lord?

Most certainly! The early church is our example: "They gave themselves first to the Lord and then by the will of God to us" (2 Corinthians 8:5). Only when we have given ourselves to the Lord will we have a proper perspective on money.

We also read in Romans 12:1, "Present your bodies as a living sacrifice, holy and acceptable to God, which is your spiritual worship." The first sacrifice we make to God is not financial. Our first sacrifice is that of our own lives. As we give ourselves unconditionally to the Lord for His service, our attitude toward money will be what it should be. God is not interested in your money until He first has your heart.

Some believers who are unreservedly committed to God may only be able to afford giving two or three percent of their income. But others might be able to afford twenty-five percent or more. Whatever amount you tithe, just remember that God primarily looks upon your heart.

Is church discipline a biblical mandate?

I believe so. The motive for discipline should be love and the restoration of the offender. According to 1 Corinthians 5, discipline is always for the good of the offender (verses 1-5), the church (verses 6-8), and for everyone, as this is a witness to the unsaved world (verses 9-13).

I believe the pastor should make the initial approach in disciplining the offender (see 1 Timothy 5:1-2; Matthew 18:15). If this fails, the pastor should make a second attempt accompanied by other spiritual men (Matthew 18:16). Finally, if this fails, the whole church must become involved (Matthew 18:17; see also 1 Corinthians 5:1-5).

What are the different views of the Lord's Supper?

There are four primary views:

The Roman Catholic view is known as transubstantiation. The advocates of this view say that the elements actually change into the body and blood of Jesus Christ at the prayer of the priest. They say that partaking of the elements imparts grace to the recipient. They view Jesus Christ as literally present. The *appearance* of the elements do not change, but the *elements* do change.

This view has some notable problems. First, note that Jesus was present with the disciples when He said the bread and wine were His body and blood (Luke 22:17-19). Obviously He intended that His words be taken figuratively. Further, one must keep in mind the scriptural teaching that drinking blood is forbidden to anyone (Acts 15:29).

The Lutheran view is labeled consubstantiation. According to this view, Christ is present *in, with,* and *under* the bread and wine. Christ is truly present, but no change occurs in the elements. The mere partaking of the elements after the prayer of consecration communicates Christ to the participant along with the elements.

The Reformed view is that Christ is spiritually present at the Lord's Supper. It is a means of grace. The proponents of this view say that the elements contain a dynamic presence of Jesus, and it is made effective in the believer as he partakes. The partaking of His presence is not a physical eating and drinking, but an inner communion with His person.

The memorial view (my view) is that the elements do not change. The ordinance is not intended as a means of communicating grace to the participant. The bread and wine are symbols and reminders of Jesus in His death and resurrection (1 Corinthians 11:24-25). It also reminds us of the basic facts of the gospel and our anticipation of the second coming (11:26), as well as our oneness as the body of Christ (10:17).

Should foot washing be practiced in churches today?

In John 13:14 Jesus said to the disciples, "If I then, your Lord and Teacher, have washed your feet, you also ought to wash one another's feet." Does this mean that churches today should be engaged in this practice?

In the broader context of John 13:1-17, Jesus was teaching about humility and servanthood, and He does so through a living parable— an *acted-out* parable. Normally when one entered someone's house in New Testament days, it would be the job of the servant of that household to wash that person's feet, not the job of the master of the household. By washing the disciples' feet, Jesus placed Himself in the role of a servant. The Son of God was a servant, so the disciples were also to be servants to each other.

This was a tremendous lesson in humility and servanthood for the disciples. Instead of trying to exalt themselves over others (the normal human tendency), they were to become each other's servants. This is right in line with Jesus' teaching elsewhere that he who is greatest in the kingdom of heaven is the one who becomes the servant of all (Matthew 20:26).

Was Jesus teaching that foot washing should become an ordinance in the church—like baptism and the Lord's Supper? Christians have different views on this matter. Some denominations believe foot washing is an ordinance of humility that reminds believers of the need for continual cleansing from sin. In these churches, male believers wash the feet of other males, while female believers wash the feet of other females.

Other Christians feel that John 13:14 was *descriptive*, not *prescriptive*. That is, they feel the verse *describes* something that Jesus did with the disciples but was not intended to be something *prescribed* for all Christians throughout the rest of church history. The evidence suggests that foot washing was not even common in church gatherings of the first century. Certainly the principle behind foot washing—humility and servanthood—is something all Christians should seek to emulate.

Part 7

Questions About Angels and Demons

Angels Among Us
The Devil and His Fallen Angels

26
Angels Among Us

Why are angels called "sons of God" in the Old Testament?

Angels are sometimes referred to as "sons of God" (Job 1:6; 2:1; 38:7). The term "son of" can carry different meanings in different contexts. A look at any Hebrew or Greek lexicon makes this clear. Therefore, the term can be used in one way in regard to angels and in quite another way when used of the person of Jesus Christ.

Angels are sons of God in the sense of being created directly by the hand of God. They were brought into existence by a direct creative act of God.

One must keep in mind that angels do not give birth to other baby angels (Matthew 22:30). Therefore, we never read of "sons of angels." Since every single angel was directly created by the hand of God, it is appropriate that they be called "sons of God."

How does this relate to Christ being called the "Son of God"? This is an important question, for Christ is not in the same league as the angels. One will go far astray unless one sees a clear distinction between Christ as the *Son of God* and angels as *sons of God*. The Bible indicates that Christ is *eternally* the Son of God in the sense that He eternally has the nature of God. He is just as divine as the Father is.

When were the angels created?

The angels were apparently created some time prior to the creation of the earth. Job 38:7 makes reference to the "sons of God" (angels) singing at the time the earth was created. So, even before the creation of the material universe there was a vast world of spirit beings. These angelic spirit beings sang as a massive choir when God created the earth. What a moment that must have been!

How many angels are there?

Many commentators have speculated regarding just how many angels there are. The great logician Thomas Aquinas believed that more angels exist than human beings do.[1] Saint Albert the Great calculated that there were exactly 399,920,004 angels.[2] The Kabbalists of medieval Judaism determined there were precisely 301,655,722 angels.[3]

Clement of Alexandria in the second century AD suggested that there are as many angels as there are stars in the stellar heavens.[4] This line of thinking is based on the idea that angels are associated with the stars in Scripture (Job 38:7; Psalm 148:1-3). If Clement is correct, the number of angels would exceed the stars visible to the human eye. Scientists say the total number of stars in the universe may run into the billions.[5]

Actually Scripture does not tell us precisely how many angels there are. Nevertheless, it indicates that their number is vast indeed. Scripture makes reference to "a multitude of the heavenly host" (Luke 2:13), and the angels are spoken of as "twice ten thousand, thousands upon thousands" (Psalm 68:17). Their number is elsewhere described as "myriads of myriads and thousands of thousands" (Revelation 5:11). (The word *myriad* means "vast number," "innumerable.")

Daniel 7:10, speaking of God, says that "a thousand thousands [of angels] served him, and ten thousand times ten thousand stood before him." The number "ten thousand times ten thousand" is 100,000,000 (one hundred million). This is a number almost too vast to fathom. Job 25:3 understandably asks, "Is there any number to his armies?"

What are angels like?

We learn a great deal about the nature of angels by studying what the Bible says about their characteristics:

Angels are incorporeal and invisible (Hebrews 1:14). The word *incorporeal* means "lacking material form or substance." Angels, then, are not material, physical beings. They are spiritual beings and are therefore invisible.

Angels are also localized beings. Scripture portrays them as having to move from one place to another (Daniel 9:21-23). Angels are powerful beings. Psalm 103:20 calls them "mighty ones," while 2 Thessalonians 1:7 calls them "mighty angels." Angels are holy. Angels are often called God's "holy ones" (Job 5:1; 15:15; Psalm 89:7). Angels are obedient. They always do only God's bidding (Psalm 103:20).

Angels have great knowledge. Angels were created as a higher order of creatures than humans are (see Psalm 8:5), and innately possess a greater knowledge. Angels also gain ever-increasing knowledge through long observation of human activities. Angels are also immortal. Angels are not subject to death (Luke 20:36), and they do not propagate (Matthew 22:30). Therefore, the number of angels remains constant.

Are angels personal beings?

Yes. Angels are persons—spirit persons (Hebrews 1:14)—with all the attributes of personality: mind, emotions, and will. We know the angels have a mind because the Scriptures say they possess great wisdom (2 Samuel 14:20), great discernment (2 Samuel 14:17), and they use their minds to look into matters (1 Peter 1:12).

We know the angels have emotions because they are said to be gathered in "joyful assembly" in the presence of God in heaven (Hebrews 12:22). We are also told that they "shouted for joy" at the Creation (Job 38:7), and there is "joy in heaven" whenever a sinner repents (Luke 15:7).

Angels certainly give evidence of having a moral will in the many moral decisions they make. For example, an angel exercised his moral will in forbidding John to worship him, acknowledging that worship belongs only to God and no one else (Revelation 22:8-9).

Beyond having the basic attributes of personality, angels are also seen to engage in personal actions. For example, angels are said to love and rejoice (Luke 15:10), they express desire (1 Peter 1:12), they contend (Jude 9; Revelation 12:7), they engage in worship (Hebrews 1:6), they talk (Luke 1:13), and they come and go (Luke 9:26). Angels also have personal names, such as Michael and Gabriel.

In what ways are angels "ministering spirits" (Hebrews 1:14)?

Hebrews 1:14 asks, Are not the angels "all ministering spirits sent out to serve for the sake of those who are to inherit salvation?" This brief statement is packed with meaning.

The word "ministering" comes from a Greek word meaning "serve." Angels are spirit servants who render aid, and this aid is rendered to the heirs of salvation in the outworking of God's purposes on the earth. What form does this service take? Such ministry can involve protection (Psalm 91:11), guidance (Genesis 19:17), encouragement (Judges 6:12), deliverance (Acts 12:7), supply (Psalm 105:40), empowerment (Luke 22:43), as well as occasional rebuke (Numbers 22:32) and judgment (Acts 12:23). And angelic service is rendered largely unseen and often unrecognized (2 Kings 6:17; Hebrews 13:2).

Notice that Hebrews 1:14 says angels are "sent" by God to render service to the *heirs of salvation.* God has specifically sent and appointed angels to carry out tasks on behalf of believers. Humans do not invoke or manipulate them. We must never forget that angels assist us because God has ordained it that way. Scripture never indicates that the *sent one* is more significant than (or takes the place of) the *divine Sender.*

In keeping with this, angels are most often described in relation to God as *His* angels (for example, Psalm 91:11). It is of great significance that two angelic names mentioned in the Bible—Michael and Gabriel—emphasize this relationship with God with the *'el* ending, which in the Hebrew means "God." (*Michael* means "Who is like God?" while *Gabriel* means "Mighty one of God.") Angels belong to *God*, and they exist to carry out *His* purposes. Psalm 103:20 makes reference to God's angels "who do his word, obeying the voice of his word."

Do all angels have wings?

Scripture indicates that many (if not all) angels have wings. The seraphim described in Isaiah 6:1-5 have wings. The cherubim Ezekiel saw in his vision have wings (Ezekiel 1:6). The angels the apostle John saw in his vision have wings (Revelation 4:8). But many other Bible verses about angels make no specific mention of wings (for example, Hebrews 13:2). What can we conclude from this?

Though it is possible that all of God's angels have wings, this is not a necessary conclusion. Though many angels are described as winged, we have no assurance that what is true of them is true of all angels. Since there is no explicit reference indicating that angels *as a whole* are winged, we must regard this as, at best, an inference.

Are there ranks among the angels?

Yes. Scripture indicates that the angels are organized by rank. In Colossians 1:16 we read, "By him [Christ] all things were created, in heaven and on earth, visible and invisible, whether *thrones* or *dominions* or *rulers* or *authorities*—all things were created through him and for him." Ephesians 1:21 speaks of Christ's authority as being "far above all *rule* and *authority* and *power* and *dominion*, and above every name that is named, not only in this age but also in the one to come."

What do the terms *thrones, dominions, rulers,* and *authorities* mean in these and other such verses? In the rabbinic (Jewish) thought of the first century, these terms were used to point to the hierarchical organization in the angelic realm. These appellations do not point to different kinds of angels, but simply to differences of rank among them.

Scripture also speaks of other angels who have varying levels of authority and dignity—including the archangel Michael, the cherubim, the seraphim, and Gabriel. The archangel is the highest ranking angel of all (the Greek word *arche* means first). The cherubim and seraphim rank very high, though we are not told how they relate to the other angels mentioned previously. Because Gabriel is the angel God always used in biblical times to deliver important revelations to human beings, we must assume that he is very high ranking as well.

Does God need angels in order to accomplish His work in the universe?

No! God does not *need* angels. In saying this, my intention is not to minimize the importance of what the Bible teaches about angels. I am personally very thankful that God created angels. My point is simply that God does not *need* them as if He could not accomplish His ends without their assistance.

Reformer John Calvin says God does not use angels "out of necessity as if he could not do without them, for as often as he pleases, he disregards them and carries out his work through his will alone."[6] Though God does not need angels, He nevertheless created them—for His own pleasure and for His own glory—to carry out various functions in His universe and before His throne.

Does God always answer our prayers by Himself, or does He sometimes use angels?

God often does answer prayers apart from any involvement of the angels (see 1 Chronicles 5:20; 1 Peter 3:12). Nevertheless, it is sometimes God's sovereign choice to use angels in answering people's prayers.

One example of this is in Acts 12 where we find Peter wrongfully imprisoned. We read that while Peter was in prison, "earnest prayer for him was made to God by the church" (verse 5). What happened next? All of a sudden an angel appeared in Peter's prison cell and helped him escape (verses 7-10).

It is interesting to observe that just as God's angels are sometimes used to answer prayers, so demons (fallen angels) sometimes seek to thwart the angels God uses in the process of answering a particular prayer. This happened when the prophet Daniel prayed.

According to Daniel 10:13 an angel that had been sent by God to answer Daniel's prayer was detained by a more powerful fallen angel (a demon). It was only when the archangel Michael showed up to render aid that the lesser angel was freed to carry out his task. One thing we learn from this is that we must be fervent in our prayers and not think that God is not listening simply because there seems to be a delay in God's answer.

Do Christians have a single guardian angel that stays with them throughout life?

Two primary passages in the New Testament relate to the idea of guardian angels. Matthew 18:10 says, "See that you do not despise one of these little ones. For I tell you that in heaven their angels always see the face of my Father who is in heaven." Then, in Acts 12:15, we find a woman named Rhoda recognizing Peter's voice outside the door of the house. The others inside the house—thinking Peter was still in jail—replied, "You are out of your mind...It is his angel!" A number of theologians have concluded from these two verses that every believer must have his or her own guardian angel.

Based upon Matthew 18:10 and Acts 12:15, it is certainly *possible* that each believer has a specific guardian angel assigned to him or her. However, many theologians argue that this is flimsy support for such an idea. (For example, the angels of the little ones in Matthew 18:10 are said to be *in heaven,* not specifically *with* the little ones.) These theologians argue that Scripture seems to indicate that *many multitudes of angels* are always ready and willing to render help and protection to each individual Christian whenever there is a need.

For example, we read in 2 Kings 6:17 that Elisha and his servant were surrounded by *many* glorious angels. Luke 16:22 indicates that several angels were involved in carrying Lazarus's soul to Abraham's side. Jesus could have called on twelve legions of angels to rescue Him if He had wanted (Matthew 26:53). Psalm 91:9-11 tells us, "Because you have made the LORD your dwelling place—the Most High, who is my refuge—no evil shall be allowed to befall you, no plague come near your tent. For he will command his angels concerning you to guard you in all your ways."

How do we reconcile the doctrine of guardian angels with the fact that bad things sometimes happen to us?

If something bad should happen to you (such as a car wreck), you may be tempted to ask, "Where was my guardian angel?" God sometimes has a purpose in allowing us to go through tough times. It is good for us to keep in mind that God sometimes uses adversities in our lives to help develop our faith muscles and to make us strong, mature believers (James 1:2-4). Also, even though God may not always remove us from the midst of adversity, He will always walk with us *through* the adversity (Psalm 23:4).

So—your guardian angel is not asleep. He is there. But God may choose to allow a difficult circumstance to come into your life in order to accomplish a greater good. *Trust God no matter what!*

Do humans become angels at the moment of death?

No! Scripture tells us that Christ created the angels—and He created them *as* angels (Colossians 1:16).

We see the distinction between humans and angels reflected in a number of biblical passages. For example, Psalm 8:5 indicates that man was made lower than the angels. In Hebrews 12:22-23 the "innumerable angels" are clearly distinguished from the "spirits of the righteous made perfect" (redeemed humans). First Corinthians 6:3 tells us that a time is coming when believers (in the afterlife) will judge over the angels. Also, 1 Corinthians 13:1 draws a distinction between the languages of human beings and those of angels. Clearly, human beings and angels are portrayed as different classes of beings in the Bible.

Can angels take on the appearance of human beings?

Yes indeed. Though angels are by nature incorporeal and invisible, they can nevertheless appear as men. In fact, their resemblance to men can be so realistic that they are actually taken to be human beings. Hebrews 13:2 instructs us, "Do not neglect to show hospitality to strangers, for thereby some have entertained angels unawares."

To illustrate, Abraham once welcomed three "men" in the plains of Mamre (Genesis 18:1-8). These "men" walked, talked, sat down, and ate—just like normal men—but they were not men. They were angels (see Genesis 18:22; 19:1; compare with Psalm 78:25).

What is the distinction between evil and elect angels?

All the angels in God's universe were originally created good and holy (Jude 6; Genesis 1:31; 2:3). It is inconsistent with the holy character of God that He could create anything wicked such as evil angels.

All the angels, however, were subjected to a period of probation. Some retained their holiness and did not sin, while others—following Lucifer's lead—rebelled against God and fell into great sin (Isaiah 14:12-17; Ezekiel 28:12-16; Revelation 12:4).

Once the angels were put to the test, their decision seems to have been made permanent in its effect. Those who passed the probationary test are permanently confirmed in that original holy state. Those who failed are now permanently confirmed in their evil, rebellious state.

The good angels are called "elect" angels in 1 Timothy 5:21, not because they sinned and then were elected unto redemption (remember, these angels never sinned during the probationary period). Rather they are called "elect" because God intervened to permanently confirm (or "elect") them in their holiness so there would be no possibility of future sin on their part. Good angels are therefore now incapable of sinning.

The lines have been drawn, and the lines are now absolute. The evil angels who rebelled against God are nonredeemable. Those that followed Satan's rebellion fell decisively, and are permanently locked in their evil state without the possibility of redemption. They are destined for eternal suffering (Matthew 25:41).

27

The Devil and His Fallen Angels

Is Ezekiel 28:11-17 a reference to the fall of Lucifer?

I believe so. It would seem from the context of Ezekiel 28 that the first ten verses of this chapter are dealing with a human leader. Then, starting in verse 11 and on through verse 19, Lucifer is the focus of discussion.

What is the rationale for the conclusion that these latter verses refer to the fall of Lucifer? Whereas the first ten verses in this chapter speak about the *ruler* of Tyre (who was condemned for claiming to be a god though he was just a man), the discussion moves to the *king* of Tyre starting in verse 11. Many scholars believe that though there was a human "ruler" of Tyre, the *real* "king" of Tyre was Satan, for it was he who was ultimately at work in this anti-God city and it was he who worked through the human ruler of the city.

Some have suggested that these verses may actually be dealing with a human king of Tyre who was *empowered* by Satan. Perhaps the historic king of Tyre was a tool of Satan, possibly even indwelt by him. In describing this king, Ezekiel also gives us glimpses of the superhuman creature, Satan, who was using, if not indwelling, him.

What descriptive characteristics in Ezekiel 28:11-17 lead Bible expositors to believe this may be a reference to Lucifer?

Bible expositors have noticed that there are things that are said of this "king" that—at least ultimately—cannot be said to be true of human beings. For example, the king is portrayed as having a *different nature* from man (he is a cherub, verse 14), being in a *different realm* from man (the holy mount of God, verses 13-14), having received a *different judgment* from man (he was cast out of the mountain of God and thrown to the earth, verse 16), and having superlatives ascribed to him that do not seem to fit that of a normal human being ("signet of perfection, full of wisdom and perfect in beauty," verse 12).

What does Ezekiel 28:11-17 reveal about Lucifer's actual fall?

Our text reveals that Lucifer was a created being and left the creative hand of God in a perfect state (Ezekiel 28:12,15). He remained perfect in his ways until iniquity was found in him (verse 15). What was this iniquity? We read in verse 17, "Your heart was proud because of your beauty; you corrupted your wisdom for the sake of your splendor." Lucifer apparently became so impressed with his own beauty, intelligence, power, and position that he began to desire for himself the honor and glory that belonged to God alone. The sin that corrupted Lucifer was self-generated pride.

Apparently, this represents the actual beginning of sin in the universe, preceding the fall of the human Adam by an indeterminate time. Sin originated in the free will of Lucifer, who chose to rebel against the Creator with full understanding of the issues involved.

What does it mean that Lucifer was "cast" down to the ground (Ezekiel 28:17)?

This mighty angelic being was rightfully judged by God: "I cast you to the ground" (on the earth—see Ezekiel 28:17). This does not mean that Satan had no further access to heaven, for other Scripture verses clearly indicate that Satan maintained this access even after his fall (for example, see Job 1:6-12; Zechariah 3:1-2). However, Ezekiel 28:18 indicates that Satan was absolutely and completely cast out of God's heavenly government and his place of authority (Luke 10:18).

Does Isaiah 14:12-17 refer to the fall of Lucifer?

Some Bible scholars see no reference whatsoever to Lucifer in this passage. They argue that this passage refers to a man (Isaiah 14:16).

They say that he is compared with other kings on the earth (verse 18). And they allege that the words "How you are fallen from heaven" (verse 12) refer to a fall from great political heights.

Other scholars interpret this passage as referring *only* to the fall of Lucifer, with no reference whatsoever to a human king. The argument here is that the description of this being is beyond humanness and therefore could not refer to a mere mortal man.

I think a third view is preferable to the two previous views. This view sees Isaiah 14:12-17 as having a dual reference. It may be that verses 4 through 11 deal with an actual king of Babylon. Then, in verses 12 through 17, we find a *dual* reference that includes not just the king of Babylon but a typological description of Lucifer as well.

If this passage contains a reference to the fall of Lucifer, then the pattern of this passage would seem to fit that of the Ezekiel 28 reference—that is, first a human leader is described, and then dual reference is made to a human leader *and* Lucifer (Satan). Also, the language used to describe this being fits other passages that speak about Satan. For example, the five "I wills" in Isaiah 14 indicate an element of pride, which was also evidenced in Ezekiel 28:17.

As a result of this heinous sin against God, Lucifer was kicked out of heaven (Isaiah 14:12). He became corrupt, and his name changed from *Lucifer* ("morning star") to *Satan* ("adversary"). His power became completely perverted (Isaiah 14:12,16-17).

Where did the demons come from?

Many scholars believe the first five verses of Revelation 12 contain a mini-history of Satan. In keeping with this, it would seem that Revelation 12:4 refers to the fall of the angels who followed Satan: "His [Satan's] tail swept down a third of the stars of heaven and cast them to the earth." It has long been recognized that the word "stars" is sometimes used of angels in the Bible (see Job 38:7). If "stars" refers to angels in Revelation 12:4, it would appear that after Lucifer rebelled against God, he was able to draw a third of the angelic realm after him in this rebellion. When he sinned, he apparently led a massive angelic revolt against God.

What do we learn about Satan from the titles used of Him in the Bible?

Satan is our adversary (1 Peter 5:8), and he opposes us in every way he can. He is called "Beelzebub" (Matthew 12:24), a term meaning "lord of the flies"—he corrupts everything he touches. He is the devil (Matthew 4:1), meaning he is our "adversary" and "slanderer." He truly is the evil one (1 John 5:19), opposing all that is good.

Satan is the "father of lies" and a "murderer" (or, more literally, "man-killer"—see John 8:44; see also 1 John 3:12,15). He is a roaring lion (1 Peter 5:8-9), strong and destructive, seeking to devour Christians. Toward this end, he is the tempter (Matthew 4:3), seeking to incite Christians to sin. He truly is our enemy (Matthew 13:39), full of hate for God and His children.

Satan is a serpent (Genesis 3:1; Revelation 12:9), characterized by treachery, deceitfulness, venom, and murderous proclivities. He is the accuser of the brethren (Revelation 12:10), accusing them before God (see Zechariah 3:1; Romans 8:33).

Satan is the god (or head) of this evil age (2 Corinthians 4:4). He is the prince of this world (John 12:31; 14:30; 16:11), promoting an anti-God system which conforms to his ideals, aims, and methods.

Can Christians become demon-possessed?

I don't think so. Let's begin by defining demon possession:

> [Demon possession is when] a demon [is] residing in a person, exerting direct control and influence over that person, with certain derangement of mind and/or body. Demon possession is to be distinguished from demon influence or demon activity in relation to a person. The work of the demon in the latter is from the outside; in demon possession it is from within.[1]

According to the definition given above, a Christian cannot be possessed by a demon since he is perpetually indwelt by the Holy Spirit (1 Corinthians 6:19). I like the way Walter Martin once put it. He said that when the devil knocks on the door of the Christian's heart, the Holy Spirit opens it and says, "Get lost!"

In keeping with this, not once does Scripture record a Christian being demon-possessed. For sure, there are examples of Christians being *afflicted* by the devil, and *tempted* by the devil, but not *possessed* by the devil.

Christians have been delivered from Satan's domain. As Colossians 1:13 puts it, Christ "has delivered us from the domain of darkness and transferred us to the kingdom of his beloved Son." Further, we must remember that "he who is in you [the Holy Spirit] is greater than he who is in the world [the devil]" (1 John 4:4). This statement would not make much sense if Christians could be possessed by the devil.

What can Satan and demons do to Christians?

Satan and his host of demons are very active in seeking to harm believers in various ways. Satan tempts believers to sin (Ephesians 2:1-2; 1 Thessalonians 3:5), to lie (Acts 5:3), and to commit sexually immoral acts (1 Corinthians 7:5). He accuses and slanders believers (Revelation 12:10), hinders their work in any way he can (1 Thessalonians 2:18), sows weeds among them (Matthew 13:38-39), and incites persecutions against them (Revelation 2:10).

Satan seeks to wage war against believers (Ephesians 6:11-12), opposes them with the ferociousness of a hungry lion (1 Peter 5:8), seeks to plant doubt in their minds (Genesis 3:1-5), desires to foster spiritual pride in their hearts (1 Timothy 3:6), and seeks to lead them away from "a sincere and pure devotion to Christ" (2 Corinthians 11:3).

No wonder our Lord found it so necessary to provide us with spiritual armor to protect us from these insidious fallen angels (Ephesians 6:11-18).

Are all sicknesses caused by demonic spirits?

No. On the one hand, Scripture portrays Satan and demons as inflicting physical diseases on people, such as *muteness* (Matthew 9:33), *blindness* (Matthew 12:22), and *epilepsy* (Matthew 17:15-18). They can also afflict people with mental disorders (Mark 9:22; Luke 8:27-29) and can cause people to be self-destructive (Mark 5:5; Luke 9:42).

Demons can cause physical illnesses, but Scripture distinguishes natural illnesses from demon-caused illnesses (Matthew 4:24; Mark 1:32; Luke 7:21; 9:1; Acts 5:16). In the case of numerous healings, no mention is made of demons. For example, no mention is made of demon affliction in the cases where Jesus healed the centurion's servant (Matthew 8:5-13), the woman with the hemorrhage of twelve years' duration (9:19-22), the two blind men (9:27-30), the man with the withered hand (12:9-13), and those who touched the fringe of Jesus' garment (14:35-36). Therefore, every time you get sick, don't presume you are being afflicted by a demon. You may have just caught a bad bug!

Does Satan have the ability to read our thoughts?

I don't think so. Scripture indicates that only God has the ability to "know the hearts of all the children of mankind" (1 Kings 8:39). God is portrayed in Scripture as being omniscient (Psalm 139:1-3), and He certainly knows our thoughts: "Even before a word is on my tongue, behold, O LORD, you know it altogether" (Psalm 139:4). Satan, by contrast, is a creature with creaturely limitations.

Nevertheless, Satan is a highly intelligent being (Ezekiel 28:12) who has had virtually thousands of years of experience in dealing with human beings. Therefore, he may give the appearance of knowing your thoughts. Satan is also the head of a vast network of demonic spirits who answer to him (Revelation 12:4,7), and this too may give the appearance of Satan being omniscient. But again, he is just a creature with creaturely limitations. Scripture certainly gives no indication anywhere that he has the capability of reading our minds.

In what way is Satan a counterfeiter?

Scripture reveals that Satan and his fallen angels seek to thwart the purposes of God and Christ (Matthew 13:39; Ephesians 6:11; 1 Timothy 4:1; 1 Peter 5:8; Revelation 2:10). We also know that they seek to blind the minds of people to spiritual truth (2 Corinthians 4:4; 11:14; 2 Thessalonians 2:9-10).

Some in the church are said to possess the ability to "distinguish between spirits" (1 Corinthians 12:10). The need for this gift reminds us that not all spirits are good. This is why we are called to test everything against Scripture (Acts 17:11; 1 Thessalonians 5:21).

One reason this is necessary is that Satan is a masterful counterfeiter. For example, Scripture reveals that Satan has his own church—the "synagogue of Satan" (Revelation 2:9). Satan has his own ministers—ministers of darkness that bring false sermons (2 Corinthians 11:4-5). He has formulated his own system of theology, which is called "teachings of demons" and "the deep things of Satan" (1 Timothy 4:1; Revelation 2:24). His ministers proclaim a counterfeit gospel—"a gospel contrary to the one...preached to you" (Galatians 1:7-8).

Satan has his own throne (Revelation 13:2) and his own worshippers (13:4). He inspires false Christs and self-constituted messiahs (Matthew 24:4-5). He employs false teachers who bring in "destructive heresies" (2 Peter 2:1). He sends out false prophets (Matthew 24:11) and sponsors false apostles who imitate the true ones (2 Corinthians 11:13).

What defenses does the Christian have against Satan and the powers of darkness?

The Lord Jesus lives in heaven to make intercession for us (Romans 8:34; Hebrews 7:25). Certainly Christ's intercession for us includes the kind of intercession He made for His disciples in John 17:15, where He specifically asked the Father to keep them safe from the evil one (Satan).

Beyond this, God has provided spiritual armor for our defense (Ephesians 6:11-18). "Wearing" this armor means that our lives will be characterized by such things as righteousness, obedience to the will of God, faith in God, and an effective use of the Word of God. These things spell *defeat* for the devil in your life.

Effective use of the Word of God is especially important for spiritual victory. Jesus used the Word of God to defeat the devil during His wilderness temptations (Matthew 4). We must learn to do the same. Obviously, the greater exposure we have to Scripture, the more God's Spirit can use this mighty sword in our lives.

Of course, Scripture specifically instructs us that each believer must be informed and thereby alert to the attacks of Satan (1 Peter 5:8). A prerequisite to defeating an enemy is to know as much as possible about the enemy, including his tactics (2 Corinthians 2:11).

We are also instructed to take a decisive stand against Satan. James 4:7 says, "Resist the devil, and he will flee from you." This is not a one-time resistance. Rather, on a day-to-day basis we must steadfastly resist the devil. And when we do, he will flee from us. Ephesians 6:13-14 tells us to "stand firm" against the devil.

We must not give place to the devil by letting the sunset pass with us having unrighteous anger in our hearts toward someone (Ephesians 4:26-27). An excess of wrath in our heart gives opportunity to the devil to work in our lives.

We are instructed to rely on the indwelling Spirit of God, remembering that "he who is in you is greater than he who is in the world" (1 John 4:4).

We should pray for ourselves and for each other. Jesus set an example for us in the Lord's Prayer by teaching us to pray, "Deliver us from evil" (Matthew 6:13), which can also be translated, "Deliver us from the evil one." Jesus also set an example of how to pray for others in His prayer for Peter: "Simon, Simon, behold, Satan demanded to have you, that he might sift you like wheat, but I have prayed for you *that your faith may not fail*" (Luke 22:31-32). We should pray for each other that we will maintain a strong faith in the face of adversity.

Of course, the believer should never dabble in the occult, for this gives the devil opportunity to work in his life (Deuteronomy 18:10-11; see also Romans 16:19).

Finally, we must remember that Satan is "on a leash." He cannot go beyond what God will allow him (the book of Job makes this abundantly clear). So we should rest secure in the fact that God is in control of the universe and realize that Satan cannot simply do as he pleases in our lives.

Does the reference to "binding" and "loosing" in the New Testament indicate that we have authority over the powers of darkness (Matthew 18:18)?

This is a common misconception. While it is true that God has given us all we need to have victory over the devil (see Ephesians 6:11-18), it is also true that the New Testament verses which speak of binding and loosing have nothing to do with spiritual warfare.

In Matthew 18:18, for example, Jesus said, "Whatever you bind on earth shall be bound in heaven, and whatever you loose on earth shall be loosed in heaven." The terms "bind" and "loose" were Jewish idioms indicating that what is announced on the earth has already been determined in heaven. To *bind* meant to forbid, refuse, or prohibit. To *loose* meant to permit or allow. We can announce the prohibition or allowance of certain things on the earth because heaven (or God) has already made an announcement on these matters.

In the context of Matthew 18, Jesus was speaking only about church discipline. The basic idea He was communicating is that those members of the church who sin and repent are to be "loosed" (that is, they are to be restored to fellowship) while those who are unrepentant are to be "bound" (that is, they are to be removed from fellowship). These ideas can be declared on the earth because heaven (God) has already declared it.

Part 8

Questions About Prophecy and the Afterlife

The Prophetic Future
The Wonder of Heaven
The Judgment of Humankind
Erroneous Views of the Afterlife
Near-Death Experiences

28
The Prophetic Future

What is dispensationalism?

Dispensationalism is a system of theology that is characterized by (1) a consistent literal method of interpreting the Bible, (2) a clear distinction between Israel and the church, and (3) the glory of God as God's ultimate purpose in the world.

The word *dispensation*—from the Greek *oikonomia* (meaning "stewardship")—refers to a distinguishable economy in the outworking of God's purpose. This system of theology views the world as a household run by God. In this "household" God delegates duties and assigns humankind certain responsibilities. If human beings obey God during that dispensation, God promises blessing. If human beings disobey, He promises judgment. In each dispensation, we generally see (1) the testing of humankind, (2) the failure of humankind, and (3) judgment as a consequence. As things unfold, God provides progressive revelation of His plan for history.

The present dispensation is the church age. Prior to that was the dispensation of the law. A future dispensation is the millennial kingdom (see John 1:17; Romans 6:14; Galatians 3:19-25; Ephesians 1 and 3). These three dispensations might be categorized as Old Testament, New Testament, and Kingdom. Dispensationalism recognizes that God deals differently with people in different ages or economies, as illustrated in how God related to people in Moses' time, in our day, and in the future millennium.

What are all the dispensations in Scripture?

Traditional dispensationalism divides history into seven dispensations.

First, the dispensation of *innocence* (Genesis 1:28–3:6) relates to Adam and Eve, up till the time they fell into sin at the Fall. Then follows the dispensation of *conscience* (Genesis 3:7–8:14), which describes the time between the Fall and the flood (see Romans 2:15), after which is the dispensation of *human government* (Genesis 8:15–11:9), which God instituted to mediate and restrain evil on the earth.

The subsequent dispensation of *promise* (Genesis 11:10–Exodus 18:27) relates to God's call of Abraham and the specific promises God made to Him and His descendants, both physical and spiritual. The dispensation of *Law* or *Israel* (Exodus 19:1–John 14:30) is characterized by God's giving of the Law to Israel as a guide to live by, governing every aspect of their lives. Note that the Law was not presented as a means of salvation. Note also that the Law was temporary—lasting only until the coming of and fulfillment by Christ.

Then in the dispensation of *grace* or *church* (Acts 2:1–Revelation 19:21), the rule of life in the church is grace.

The dispensation of the *kingdom* (Revelation 20:1-15) relates to Christ's future millennial kingdom, over which He will rule for 1,000 years on the throne of David. The church will rule with Christ as His bride.

What is the rapture?

The term *rapture* comes from the Latin translation of the Bible, at 1 Thessalonians 4:17, where we read, "Then we who are alive, who are left, will be *caught up* together with them in the clouds to meet the Lord in the air, and so we will always be with the Lord." In the Latin version, "caught up" is *rapturo*.

The rapture, then, is that glorious event in which Christ will descend from heaven, the dead in Christ will be resurrected, and living Christians will be instantly translated into their resurrection bodies. Both groups will be *caught up* to meet Christ in the air and taken back to heaven (John 14:1-3; 1 Corinthians 15:51-54; 1 Thessalonians 4:13-17).

This means one generation of Christians will never pass through death's door. They will be alive on the earth one moment. The next moment they will be with Christ in the air.

What is the biblical case for the pretribulational view of the rapture?

Pretribulationism is the view that Christ will rapture the entire church before any part of the tribulation begins. This means the church will not go through the judgments prophesied in the book of Revelation (chapters 4–18).

In support of this view, Revelation 3:10 indicates that believers will be kept from the actual hour of testing that is coming on the whole world. Further, no Old Testament passage on the tribulation mentions the church (Deuteronomy 4:29-30; Jeremiah 30:4-11; Daniel 8:24-27; 12:1-2). No New Testament passage on the tribulation mentions the church (Matthew 13:30,39-42,48-50; 24:15-31; 1 Thessalonians 1:9-10; 5:4-9; 2 Thessalonians 2:1-11; Revelation 4–18).

Scripture assures us that the church is not appointed to wrath (Romans 5:9; 1 Thessalonians 1:9,10; 5:9). This means the church cannot go through the "great day of...wrath" in the tribulation period (Revelation 6:17).

Is it God's typical pattern to deliver His people before judgment falls?

Yes. All throughout Scripture God is seen protecting His people before judgment falls (see 2 Peter 2:5-9). Enoch was transferred to heaven before the judgment of the flood. Noah and his family were in the ark before the judgment of the flood. Lot was taken out of Sodom before judgment was poured out on Sodom and Gomorrah. The first-born among the Hebrews in Egypt were sheltered by the blood of the Paschal lamb before judgment fell. The spies were safely out of Jericho and Rahab was secured before judgment fell on Jericho. So, too, will the church be secured safely (via the rapture) before judgment falls upon the earth in the tribulation period.

Does Christ's second coming "with" His saints support the pretribulational rapture theory?

I believe it does. Pretribulationists believe the rapture involves Christ coming *for* His saints in the air prior to the tribulation, whereas at the second coming He will come *with* His saints to the earth to reign for a thousand years (Revelation 19; 20:1-6). The fact that Christ comes "with" His "holy ones" (redeemed believers) at the second coming presumes they've been previously raptured. (He cannot come *with* them until He has first come *for* them.)

Do pretribulationists believe there will be believers during the tribulation period?

Most certainly. Scripture is clear that there will be believers who live during the tribulation period (for example, Revelation 6:9-11; 7:9-17). But pretribulationists believe these people become believers sometime *after* the rapture. Perhaps they become convinced of the truth of Christianity after witnessing millions of Christians supernaturally vanish off the planet at the rapture. Or perhaps they become believers as a result of the ministry of the 144,000 Jewish believers introduced in Revelation 7 (who themselves apparently come to faith in Christ after the rapture). Many may become believers as a result of the miraculous ministry of the two witnesses of Revelation 11, prophets who apparently have the same powers as Moses and Elijah.

Does a pretribulational rapture relate to the apostasy that will come upon the earth in the end times?

It is highly likely. I think a case can be made that a pretribulational rapture best explains the sudden apostasy that comes upon the world by the removal of the restrainer, who is apparently the Holy Spirit (2 Thessalonians 2:3-7). Since the Holy Spirit indwells all believers (John 14:16; 1 Corinthians 3:16-17; 6:19), He will essentially be "removed" when the church is raptured, thus making possible the fast eruption of apostasy around the world.

What is the posttribulational view of the rapture?

Posttribulationism is the view that Christ will rapture the church after the tribulation at the second coming of Christ. This means the church will go through the time of judgment prophesied in the book of Revelation. However, believers will allegedly be safely "kept through" the wrath of the tribulation (Revelation 3:10).

How do posttribulationists and pretribulationists differ on some of the finer points of end-times prophecy?

Posttribulationists argue that Revelation 20:4-6 proves that all believers will be resurrected at the end of the tribulation. This is in contrast to pretribulationists, who argue that in context, only those believers who die during the tribulation will be resurrected at this time (Revelation 20:4). Pretribulationists say that believers who live prior to the tribulation will be resurrected earlier at the rapture (1 Thessalonians 4:13-17).

Posttribulationists note that "saints" are mentioned as being on the earth during the tribulation, and this must therefore mean the rapture has not yet occurred. This is in contrast to pretribulationists, who grant that there will be "saints" who live during the tribulation (for example, Revelation 6:9-11) but say these people apparently become believers sometime after the rapture.

Posttribulationists cite Matthew 24:37-40, which is in the general context of the second coming: "Two men will be in the field; one will be taken and one left." This allegedly proves that the rapture will happen after the tribulation. This is in contrast to pretribulationists, who argue that the context indicates that those who are taken are taken not in the rapture but are taken in judgment, to be punished (see Luke 17:37).

Does church history support posttribulationism?

Posttribulationists believe their view is bolstered by the reality that pretribulationism emerged late in church history, finding its origin in John Nelson Darby (AD 1800–1882), who allegedly got it from Edward

Irving (1792–1834). Thus, the majority of church history knew nothing of the "novel" pretribulational view.

Pretribulationists rebut that the argument from church history is fallacious, wrongly supposing that truth is somehow determined by time. They observe that some people in the early church held to false doctrines, such as baptismal regeneration. Just because a doctrine was early thus does not mean it is correct. Conversely, just because a doctrine was late does not mean it is incorrect.

Pretribulationists believe that with the process of doctrinal development through the centuries, it makes sense that eschatology would become a focus later in church history. Besides, many throughout church history—as early as the first century—have held to the doctrine of the imminent return of Christ, a key feature of pretribulationism.

If posttribulationism is correct, then who will populate the millennial kingdom in mortal bodies?

That is a very good question. Scripture is clear that people who become believers during the tribulation period will enter into Christ's millennial kingdom *in their mortal bodies*. Scripture says they will be married, bear children, grow old, and die (see Isaiah 65:20; Matthew 25:31-46).

This is where the problem emerges for posttribulationism. Obviously, if all believers are raptured at the second coming, no believers are left to enter the millennium in their mortal bodies. This is no problem for pretribulationism, which teaches that after the rapture, many will become believers during the tribulation.

What is the biblical case for and against the midtribulational view of the rapture?

Midtribulationism is the view that Christ will rapture the church at the midpoint in the tribulation. In this view, the last half of the seventieth week of Daniel (Daniel 9:24-27) is much more severe than the first half. (The seventieth week of Daniel is a reference to the seven-year period of tribulation.) It is this last half of the tribulation that the church will reportedly be delivered from.

The two witnesses of Revelation 11, who are caught up to heaven at the midpoint in the tribulation, are believed to be representative of the church. This is in contrast to pretribulationists, who argue that there is virtually no indication in the context that these witnesses represent the church.

Proponents of midtribulationism argue that the church will be delivered from God's wrath (1 Thessalonians 5:9), which, they say, is only in the second half of the tribulation. However, the church will not be delivered from the general tribulation in the first half. This is in contrast to pretribulationists, who argue that since the entire tribulation period is characterized by wrath (see Zephaniah 1:15,18; 1 Thessalonians 1:10; Revelation 6:17; 14:7,10; 19:2), it makes more sense to say the church is delivered from the entire seven-year period (1 Thessalonians 1:9-10; 5:9; Revelation 3:10).

Proponents of midtribulationism argue that because the rapture occurs at the last trumpet (1 Corinthians 15:52), and because the seventh trumpet sounds at the midpoint in the tribulation (Revelation 11:15-19), then the rapture must occur at the midpoint in the tribulation. Pretribulationists respond, however, that the seventh trumpet sounds at the end of the tribulation, not the middle (compare with Daniel 7:25; 12:7; Matthew 24:21). Besides, the seventh trumpet in Revelation 11 is unrelated to the rapture but rather deals with judgment. This is entirely different from the trumpet in 1 Corinthians 15, which relates to the rapture and glorification. These are two different contexts, and so the trumpets are unrelated to each other.

What is the biblical case for and against the pre-wrath view of the rapture?

The pre-wrath view argues that the rapture occurs toward the end of the tribulation before the great wrath of God falls. It is argued that the Bible indicates that the church will not experience the wrath of God (2 Thessalonians 1:5-10). Since the word *wrath* does not appear in Revelation until after the sixth seal, this must mean God's wrath will not be poured out until the seventh seal (Revelation 6:12–8:1). So the rapture must take place between the sixth and seventh seals.

Pretribulationists raise a number of problems with this view, not the least of which is that God's wrath is poured out on the earth prior to the seventh seal (Zephaniah 1:15,18; 1 Thessalonians 1:10; Revelation 6:17; 14:7,10; 19:2). Scripture pictures the seven seals as a sequence, all coming from the same ultimate source—God (Revelation 6; 8). This sequence features divine judgments which increase in intensity with each new seal. Even the unsaved who experience this wrath recognize it specifically as the "wrath of the Lamb" (Revelation 6:15-16), who Himself opens each seal that causes each respective judgment (see Revelation 6:1,3,5,7,9,12; 8:1).

What is the biblical case for the partial rapture theory?

This view is based on the parable of the ten virgins—depicting five virgins being prepared and five unprepared (Matthew 25:1-13). This is interpreted to mean that only faithful, watchful, and praying Christians will be raptured.

Only Christians who have "loved his appearing" (2 Timothy 4:8) and those "who are eagerly waiting for him" (Hebrews 9:28) will be caught up to meet the Lord in the air. Unfaithful Christians, or professed Christians who are not really Christians at all, will be "left behind" to suffer through the tribulation. In this view, multitudes who expect to be raptured will not be raptured. Unfaithful and unprepared Christians will be sifted and refined by the fiery trials of the tribulation, so that they will be made ready to meet the Lord at the second coming.

What is the biblical case against the partial rapture theory?

Pretribulationists respond that Matthew 25:1-13 has nothing to do with the rapture. Those virgins who are "unprepared" apparently represent people living during the tribulation period who are unprepared for Christ's second coming (seven years after the rapture).

Some claim the partial rapture theory amounts to a Protestant version of purgatory, in which Christians get "purged" into readiness to meet the Lord at the second coming. Such a view seems to imply that trusting in the atonement of Christ alone (2 Corinthians 5:21) is not sufficient to bring one to heaven (see also Romans 5:1; Colossians 2:13).

Scripture reveals that if one is a believer, one is "saved" (John 3:16-17; Acts 16:31). *That alone* qualifies one to participate in the rapture (1 Corinthians 15:51-52).

Moreover, the Spirit's baptism places *all* believers in Christ's body (1 Corinthians 12:13) and therefore *all* believers will be raptured (1 Thessalonians 4:16-17). The partial rapture theory denies the perfect unity in the body of Christ (1 Corinthians 12:12-13).

First Corinthians 15:51 settles the issue, for it specifically tells us that "*we* shall *all* be changed." "We" here includes even the carnal believers in the Corinthian church, to whom Paul was writing. None are excluded, for "all" will be changed.

How is the rapture to be distinguished from the second coming of Christ?

It is important to note that the "glorious appearing" (second coming) is different from the rapture. Every eye will see Jesus at the second coming (Revelation 1:7), but the rapture is never described as being visible to the whole world. At the rapture, Jesus will come *for* His church (John 14:1-3; 1 Thessalonians 4:13-17), while at the second coming Jesus will come *with* His church (Colossians 3:4; Jude 14; Revelation 19:14).

At the rapture, Christians meet Jesus in the air (1 Thessalonians 4:13-17), whereas at the second coming Jesus' feet touch the Mount of Olives (Zechariah 14:4). At the rapture, Christians are taken and unbelievers are left behind (1 Thessalonians 4:13-17), whereas at the second coming unbelievers are taken away in judgment (Luke 17:34-36), and mortal believers remain to enter into Christ's millennial kingdom (Matthew 25:31-46).

At the rapture, Jesus will receive His bride, whereas at the second coming He will execute judgment (Matthew 25:31-46). The rapture will take place in the blink of an eye (1 Corinthians 15:52), whereas the second coming will be more drawn out, and every eye will see Him (Matthew 24:30; Revelation 1:7).

What are some key verses on the rapture and the second coming of Christ?

These are some key verses on the rapture: John 14:1-3; Romans 8:19; 1 Corinthians 1:7-8; 15:51-53; 16:22; Philippians 3:20-21; 4:5; Colossians 3:4; 1 Thessalonians 1:10; 2:19; 4:13-18; 5:9,23; 2 Thessalonians 2:1,3; 1 Timothy 6:14; 2 Timothy 4:1,8; Titus 2:13; Hebrews 9:28; James 5:7-9; 1 Peter 1:7,13; 5:4; 1 John 2:28–3:2; Jude 21; Revelation 2:25; 3:10.

These are some key verses on the second coming: Daniel 2:44-45; 7:9-14; 12:1-3; Zechariah 12:10; 14:1-15; Matthew 13:41; 24:15-31; 26:64; Mark 13:14-27; 14:62; Luke 21:25-28; Acts 1:9-11; 3:19-21; 1 Thessalonians 3:13; 2 Thessalonians 1:6-10; 2:8; 1 Peter 4:12-13; 2 Peter 3:1-14; Jude 14-15; Revelation 1:7; 19:11–20:6; 22:7,12,20.

Is the rapture of the church an imminent event?

The New Testament teaches that the rapture is imminent—that is, nothing must be prophetically fulfilled before the rapture occurs (see 1 Corinthians 1:7; 16:22; Philippians 3:20; 4:5; 1 Thessalonians 1:10; Titus 2:13; Hebrews 9:28; James 5:7-9; 1 Peter 1:13; Jude 21). The rapture is a *signless* event that can occur at any moment. This is in contrast to the second coming of Christ, which is preceded by many events in the seven-year tribulation period (see Revelation 4–18).

Imminence is implied in the apostle Paul's words in Romans 13:11-12: "*Salvation is nearer to us now than when we first believed. The night is far gone; the day is at hand.* So then let us cast off the works of darkness and put on the armor of light." The word *salvation* in this context must be eschatological, referring to the rapture, for this salvation is a *specific future event* referenced by Paul. At the end of each day, the Christian is that much closer to the time when the rapture may occur.

Imminence is also implied in James 5:7-9: "*The coming of the Lord is at hand.* Do not grumble against one another, brothers, so that you may not be judged; behold, *the Judge is standing at the door.*"

Imminence only makes sense within the theology of pretribulationism. In midtribulationism, the rapture takes place three and a half years after the tribulation begins. In posttribulationism, the rapture follows the tribulation. Therefore, imminence is impossible in these systems.

How does the imminence of the rapture relate to the pursuit of personal purity among Christians?

The fact that the rapture is a signless event and could occur at any moment ought to spur the Christian to live in purity and righteousness (see Titus 2:13-14). How blessed it will be for the Christian to be living in righteousness at that moment. How embarrassing it will be for the Christian to be engaged in sin at that moment.

In what sense is the rapture a "mystery"?

A mystery, in the biblical sense, is a truth that cannot be discerned simply by human investigation. It requires special revelation from God. Generally, this word refers to a truth that was unknown to people living in Old Testament times, but is now revealed to humankind by God (Matthew 13:17; Colossians 1:26).

In 1 Corinthians 15:51-55, the apostle Paul calls the rapture a mystery:

> Behold! *I tell you a mystery.* We shall not all sleep, but we shall all be changed, in a moment, in the twinkling of an eye, at the last trumpet. For the trumpet will sound, and the dead will be raised imperishable, and we shall be changed. For this perishable body must put on the imperishable, and this mortal body must put on immortality. When the perishable puts on the imperishable, and the mortal puts on immortality, then shall come to pass the saying that is written: "Death is swallowed up in victory." "O death, where is your victory? O death, where is your sting?"

The rapture of the church is categorized as a "mystery" because it had never been revealed in Old Testament times. It was revealed for the first time in the New Testament.

What will the future tribulation period be like?

The tribulation will be a definite period of time at the end of the age that will be characterized by great hardship (Matthew 24:29-35). It is called "the great tribulation" in Revelation 7:14. It will be of such severity that no period in history past or future will equal it (Matthew 24:21). It is called the "time of distress for Jacob," for it is a judgment on Messiah-rejecting Israel (Jeremiah 30:7; Daniel 12:1-4). The nations will also be judged for their sin and rejection of Christ (Isaiah 26:21; Revelation 6:15-17). The period will last seven years (Daniel 9:24,27).

Scripture indicates that this period will be characterized by judgment (Revelation 14:7), wrath (Isaiah 26:20-21), trial (Revelation 3:10), trouble (Jeremiah 30:7), destruction (Joel 1:15), darkness (Amos 5:18), desolation (Daniel 9:27), overturning (Isaiah 24:1-4), and punishment (Isaiah 24:20-21). Simply put, no passage can be found to alleviate to any degree whatsoever the severity of this time that will come upon the earth.

Can you explain the timing of Daniel's 70 weeks (Daniel 9:25-27)?

Yes. In Daniel 9 God provided a prophetic timetable for the nation of Israel. The prophetic clock began ticking when the command went out to restore and rebuild Jerusalem following its destruction by Babylon (Daniel 9:25). According to this verse, Israel's timetable was divided into 70 groups of seven years, totaling 490 years.

The first 69 groups of seven years—or 483 years—counted the years "from the going out of the word to restore and build Jerusalem to the coming of an anointed one, a prince" (Daniel 9:25). The "anointed one," of course, is Jesus Christ. *Anointed one* means "Messiah." The day that Jesus rode into Jerusalem to proclaim Himself Israel's Messiah was exactly 483 years to the day after the command to restore and rebuild Jerusalem had been given.

At that point God's prophetic clock stopped. Daniel describes a gap between these 483 years and the *final* seven years of Israel's prophetic timetable. Several events were to take place during this "gap." According to Daniel 9:26, the Messiah would be killed, the city of Jerusalem and its temple would be destroyed (which occurred in AD 70), and the Jews would encounter difficulty and hardship from that time on.

The final "week" of seven years will begin for Israel when the antichrist will confirm a "strong covenant" for seven years (Daniel 9:27). When this peace pact is signed, this will signal the beginning of the tribulation period. That signature marks the beginning of the seven-year countdown to the second coming of Christ (which follows the tribulation period).

What is "replacement theology"?

Replacement theology is the view that the church is the new or true Israel that has permanently replaced or superseded Israel as the people of God. It is suggested that God has already fulfilled all His promises to ancient Israel. Today the church is the only people of God.

What does Joshua 21:43-45 have to do with replacement theology?

Joshua 21:43-45 reveals that when Israel finally took possession of the land of milk and honey, it was in direct fulfillment of God's promise to the nation:

> Thus the LORD gave to Israel all the land that he swore to give to their fathers. And they took possession of it, and they settled there. And the LORD gave them rest on every side just as he had sworn to their fathers. Not one of all their enemies had withstood them, for the LORD had given all their enemies into their hands. Not one word of all the good promises that the LORD had made to the house of Israel had failed; all came to pass.

Proponents of replacement theology argue that because God is said to have given the Israelites the land in Joshua 21:43-45, God's obligation regarding the land promises to Israel are completely fulfilled, and no future promises are yet to be fulfilled on the matter. After all, the text tells us that "not one word of all the good promises that the LORD had made to the house of Israel had failed; all came to pass." Such individuals thus believe the modern state of Israel has no legitimate biblical basis. They claim it is not a fulfillment of biblical prophecy. All of God's land promises to Israel were fulfilled in the past. The church now spiritually replaces Israel as the recipient of God's promises.

What is the problem with how replacement theologians interpret Joshua 21:43-45?

Joshua 21:43-45 is absolutely correct regarding God fulfilling His part in giving the Israelites the Promised Land. Israel, however, failed to take full possession of what was promised to the nation by God, and they failed to dispossess all the Canaanites, despite the fact that the gift of land had been made. It was there for the taking. God had faithfully done for Israel what He promised. Israel, by contrast, was not completely faithful. The Lord had not failed to keep His promise even though Israel had failed by faith to conquer all the land.

Are there other verses that argue against the replacement theology explanation of Joshua 21:43-45?

Yes. In fact, the idea that no further land promises need to be fulfilled for Israel is proven to be false because many prophecies written *far after* the time of Joshua speak of Israel possessing the land *in the future* (see Isaiah 60:18,21; Jeremiah 23:6; 24:5-6; 30:18; 31:31-34; 32:37-40; 33:6-9; Ezekiel 28:25-26; 34:11-12; 36:24-26; 37; 39:28; Hosea 3:4-5; Joel 2:18-29; Amos 9:14-15; Micah 2:12; 4:6-7; Zephaniah 3:19-20; Zechariah 8:7-8; 13:8-9). Every Old Testament prophet except Jonah speaks of a permanent return to the land of Israel by the Jews. One can also observe that though Israel possessed the land at the time of Joshua, it was later dispossessed, whereas the

Abrahamic covenant promised Israel that she would possess the land *forever* (Genesis 17:8).

Contrary to the claims of replacement theology, aren't the church and Israel still seen to be distinct in the New Testament?

Yes indeed. For example, we are instructed in 1 Corinthians 10:32, "Give no offense to Jews or to Greeks [Gentiles] or to the church of God." Moreover, Israel and the church are seen as distinct throughout the book of Acts, with the word "Israel" being used 20 times and the word "church" 19 times.

Does replacement theology go against a literal interpretation of biblical prophecy?

Yes, and that is an important point. The prophecies that have already been fulfilled in Scripture—such as the Old Testament messianic prophecies that refer to the first coming of Jesus Christ—have been fulfilled quite literally. From the book of Genesis to the book of Malachi, the Old Testament abounds with anticipations of the coming Messiah. Numerous predictions fulfilled to the "crossing of the *t*" and the "dotting of the *i*" in the New Testament relate to His birth, life, ministry, death, resurrection, and glory (for example, Isaiah 7:14; Micah 5:2; Zechariah 12:10).

The fact that these prophecies of the first coming have been fulfilled literally gives us strong confidence to expect that the prophecies not yet fulfilled will also be fulfilled literally. Therefore, the land promises to Israel will be fulfilled literally. As the apostle Paul indicates in Romans 9–11, God still has a plan for Israel.

Eventually, Israel will finally (wonderfully) come to recognize Jesus as the divine Messiah and come into full possession of the Promised Land. The fullness of this possession will be in the future millennial kingdom. At present, however, Israel's regathering to the land is only partial and Israel is yet in unbelief. This partial regathering in unbelief is setting the stage for Israel to eventually go through the tribulation period—the "time of Jacob's trouble" (Jeremiah 30:7 KJV)—during which time a remnant of Israel will be saved (see Romans 9–11). Israel will then come into full possession of her Promised Land in the millennial kingdom.

What is the case for America being only indirectly mentioned in Bible prophecy?

While no verses in the Bible mention America by name, theologians have come up with quite a number of theories regarding indirect references to America in Bible prophecy.

One such theory is that the U.S. is *one of the "nations."* Theologians who favor this theory say that while there are no direct references to the United States in Bible prophecy, there are a number of general prophetic references to "the nations" in the tribulation that may loosely apply to the United States (for example, Isaiah 66:18-20; Haggai 2:6-7; and Zechariah 12:2-3).

Another theory has to do with *cooperation with Europe.* That is, even though the United States is not specifically mentioned in biblical prophecy, perhaps the United States will, in the end times, be in general cooperation with Europe—the revived Roman Empire headed by a powerful leader (the antichrist).

Other interpreters have seen parallels between *Babylon the Great* (mentioned in Revelation 17–18) and the United States. After all, both Babylon and the United States are dominant, both are immoral, both are excessively rich, and both think they are invulnerable.

Some interpreters claim that the United States is *the land "divided by rivers"* mentioned in Isaiah 18:1-7 since it is divided by the Mississippi River. The obvious problem with this view is that the nation is explicitly identified in Isaiah 18:1-2 as ancient Cush, or modern Sudan.

According to Ezekiel 38:13, when the great northern military coalition invades Israel in the end times, a small group of nations—including *Tarshish*—will lamely protest the invasion. Some suggest Tarshish might represent all the western nations, including the U.S.

If America is not mentioned in Bible prophecy at all, then why not?

There are a number of possible explanations as to why America may not be mentioned in biblical prophecy:

Most nations in the world are not mentioned in Bible prophecy, so it really may be no big deal if the United States is not mentioned. Also, America may not be mentioned simply because America plays no significant role in the unfolding of God's end-time plans.

Perhaps the reason America is not mentioned in Bible prophecy is that our country may eventually implode due to ever-escalating moral and spiritual degeneration, or maybe the United States is not mentioned in Bible prophecy because it will be destroyed or at least greatly weakened by nuclear weapons. Another possibility is that the United States may not be mentioned in Bible prophecy because the country will become incapacitated due to an electromagnetic pulse (EMP) attack. Such an attack would utterly incapacitate electrical power systems, all electronic gadgets, and information systems in the U.S.

One final possible reason the United States is not mentioned in Bible prophecy is that the United States will be affected catastrophically by the rapture.

What is the biblical case for premillennialism?

As a backdrop, there are three theological views regarding the millennial kingdom: premillennialism, amillennialism, and postmillennialism. I personally subscribe to premillennialism.

Premillennialism teaches that following the second coming, Christ will institute a kingdom of perfect peace and righteousness on the earth that will last for one thousand years.

There are a number of arguments in favor of premillennialism. For one thing, it naturally emerges from a literal hermeneutic. Also, it best explains the unconditional land promises made to Abraham and his descendants, which are yet to be fulfilled (Genesis 13:14-18) and makes the best sense of the unconditional Davidic covenant in regard to the throne promise (2 Samuel 7:12). And it is most compatible with numerous Old Testament predictions about the coming messianic age.

It is also consistent with the Old Testament ending with an expectation of the messianic kingdom (for example, Isaiah 9:6; 16:5; Malachi 3:1). It best explains the scriptural teaching that Jesus and the apostles would reign on thrones in Jerusalem (Matthew 19:28). Finally, it is most consistent with the apostle Paul's promise that Israel will one day be restored (Romans 9:3-4; 11:1).

What is the biblical case for amillennialism?

Amillennialism, which takes a spiritualized approach in interpreting biblical prophecy, teaches that when Christ comes, eternity will begin with no prior literal thousand-year reign on the earth. *Amillennial* literally means "no millennium." Instead of believing in a literal rule of Christ on the earth, amillennialists generally interpret prophetic verses related to the reign of Christ metaphorically and say they refer to Christ's present (spiritual) rule from heaven. Old Testament predictions made to Israel are viewed as being fulfilled in the New Testament church.

To mount a case for their position, amillennialists often suggest that the Abrahamic and Davidic covenants were conditional and therefore do not require a future fulfillment because the conditions were not met. (Premillennial dispensationalists rebut that these covenants were actually *un*conditional, resting upon God alone for their fulfillment.)

They may also suggest that prophecy should be interpreted symbolically, for apocalyptic literature is highly symbolic in nature. (Premillennialists rebut that prophecy ought to be interpreted literally, for all the prophecies dealing with the first coming of Christ [more than 100] were fulfilled literally. Though there are symbols in Revelation and Daniel, these symbols point to literal truths, and Scripture itself guides us in how to interpret the symbols.)

Amillennialists may also claim that Israel and the church are not two distinct entities but rather one people of God united by the covenant of grace. (Premillennialists rebut that the church and Israel are viewed as distinct all throughout the New Testament—for example, see Romans 9:6, 1 Corinthians 10:32, and Hebrews 12:18-24.)

Proponents of this view say it is most compatible with the idea that the Old Testament is fulfilled in the New Testament. (Premillennialists rebut that the Old Testament promises to Israel were unconditional and await a future fulfillment.)

What is the biblical case for postmillennialism?

The postmillennial view, which takes a spiritual approach in interpreting biblical prophecy, teaches that through the church's progressive influence, the world will be Christianized before Christ returns. In postmillennialism, the millennium will basically involve a thousand years (or more) of peace and prosperity that precedes Christ's physical return.

Some postmillennialists argue that Scripture promises a universal proclamation of the gospel (Matthew 28:18-20). People from all nations, they say, will come to salvation (Revelation 7:9-10). They may also claim that Christ's throne is in heaven, and it is from this throne—not a throne on the earth—that He rules. They often argue that Jesus' parable of the mustard seed is saying that Christianity will continually spread throughout the world (Matthew 13:31-32) and that world conditions are improving morally, socially, and spiritually—all due to the church's influence.

Premillennialists challenge these points. For example, it hardly seems that the world is getting better and better. (The world seems to be plummeting ever deeper into sin.) This view seems to contradict clear biblical passages which predict a massive apostasy in the end times prior to Christ's return (Matthew 24:3-14; Luke 18:8; 1 Timothy 4:1-5; 2 Timothy 3:1-7). Moreover, the Davidic covenant and other biblical passages clearly point to a future reign of Christ on the earth (2 Samuel 7).

The premillennial view is most consistent with a literal interpretation of Scripture.

What is preterism?

The word "preterism" derives from the Latin *preter*, meaning past. In this view, the biblical prophecies in the book of Revelation (especially chapters 6–18) and Matthew 24–25 (Christ's Olivet discourse) have already been fulfilled in the past. This approach to interpreting prophecy appeared in the early writer Eusebius (AD 263–339) in his *Ecclesiastical History*. Hugo Grotius of Holland (ca. 1644), and (in modern times) David Chilton are examples of people who have taken this view.

What are the two forms of preterism?

Moderate preterism is represented by modern writers such as R.C. Sproul, Hank Hanegraaff, and Gary DeMar. While they believe the literal resurrection and second coming are yet future, the other prophecies in Revelation and Matthew 24–25 have allegedly already been fulfilled when Jerusalem fell to Rome in AD 70.

Extreme or full preterism goes so far as to say that all New Testament predictions were fulfilled in the past, including those of the resurrection and second coming. This latter view is heretical, denying two of the fundamentals of the faith: the physical resurrection and a literal second coming.

Does Matthew 24:34 support preterism?

Preterists often point to Matthew 24:34, where Jesus asserted, "This generation will not pass away until all these things take place." This verse allegedly proves the prophecies would be fulfilled in the first century.

Evangelical Christians have generally held to one of two interpretations of Matthew 24:34. One interpretation is that Christ is simply saying that those people who witness the signs stated earlier in Matthew 24—the abomination of desolation (verse 15), the great tribulation such as has never been seen before (verse 21), and the sign of the Son of Man in heaven (verse 30)—will see the coming of Jesus Christ within that very generation. Since it was common knowledge among the Jews that the future tribulation period would last only seven years (Daniel 9:24-27), it is obvious that those living at the beginning of this time would likely live to see the second coming seven years later (except for those who lose their lives during this tumultuous time).

Other evangelicals hold that the word *generation* is to be taken in its basic usage of "race, kindred, family, stock, or breed." If this is what is meant, then Jesus is here promising that the nation of Israel will be preserved—despite terrible persecution during the tribulation—until the consummation of God's program for Israel at the second coming. Many divine promises have been made to Israel—including land promises (Genesis 12; 14–15; 17) and a future Davidic kingdom (2 Samuel 7). Jesus could thus be referring to God's preservation of Israel in order to fulfill the divine promises to them (see Romans 11:11-26).

Either way, Matthew 24:34 does not support preterism.

Does Matthew 16:28 support preterism?

Preterists also argue from Matthew 16:28 that Jesus said some of His followers "standing" there would not taste death until they saw Him return, "coming in His kingdom." Therefore, prophecies of the second coming must have been fulfilled during their generation—apparently in AD 70 when Rome overran Jerusalem.

Contrary to the preterist view, many evangelicals believe that when Jesus said this, He had in mind the transfiguration, which happened precisely one week later (Matthew 17:1-13). In this view, the transfiguration served as a preview of the kingdom in which the divine Messiah would appear in glory. Moreover, against the idea that this verse refers to AD 70 is the pivotal fact that some of the disciples "standing" there were no longer alive by AD 70 (all but John had been martyred by then). Still further, no astronomical events occurred in AD 70, such as the stars falling from heaven and the heavens being shaken (Matthew 24:29). And Jesus did not return "on the clouds of heaven with power and great glory" (Matthew 24:30).

Do prophetic verses which say Jesus will come "quickly" support preterism?

Preterists point to verses which indicate that Jesus will come "quickly" (Revelation 22:12,20 NASB), and that the events of which the book of Revelation speaks will be fulfilled "soon" (1:1; 22:6 NASB). Futurists point out, however, that the Greek word for "quickly" often carries the meaning, "swiftly, speedily, at a rapid rate." Therefore, the term could simply indicate that when the predicted events first start to occur, they will progress swiftly, in rapid succession. Likewise, the phrase translated "soon" can simply mean "suddenly," not necessarily soon.

Was the book of Revelation written prior to AD 70, as preterists claim?

A favorite argument among preterists is that the book of Revelation was written prior to AD 70, and so the book must have been fulfilled *in* AD 70 when Rome overran Jerusalem. Futurists point out, however, that some of the earliest church Fathers confirmed a late date of Revelation, including Irenaeus who claimed the book was written at the close of the reign of Domitian (which took place from AD 81–96). Victorinus confirmed this date in the third century, as did Eusebius (263–340). Therefore, because the book was written *after* AD 70, it could hardly have been referring to events that would be fulfilled in AD 70.

Against the idea that the book of Revelation was fulfilled when Jerusalem was overrun by the Romans is the fact that key events described in the book of Revelation did not occur in AD 70. For example, in AD 70 "a third of mankind" was not killed (Revelation 9:18). Nor has "every living thing died that was in the sea" (16:3). Preterists must resort to an allegorical interpretation to explain away these texts.

Will the second coming of Christ be a physical, visible event, or will it be a spiritual, invisible event, as some cultists argue?

The second coming will be a physical, visible event. One Greek word used to describe the second coming is *apokalupsis,* which carries the basic meaning of "revelation," "visible disclosure," "unveiling," and "removing the cover" from something that is hidden. The word is used of pulling a cover off a sculpture for everyone to see and of Christ's second coming in 1 Peter 4:13.

Also used of Christ's second coming is the word *epiphaneia,* which carries the basic meaning of "appearing." It literally means "a shining forth" and is used several times by the apostle Paul in reference to Christ's visible second coming. For example, in Titus 2:13 Paul speaks of "*the appearing* of the glory of our great God and Savior Jesus Christ." In 1 Timothy 6:14 Paul urges Timothy to "keep the commandment unstained and free from reproach until *the appearing* of our Lord Jesus Christ." Significantly, Christ's *first* coming—which was both *bodily* and *visible*—was called an *epiphaneia* (2 Timothy 1:10). In the same way, Christ's second coming will be both *bodily* and *visible*.

In support of a visible coming of the Lord we must not forget the clear teaching of Matthew 24:29-30:

> Immediately after the tribulation of those days the sun will be darkened, and the moon will not give its light, and the stars will fall from heaven, and the powers of the heavens will be shaken. Then will appear in heaven the sign of the Son of Man, and then all the tribes of the earth will mourn, and they will see the Son of Man coming on the clouds of heaven with power and great glory.

Should Christians be involved in setting dates for the rapture or the second coming of Christ?

No. Christians can certainly be excited to be living in the general season of the Lord's return. But they should never set dates.

I can think of several good reasons for this: Over the past 2,000 years, the track record of those who have predicted and/or expected "the end" has been 100 percent wrong. The history of doomsday predictions is little more than a history of dashed expectations. Though it is possible we are living in the last days, it is also possible that Christ's second coming is a long way off.

Also, date-setters may end up making harmful decisions for their lives. Selling one's possessions and heading for the mountains, purchasing bomb shelters, stopping education, leaving family and friends—these are destructive actions that can ruin or at least injure one's life or even one's faith. Expecting the rapture to occur by a specific date, for example, may end up damaging a date-setter's faith in the Bible (especially prophetic sections) when those expectations fail. And if someone loses confidence in the prophetic portions of Scripture, biblical prophecy ceases to be a motivation to purity and holiness in that person's daily life (see

Titus 2:12-14). Further, the faith of new and immature believers may be damaged when predicted events by date-setters fail to materialize.

Date-setters also tend to be sensationalistic, which is unbefitting to a Christian. Christ calls His followers to live soberly and alertly as they await His coming (Mark 13:32-37). For this reason, Christians who get caught up in date-setting can do damage to the cause of Christ. Humanists enjoy scorning Christians who have put stock in end-time predictions (especially when specific dates have been attached to specific events). Why give "ammo" to the enemies of Christianity?

The timing of end-time events is in God's hands, and we haven't been given the precise details (Acts 1:7). As far as the second coming is concerned, it is better to live as if Jesus were coming today and yet prepare for the future as if He were not coming for a long time. This way you are ready for time and eternity.

29
The Wonder of Heaven

What actually happens at the moment of death?

From a biblical perspective, human beings have both a material aspect (the physical body) and an immaterial aspect (the soul or spirit). The New Testament word for "death" carries the idea of *separation*. At the moment of physical death, the human spirit separates or departs from the body (2 Corinthians 5:8).

This is why, when Stephen was being put to death by stoning, he prayed, "Lord Jesus, receive my spirit" (Acts 7:59). At the moment of death "the spirit returns to God who gave it" (Ecclesiastes 12:7).

These verses indicate that death for the believer involves his or her spirit departing from the physical body and immediately going into the presence of the Lord in heaven. Death for the believer is thus an event that leads to a supremely blissful existence (see Philippians 1:21-23). For the unbeliever, however, death holds grim prospects. At death the unbeliever's spirit departs from the body and goes not to heaven but to a place of great suffering (Luke 16:19-31; see also 2 Peter 2:9).

How long will people remain in a bodiless state?

Both believers and unbelievers remain as spirits—that is, they remain in a disembodied state—until the future day of resurrection. For believers, this will be on the day of the rapture. On that day, the dead in Christ will be resurrected and believers still alive on the earth will be instantly transformed with resurrection bodies. In a blink of an eye, dead and living Christians will be caught up to meet Jesus in the air (1 Thessalonians 4:13-17). What a glorious day that will be! Our new bodies will be specially suited to dwelling in heaven in the direct presence of God. The perishable will be made imperishable and the mortal will be made immortal (1 Corinthians 15:53).

Unbelievers, too, will be resurrected, but not until after Christ's millennial kingdom. They will be resurrected in order to participate in the great white throne judgment (Revelation 20:11-13). Following this judgment, they will be cast into the lake of fire, where they will suffer forever in their eternal resurrection bodies (verses 14-15).

The Bible speaks of three different heavens. What are we to make of this?

The Scriptures make reference to the "third heaven" (2 Corinthians 12:2). This is the indescribable and glorious dwelling place of God in all His glory. It is elsewhere called the "heaven of heavens" (Nehemiah 9:6) and the "highest heaven" (1 Kings 8:27; 2 Chronicles 2:6).

If God's abode is the "third" heaven, then what are the first and the second heavens? Scripture gives us the answer. The first heaven is the earth's atmosphere (Job 35:5). The second heaven is the stellar universe (Genesis 1:17; Deuteronomy 17:3).

Will our present earth and universe be destroyed? If so, why?

Yes. Recall that after Adam and Eve sinned against God in the Garden of Eden, a curse was placed upon the earth by God (Genesis 3:17-18). So before the eternal kingdom can be made manifest, God must deal with this cursed earth. Indeed, the earth—along with the first and second heavens (the earth's atmosphere and the stellar universe)—must be dissolved by fire. The old must make room for the new.

The Scriptures often speak of the passing of the old heaven and earth. Psalm 102:26, for example, speaking of the earth and stellar heavens, says, "They will perish, but you [Oh God] will remain; they will all wear out like a garment. You will change them like a robe, and they will pass away."

What does the Bible say about the new heaven and new earth?

In the book of Revelation we read, "Then I saw a new heaven and a new earth, for the first heaven and the first earth had passed away, and the sea was no more...And he who was seated on the throne said, 'Behold, I am making all things new'" (Revelation 21:1,5).

The Greek word used to designate the newness of the cosmos is *kainos*. This word means "new in nature" or "new in quality." So the phrase "new heavens and a new earth" refers not to a cosmos that is totally other than the present cosmos. Rather, the new cosmos will stand in continuity with the present cosmos, but it will be utterly renewed and renovated. In keeping with this, Matthew 19:28 speaks of "the new world." Acts 3:21 speaks of a coming restoration.

Will we live forever on this new earth?

Yes, and it will be glorious. The new earth, being a renewed and an eternal earth, will be adapted to the vast moral and physical changes which the eternal state necessitates. Everything is new in the eternal state and will be according to God's own glorious nature. The new heavens and the new earth will be brought into blessed conformity with all that God is—in a state of fixed bliss and absolute perfection.

An incredible thing to ponder is that in the next life heaven and earth will no longer be separate realms, as they are now, but will be merged. Believers will thus continue to be *in heaven* even while they are *on the new earth*. The new earth will be utterly sinless, and therefore bathed and suffused in the light and splendor of God, not obscured by evil of any kind or tarnished by evildoers of any description.

"Heaven" will thus encompass the new heaven and the new earth. And the New Jerusalem—the eternal city that measures 1,400 by 1,400 by 1,400 miles—will apparently "come down" and rest upon the newly renovated earth (see Revelation 21:2). This city will be the eternal dwelling place of the saints of all ages.

Does the fact that "flesh and blood" cannot enter into God's kingdom mean that our resurrection bodies will not be physical?

No. It is true that 1 Corinthians 15:50 says, "I tell you this, brothers: flesh and blood cannot inherit the kingdom of God, nor does the perishable inherit the imperishable." However, the term "flesh and blood" is simply a Jewish idiom used in Scripture to refer to mortal, perishable humanity. This verse is saying that mortal human beings in their present perishable bodies cannot inherit heaven.

Mortal humanity must be made immortal humanity in order to survive in heaven. The resurrection body will be endowed with special qualities that will enable it to adapt perfectly to life in God's presence. As 1 Corinthians 15:53 puts it, "This perishable body must put on the imperishable, and this mortal body must put on immortality."

What will worship be like in the eternal state?

The book of Revelation portrays believers in the eternal state as offering worship and praise before the throne of God and Christ (Revelation 19:1-6). The worship that takes place in heaven will be ultimately fulfilling. It will not be confining or manipulated, but spontaneous and genuine. We will not find ourselves nodding off to sleep, as we're often tempted to do in church services. (In fact, our resurrection bodies won't need any sleep at all!) Rather, we will virtually lose ourselves in the sheer joy of expressing with our lips the adoration and love we feel for God in our hearts.

Will we serve God in the afterlife?

Yes, we will serve God in various capacities (Revelation 1:5-6; see also 22:3). This will not be a tedious kind of service but a joyous one—fully meeting our heart's every desire. There will be no boredom in eternity. Because we will be servants of the Most High, and because there will be an endless variety of tasks to perform, the prospect of heaven is entrancingly attractive. We definitely won't be sitting on clouds playing harps for all eternity!

It would seem that one aspect of our service will involve reigning with Christ. In Revelation 22:5 we are told that believers "will reign forever and ever." We will be involved in some capacity in the heavenly government.

Also, part of our service will involve judging the angels in some capacity. "Do you not know that we are to judge angels?" Paul asks in 1 Corinthians 6:3. This is noteworthy because human beings at present are lower than the angels (see Psalm 8). The situation will be reversed in the eternal state. Angels will be lower than redeemed humanity in heaven.

Will we be able to study God's glorious nature throughout eternity?

I believe so. Throughout our eternal future, we will continuously be shown "the immeasurable riches of his grace" (Ephesians 2:7). God is so infinite—with matchless perfections that are beyond us in every way—that we will never come to the end of exploring Him and His marvelous riches. It will be wondrous.

Do babies and little children go to heaven at the moment of death?

Yes. I believe the Scriptures teach that every infant and young child who dies is immediately ushered into God's glorious presence in heaven. I believe that at the moment of death, Jesus applies the benefits of His death on the cross to that child, thereby saving him or her.

At the outset, we must recognize that the whole of Scripture points to the universal need of salvation—even among little children. All of us—including infants who can't believe—are lost (Luke 19:10), perishing (John 3:16), condemned (John 3:18), and under God's wrath (John 3:36). In view of this, we cannot say that little children are in a sinless state. That's why Christ must apply the benefits of His death on the cross to each child that dies.

Also, God's primary purpose in saving human beings is to display His wondrous grace. One must ask, would "the riches of his grace" be displayed in "wisdom and insight" (Ephesians 1:7-8) in sending little children to hell? I think not. It would be a cruel mockery for God to call upon infants to do—and to hold them *responsible* for doing—what they *could not* do. At that young age children simply do not have the capacity to exercise saving faith in Christ.

I believe it is the uniform testimony of Scripture that those who are not capable of making a decision to receive Jesus Christ and have died are now with Christ in heaven, resting in His tender arms, enjoying the sweetness of His love. It is highly revealing that in all the descriptions of hell in the Bible, we *never* read of infants or little children there. Only adults capable of making decisions are seen there. Nor do we read of infants and little children standing before the great white throne judgment, which is the judgment of the wicked dead and the precursor to the lake of fire (Revelation 20:11-15). The complete silence of Scripture regarding the presence of infants in eternal torment strongly suggests they will not be there.

Another consideration that points to the assurance of infant salvation relates to the basis of the judgment of the lost. We read in Revelation 20:12 that the lost are judged "according to what they had done." The basis of the judgment of the wicked is clearly *deeds done while on the earth.* So infants cannot possibly be the objects of this judgment because they are not responsible for their deeds. Such a judgment against infants would be a travesty.

As we examine instances in which Christ encountered children during His earthly ministry, it would seem that children have a special place in His heart and His kingdom. Jesus even said, "Truly, I say to you, unless you turn and become like children, you will never enter the kingdom of heaven" (Matthew 18:3). He also said, "Whoever receives one such child in my name receives me" (verse 5). I don't think anyone could read through Matthew 18 and conclude that it is within the realm of possibility that Jesus could damn such little ones to hell!

King David in the Old Testament certainly believed he would again be with his young son who had died (2 Samuel 12:22-23). David firmly believed in life after death. He had no doubt that he would spend eternity with his beloved little one.

These and other scriptural factors are sufficient to establish that babies and young children go straight to heaven at the moment of death.

Will we recognize our Christian loved ones in the afterlife?

Yes. The Thessalonian Christians were apparently very concerned about their Christian loved ones who had died. They expressed their concern to the apostle Paul. So, in 1 Thessalonians 4:13-17, Paul deals with the "dead in Christ" and assures the Thessalonian Christians that a reunion will indeed take place. And yes, believers will recognize their loved ones in the eternal state.

We are told in 2 Samuel 12:23 that David knew he would be reunited with his deceased son in heaven. He had no doubt about recognizing him. Likewise, in Jesus' parable of the rich man and Lazarus in Luke 16:19-31, the rich man, Lazarus, *and* Abraham were all recognized by each other in the intermediate state.

Will our children still be our children in the afterlife?

Yes. It will always be true that your daughter is your daughter and your son is your son. Receiving a glorified body does not obliterate the fact that in earth-time history a husband and wife conceived and gave birth to a son or daughter.

But in the eternal state, we are all equally "sons" and "daughters" in God's eternal family. We have each become adopted into His forever family (Ephesians 1:5). We are all children of God!

Will husbands and wives still be married in the afterlife?

Believers will no longer be in a married state in the afterlife. Jesus said, "In the resurrection they neither marry nor are given in marriage, but are like angels in heaven" (Matthew 22:30).

Of course, it will always be true that my wife, Kerri, and I were married on this earth. *Nothing will ever change that.* And in the eternal state, in the new heavens and the new earth, we will apparently retain our memory that we were married on the old earth. It will be an eternal memory. And what a precious memory it will be.

We should not think of this as a deprivation. It may be very difficult for us to conceive how we could be happy and fulfilled if we were not still married to our present spouse. But God Himself has promised that there will *not* be any sense of deprivation. There will be only bliss, and there will be no more sorrow or pain.

My wife and I are part of the glorious church, which, the Scriptures reveal, will one day be married to Christ. This event is referred to as the marriage of the Lamb (Revelation 19:7-9). It is an event to look forward to with great anticipation.

Is it possible that animals have an afterlife like humans do?

Some theologians seem quite sure that our pets will not be in heaven. Others, such as R.C. Sproul, have questioned that thinking. It is true that only human beings are created in the image of God (Genesis 1:26). Even though animals are not created in God's image, however, Sproul thinks it is possible that they may have souls.[1]

Sproul and other theologians think that redemption involves far more than just human beings—that is, in some sense God will redeem the entire creation. As Romans 8:21 puts it, "the creation itself will be set free from its bondage to decay and obtain the freedom of the glory of the children of God." Perhaps this cosmic redemption includes the animal kingdom. If the entire creation is set free from its "bondage to decay," then maybe we'll see our pets in heaven!

How can we be happy in heaven knowing that some people are suffering in hell?

This is a difficult question to answer. In fact, on this side of eternity, we do not have all the wisdom and insight we need to fully answer it. But some scriptural considerations help us keep this question in perspective.

First, God Himself has promised that He will take away all pain and remove all our tears (Revelation 21:4). It is in His hands. We can rest assured that God has the power and ability to do as He has promised. It is a fact that we will be happy in heaven. God has promised it.

Second, we will be aware of the full justice of God's decisions. We will clearly see that those who are in hell are there precisely because they rejected God's only provision for escaping hell. They are those to whom God ultimately says, "Thy will be done."

Third, we will recognize that hell has degrees of punishment, just as heaven has degrees of reward. This gives us an assurance that the Hitlers of human history will be in a much greater state of suffering than, for example, a non-Christian moralist (Luke 12:47-48).

Finally, it is entirely possible that God may remove the memories of non-Christians (including family members) from our minds. God promises in Isaiah 65:17, "Behold, I create new heavens and a new earth, and the former things shall not be remembered or come into mind."

Let us never forget that God is perfectly wise and just. He knows what He is doing! You and I can rest with quiet assurance in God's wisdom and justice.

30
The Judgment of Humankind

Is it true that Christians will stand before the judgment seat of Christ?

Yes. All believers will one day stand before the judgment seat of Christ (Romans 14:10-11). At that time each believer's life will be examined in regard to the things done while in the body. Personal motives and intents of the heart will also be weighed.

The idea of a "judgment seat" relates to the athletic games of Paul's day. After the races and games concluded, the emperor himself often took his seat on an elevated throne, and one by one, the winning athletes came up to the throne to receive a reward. This reward was usually a wreath of leaves, a "victor's crown." In the case of Christians, each of us will stand before Christ the Judge and receive (or lose) rewards.

This judgment has nothing to do with whether or not the Christian will remain saved. Those who have placed faith in Christ *are* saved, and nothing threatens that. Believers are eternally secure in their salvation (Romans 8:29-30; Ephesians 4:30). This judgment rather has to do with the reception or loss of rewards.

Will the Christian be judged on his or her actions while on the earth?

Yes. Broadly speaking, the Christian's judgment will focus on his personal stewardship of the gifts, talents, opportunities, and responsibilities given to him in this life. The very character of each Christian's life and service will be utterly laid bare before the unerring and omniscient vision of Christ, whose eyes are "like a flame of fire" (Revelation 1:14).

Each of our actions will be judged before the Lord. The psalmist said to the Lord, "You will render to a man according to his work" (Psalm 62:12; see also Matthew 16:27). In Ephesians 6:7-8 we read that "whatever good anyone does, this he will receive back from the Lord, whether he is a slave or free."

Will our thoughts come under scrutiny at the judgment seat of Christ?

Yes, I believe so. In Jeremiah 17:10 God said, "I the LORD search the heart and test the mind, to give every man according to his ways, according to the fruit of his deeds." The Lord "will bring to light the things now hidden in darkness and will disclose the purposes of the heart" (1 Corinthians 4:5). The Lord is the one "who searches mind and heart" (Revelation 2:23). All our motives will be laid bare.

Will the words we spoke on the earth be judged?

Yes indeed. Christ once said that "people will give account for every careless word they speak, for by your words you will be justified, and by your words you will be condemned" (Matthew 12:36-37). If even our careless words are carefully recorded, *how much more* will our calculated boastful claims, our cutting criticisms of others, our off-color jokes, and our unkind comments be taken into account.

What kinds of rewards will believers receive at the judgment seat of Christ?

Scripture often speaks of these rewards in terms of crowns that we wear. In fact, a number of different crowns symbolize the various spheres of achievement and award in the Christian life.

The *crown of life* is given to those who persevere under trial, and especially to those who suffer to the point of death (James 1:12; Revelation 2:10). The *crown of glory* is given to those who faithfully and sacrificially minister God's Word to the flock (1 Peter 5:4). The *crown incorruptible* is given to those who win the race of temperance and self-control (1 Corinthians 9:25). The *crown of righteousness* is given to those who long for the second coming of Christ (2 Timothy 4:8).

Are our "crowns" intended to glorify us or God?

That's an important question. I think it is highly revealing that in Revelation 4:10 we find believers casting their crowns before the throne of God in an act of worship and adoration. This teaches us something very important. Clearly the crowns (as rewards) are bestowed on us not for our own glory but ultimately for the glory of God. We are told elsewhere in Scripture that believers are redeemed in order to bring glory to God (1 Corinthians 6:20). It would seem that the act of placing our crowns before the throne of God is an illustration of this.

Here's something else to think about. The greater reward or crown one has received, the greater capacity one has to bring glory to the Creator. The lesser reward or crown one has received, the lesser his capacity to bring glory to the Creator. Because of the different rewards handed out at the judgment seat of Christ, believers will have differing capacities to bring glory to God.

How can we be happy throughout eternity if we don't fare well at the judgment seat of Christ?

It seems to be the testimony of Scripture that some believers at the judgment seat of Christ may have a sense of deprivation and suffer some degree of forfeiture and shame. Second John 8 warns us, "Watch yourselves, so that you *may not lose* what we have worked for, but may win a full reward." In 1 John 2:28 John wrote about the possibility of a believer actually being *ashamed* at Christ's coming.

But we must keep all this in perspective. Christ's coming for us at the rapture and the prospect of living eternally with Him is something that should give each of us joy. And our joy will last for all eternity. How, then, can we reconcile this eternal joy with the possible loss of reward and perhaps even some level of shame at the judgment seat of Christ?

I think Herman Hoyt's explanation is the best I've seen:

> The Judgment Seat of Christ might be compared to a commence-ment ceremony. At graduation there is some measure of disap-pointment and remorse that one did not do better and work harder. However, at such an event the overwhelming emotion is joy, not remorse. The graduates do not leave the auditorium weeping because they did not earn better grades. Rather, they are thankful that they have been graduated, and they are grateful for what they did achieve. To overdo the sorrow aspect of the Judgment Seat of Christ is to make heaven hell. To underdo the sorrow aspect is to make faithfulness inconsequential.[1]

I think that each believer will be glorifying God to the fullness of his capacity in the next life. All of our "cups" will be "running over," but some cups will be larger than others. Perhaps the most important thing to ponder is that each one of us will be able to perpetually and forever "proclaim the excellencies of him who called you out of dark-ness into his marvelous light" (1 Peter 2:9).

What is the great white throne judgment?

The great white throne judgment is the judgment that unbeliev-ers must face (Revelation 20:11-15). (Believers will not participate in this horrific judgment.) Christ is the divine Judge, and those that are judged are the unsaved dead of all time. The judgment takes place after the millennial kingdom, Christ's 1,000-year reign on planet earth.

Those who face Christ at this judgment will be judged on the basis of their works (Revelation 20:12-13). It is critical to understand that they actually get to this judgment because they are *already unsaved.* This judgment will not separate believers from unbelievers, for all who will experience it will have already made the choice during their lifetimes to reject God. Once they are before the divine Judge, they are judged according to their works not only to justify their condemnation but also to determine the degree to which each person should be punished throughout eternity in hell.

Is there really such a thing as hell?

The Scriptures assure us that hell is a real place. But hell was not part of God's original creation, which He called "good" (Genesis 1). Hell was created later to accommodate the banishment of Satan and his fallen angels who rebelled against God (Matthew 25:41). Human beings who reject Christ will join Satan and his fallen angels in this infernal place of suffering.

The Scriptures use a variety of words to describe the horrors of hell—including fire, fiery furnace, unquenchable fire, the lake of burning sulfur, the lake of fire, everlasting contempt, perdition, the place of weeping and gnashing of teeth, eternal punishment, darkness, the wrath to come, exclusion, torments, damnation, condemnation, retribution, woe, and the second death (see, for example, Mark 9:47-48; Luke 16:23; James 3:6; 2 Peter 2:4; Revelation 20:13-15). Hell is a horrible destiny.

Why is hell sometimes called Gehenna?

One of the more important New Testament words for hell (in Greek) is "Gehenna" (Matthew 10:28). This word has an interesting history. For several generations in ancient Israel, atrocities were committed in "the Valley of the Son of Hinnom"—atrocities that included human sacrifices, even the sacrifice of children (2 Kings 23:10; 2 Chronicles 28:3; 33:6; Jeremiah 32:35). These unfortunate victims were sacrificed to the false Moabite god Molech. Jeremiah appropriately called this valley "the Valley of Slaughter" (Jeremiah 7:31-34).

Eventually the valley came to be used as a public rubbish dump into which all the filth in Jerusalem was poured. Not only garbage but also the bodies of dead animals and the corpses of criminals were thrown on the heap where they—like everything else in the dump—would perpetually burn. The valley was a place where the fires never stopped burning. And a hungry worm could always find a good meal there.

This place was originally called (in the Hebrew) *Ge-ben-hinnom* ("the Valley of the Son of Hinnom"—see Joshua 15:8). It was eventually shortened to the name *Ge-Hinnom*. The Greek translation of this

Hebrew phrase is *Gehenna*. It became an appropriate and graphic term for the reality of hell. Jesus Himself used the word eleven times as a metaphorical way of describing the eternal place of suffering of unredeemed humanity.

Does God really send anyone to hell?

God doesn't want to send anyone to hell. Scripture tells us that God is "not wishing that any should perish, but that all should reach repentance" (2 Peter 3:9). God sent Jesus into the world specifically to pay the penalty for our sins by dying on the cross (John 3:16-17). Unfortunately, not all people are willing to admit that they sin and ask for forgiveness. They don't accept the payment of Jesus' death for them. So God lets them experience the results of their choice (see Luke 16:19-31).

C.S. Lewis once said that in the end there are two groups of people. One group of people says to God, "Thy will be done." These are those who have placed their faith in Jesus Christ and will live forever with God in heaven. The second group of people are those to whom God says, sadly, "*Thy* will be done!" These are those who have rejected Jesus Christ and will spend eternity apart from Him.

Is the fire of hell literal, or is it a metaphorical way of describing punishment?

Scholars are divided on this issue. Some believe the "fire" of hell is quite literal—and that may very well be the case. Others believe "fire" is a metaphorical way of expressing the great wrath of God. Scripture tells us, "The LORD your God is a consuming fire, a jealous God" (Deuteronomy 4:24). "God is a consuming fire" (Hebrews 12:29). "His wrath is poured out like fire" (Nahum 1:6). "Who can stand when he appears? For he is like a refiner's fire" (Malachi 3:2). God said His wrath will "go forth like fire, and burn with none to quench it, because of the evil of your deeds" (Jeremiah 4:4). Whether the fire of hell is literal or metaphorical, it will entail horrible, horrible suffering for those who are there.

Are there degrees of punishment in hell?

Yes. The degree of punishment will be commensurate with one's sin against the light that one has received.

One good passage that indicates degrees of punishment is Luke 12:47-48: "That servant who knew his master's will but did not get ready or act according to his will, *will receive a severe beating*. But the one who did not know, and did what deserved a beating, *will receive a light beating*. Everyone to whom much was given, of him much will be required, and from him to whom they entrusted much, they will demand the more." Other verses on this issue include Matthew 10:15; 16:27; Revelation 20:12-13; 22:12.

Will the punishment of the wicked in hell be an eternal punishment, or is it just temporary?

Jesus affirmed that the wicked will "go away into *eternal* punishment, but the righteous into *eternal* life" (Matthew 25:46). Notice that the eternality of the punishment of the wicked equals the eternality of the eternal life of the righteous. One is just as long as the other. This points to the "forever" nature of the punishment of the wicked. It never ceases.

The eternal nature of this punishment is emphasized all throughout Scripture. The fire of hell, for example, is called an "unquenchable fire" (Mark 9:43). "The smoke of their [sinners'] torment goes up forever and ever" (Revelation 14:11).

What is the "intermediate state" like for the unsaved? If they're not in hell yet, are they in a place of suffering?

At the moment of death unbelievers go as disembodied spirits to a temporary place of suffering (Luke 16:19-31). There they await their future resurrection and judgment (at the great white throne judgment), with an eventual destiny in the lake of fire.

The state of the ungodly dead in the intermediate state is described in 2 Peter 2:9: "The Lord knows how to...keep the unrighteous under punishment until the day of judgment." The word "keep" in this verse is a present tense, indicating that the wicked (nonbelievers) are held captive *continuously*. Peter is portraying them as condemned prisoners being closely guarded in a spiritual jail while awaiting future sentencing and final judgment.

While God holds them there, their punishment continues. The present tense used in this verse points to the perpetual, ongoing nature of the punishment. But this punishment in the intermediate state is only temporary. As noted previously, the wicked dead will eventually be resurrected and then judged at the great white throne judgment, after which time their *eternal* punishment will begin in the lake of fire (Revelation 20:11-15).

Will unbelievers be resurrected as believers will be?

Yes. Those who participate in the great white throne judgment (the unsaved) are resurrected *unto judgment*. Jesus Himself affirmed that "an hour is coming when all who are in the tombs will hear his voice and come out, those who have done good to the resurrection of life, and those who have done evil to the resurrection of judgment" (John 5:28-29).

The Scriptures speak of two types of resurrection: the first and second resurrection, respectively (Revelation 20:5-6,11-15). The first resurrection is the resurrection of Christians, and the second resurrection is the resurrection of the wicked.

The second resurrection will be an awful spectacle. All the unsaved of all time will be resurrected at the end of Christ's millennial kingdom, judged at the great white throne judgment, and then cast alive into the lake of fire (Revelation 20:11-15). They will receive resurrection bodies subject to pain and suffering, and they will suffer there forever with the devil and his angels.

31
Erroneous Views of the Afterlife

What is annihilationism?

The doctrine of annihilationism teaches that man was created immortal. But those who continue in sin and reject Christ are, by a positive act of God, deprived of the gift of immortality and are ultimately destroyed. Consciousness is snuffed out.

How do we know annihilationism is not correct?

In Matthew 25:46 we read that the unsaved "will go away into eternal punishment, but the righteous into eternal life." By no stretch of the imagination can the punishment spoken of in Matthew 25:46 be defined as any kind of nonsuffering extinction of consciousness. If actual suffering is lacking, then so is punishment. Punishment entails suffering. And suffering necessarily entails consciousness.

Certainly one can exist and not be punished. But no one can be punished and not exist. Annihilation means the obliteration of existence and anything that pertains to existence, such as punishment. Instead of producing punishment, annihilation *avoids* it.

Notice that the punishment in Matthew 25:46 is said to be "eternal." The adjective *aionion* in this verse literally means "everlasting, without end." This same adjective is predicated of God (the "eternal" God) in Romans 16:26, Hebrews 9:14, 13:8, and Revelation 4:9. The punishment of the wicked is just as eternal as our eternal God.

Is it correct to say that annihilationism is ultimately unjust as a punishment?

I believe so. Notice that there are no degrees of annihilation. One is either annihilated, or one is not. (Whether you're a Hitler or a non-Christian moralist, you both get annihilated.) The Scriptures, by contrast, teach that there will be degrees of conscious punishment in hell (see Matthew 10:15; 11:21-24; 16:27; Luke 12:47-48; Hebrews 10:29; Revelation 20:11-15; 22:12). These degrees of punishment are commensurate with the level of one's wickedness. Such a punishment is therefore completely just.

Does annihilationism ultimately provide an escape from punishment?

Yes. One can hardly deny that for one who is suffering excruciating pain, the extinction of his or her consciousness would actually be a blessing—not a punishment (see Luke 23:30; Revelation 9:6). Any honest seeker after truth must admit that one cannot define "eternal punishment" as an extinction of consciousness. "It is an odd use of language to speak of an insensate (that is, unfeeling), inanimate object receiving punishment. To say, 'I punished my car for not starting by slowly plucking out its sparkplug wires, one by one,' would evoke laughter, not serious consideration."[1]

Does consciousness vanish at the moment of death?

No. The Scriptures are clear that the souls of both believers and unbelievers are fully conscious between death and the future day of resurrection. Unbelievers are in conscious woe (see Mark 9:47-48; Luke 16:22-23; 2 Peter 2:9; Revelation 19:20), and believers are in conscious bliss (2 Corinthians 5:8; Philippians 1:21-23).

A number of theological factors challenge this "soul sleep" theory. For example, Lazarus, the rich man, and Abraham—all of whom had died—were fully conscious and fully aware of all that was transpiring around them (Luke 16:19-31). Moses and Elijah (who had died long ago) were conscious on the Mount of Transfiguration with Jesus (Matthew 17:3). Jesus promised that the repentant thief would be with Him (consciously) in paradise the very day he died (Luke 23:43). The "souls" of those martyred during the tribulation period are portrayed as being conscious in heaven, talking to God (Revelation 6:9-10).

Jesus, in speaking about the Old Testament saints Abraham, Isaac, and Jacob, said that God "is not God of the dead, but of the living" (Luke 20:38). In effect, Jesus was saying, "Even though Abraham, Isaac, and Jacob died physically many years ago, they are actually living today. For God, who calls Himself the God of Abraham, Isaac, and Jacob, is not the God of the dead but of the living."

What is purgatory?

The Roman Catholic Church teaches that God admits to heaven those who are perfect at death. But those who are not perfectly cleansed and are still tainted with the guilt of venial sins do not go to heaven. Instead, they go to purgatory where they allegedly go through a process of cleansing (or "purging"). Such souls are oppressed with a sense of deprivation and suffer certain pain. How long they stay in purgatory—and how much suffering they undergo while there—depends upon their particular state of sin. Once their prescribed time is up, they go to heaven.

Roman Catholics teach that a person's time in purgatory may be shortened and his pains alleviated by the faithful prayers and good works of those still alive. The sacrifice of the Mass is viewed as especially important in this regard. Catholics find support for this doctrine in the Apocrypha (2 Maccabees 12:42-45).

Is purgatory a biblical doctrine?

No. The backdrop is that when Jesus died on the cross, He said "It is finished" (John 19:30). Jesus completed the work of redemption at the cross. In keeping with this, Jesus in His high priestly prayer to the Father said, "I glorified you on earth, having accomplished the work that you gave me to do" (John 17:4).

Hebrews 10:14 also tells us that "by a single offering he has perfected for all time those who are being sanctified." Therefore, those who believe in Christ are "perfect for all time"—no further "purging" is necessary.

Likewise, we are told in 1 John 1:7 that "the blood of Jesus his Son cleanses us from all sin." Romans 8:1 says, "There is therefore now no condemnation for those who are in Christ Jesus." Such verses make the doctrine of purgatory impossible. Jesus Himself purged all our sin at the cross.

What is reincarnation?

The word *reincarnation* literally means to "come again in the flesh." The process of reincarnation—continual rebirths in human bodies—allegedly continues until the soul has reached a state of perfection and merges back with its source (God or the "Universal Soul").

One's lot in life, according to those who believe in reincarnation, is based on the law of karma. This law says that if bad things happen in one's life, this is an outworking of bad karma. If good things happen in one's life, this is an outworking of good karma.

"Karma" refers to the "debt" a soul accumulates because of good or bad actions committed during one's life (or past lives). If one accumulates good karma by performing good actions, he or she will be reincarnated in a desirable state. If one accumulates bad karma, he or she will be reincarnated in a less desirable state.

What are some practical problems in believing in reincarnation?

The salvation-by-works doctrine of reincarnation has many practical problems:

We must ask, why does one get punished for something he or she cannot remember having done in a previous life? If the purpose of karma is to rid humanity of its selfish desires, then why hasn't there been a noticeable improvement in human nature after all the millennia of reincarnations? If reincarnation and the law of karma are so beneficial on a practical level, then how do advocates of this doctrine explain the immense and ever-worsening social and economic problems—including widespread poverty, starvation, disease, and horrible suffering—in India, where reincarnation has been systematically taught throughout its history?

Reincarnation makes one socially passive. It teaches that one should not interfere with someone else's bad karma (bad circumstances). Also, reincarnation is fatalistic. The law of karma guarantees that whatever we sow in the present life, we will invariably reap in the next life. It works infallibly and inexorably. There is no room for grace!

Reincarnation offers little to look forward to. Absorption into Brahman (the Universal Soul) has little appeal when compared to the possibility of living eternally with the living and personal God (Revelation 22:1-5).

What are some biblical problems with the doctrine of reincarnation?

In 2 Corinthians 5:8 the apostle Paul states, "We are of good courage, and we would rather be away from the body and at home with the Lord." At death, the Christian immediately goes into the presence of the Lord, not into another body. Unbelievers at death go to a place of suffering, not into another body (Luke 16:19-31; see also 2 Peter 2:9).

Most important, Hebrews 9:27 assures us that "it is appointed for man to die once, and after that comes judgment." Each human being *lives once* as a mortal on the earth, *dies once,* and *then faces judgment.* No one has a second chance by reincarnating into another body. For this reason, the apostle Paul urged, "Now is the day of salvation" (2 Corinthians 6:2).

Why do New Agers say that Matthew 11:14 proves that Jesus taught reincarnation?[2]

Matthew 11:14 says, "If you are willing to accept it, he [John the Baptist] is Elijah who is to come." Some New Agers claim that John the Baptist was a reincarnation of Elijah.

Luke 1:17 (a cross reference) clarifies any possible confusion on the proper interpretation of Matthew 11:14 by pointing out that the ministry of John the Baptist was carried out "in the spirit and power of Elijah." Nowhere does it say that John the Baptist was a reincarnation of Elijah. New Agers conveniently forget that John the Baptist, when asked if he was Elijah, flatly answered, "I am not" (John 1:21).

Why do New Agers say that John 3:3 proves that Jesus taught reincarnation?

In John 3:3 Jesus said to Nicodemus, "Truly, truly, I say to you, unless one is born again he cannot see the kingdom of God." New Agers argue that Jesus was referring to "cyclical rebirth" in this verse.

The context of John 3, however, clearly shows that Jesus was referring to a *spiritual rebirth* or regeneration. In fact, the phrase "born again" carries the idea of "born from above" and can even be translated that way. Nicodemus could not have understood Jesus' statement in any other way, for Jesus clarified His meaning: "That which is born of the flesh is flesh, and that which is born of the Spirit is spirit" (verse 6).

32
Near-Death Experiences

What kinds of things happen in a so-called near-death experience (NDE)?

Based on thousands of interviews with people who have gone through *alleged* near-death experiences, researchers say fifteen characteristics commonly occur in a near-death experience.[1]

First, most people say that *no words can describe the near-death experience*. Human language is insufficient to depict what occurred. Second, individuals typically report *hearing themselves pronounced dead* by medical personnel. To the doctors and nurses present, death seemed real because the heart and breathing had stopped, and the person appeared to be physiologically dead. But such individuals nevertheless claim to have heard themselves pronounced dead.

Third, most people who have had a near-death experience say they had *sensations of extreme pleasure, peace, and quiet*, which often motivate the individual to want to stay "dead" and not return to earthly life. Fourth, a person often *hears a noise* during a near-death experience. Sometimes the noise is pleasant, like rapturous music. In other (most) cases, the noise is harsh and disturbing, like a continuous buzzing or ringing sound.

Fifth, people often feel they are being pulled through *a dark passageway or tunnel*, usually while hearing the noise described above. Sixth, people typically say that they *depart from their physical bodies* and observe themselves lying on the operating table, while doctors and nurses attempt resuscitation or pronounce death. Seventh, those who have these experiences often claim that *spiritual entities were present to help them* through the experience. Sometimes these spiritual entities are loved ones who have already passed away.

Eighth, one of the most common characteristics of the near-death experience is encountering *a being of light*. Even though the light emanating from this being is brilliant, it does not hurt the eyes. This being also seems to emanate love and warmth. He communicates not with words but through thoughts. Often the communications deal with the meaning of life. Ninth, sometimes individuals in a near-death experience come upon an instant moment in which they *witness a vivid review of their entire life*. This life-review is said to provoke in them a recognition of the importance of loving other people. The review ends up helping them to understand the true meaning of life.

Tenth, individuals in a near-death experience often *come upon an obstruction* that prevents them from going any further in their journey or actually reaching the being of light. Sometimes this border is described as a fence, a door, or a body of water. Eleventh, because of the incredible feelings of peace and tranquility, and because of the love and warmth emanating from the being of light, many individuals in a near-death experience *want to stay in the presence of the being of light and not come back*. They nevertheless return because they are told they haven't finished their tasks on the earth. Other people say they felt obliged to return (without being asked) to complete unfinished tasks on the earth. The "return trip" is said to be instantaneous, back through the dark tunnel.

Twelfth, most people who go through this experience say they are *reticent about disclosing the experience to others because they feel their experience is inexpressible*. Moreover, they feel others would be skeptical upon hearing of their experience. Therefore, most people choose to remain quiet about what happened.

Thirteenth, many researchers claim that people who go through a near-death experience typically end up *having a more loving attitude toward other people, a greater zeal for living, and a belief that they have a better understanding of the meaning of life*. Fourteenth, most people who go through a near-death experience *say they no longer fear death*. But neither do they seek it. They typically come to view death as a simple transition to another form of life. They do not fear any judgment or punishment in the next life.

A fifteenth and final characteristic of the near-death experience is that the individual is *later able to corroborate specific events—for example, in the hospital operating room—that would have been impossible for him to know about unless he had been consciously observing things.*[2]

Do all people who claim this experience have all these characteristics?

No. Most people experience just *some* of these characteristics. No two stories are identical. How many elements a person experiences seems to relate to how deep and how long he or she was apparently "dead."[3] It should also be noted that people often experience the above characteristics in varying order.

Can near-death experiences be explained as a result of a lack of oxygen to the brain?

Some experts say these experiences can be explained as a result of a lack of oxygen to the brain. This is known as *hypoxia*. It is argued that this lack of oxygen to the brain accounts for sensations like going through a tunnel and seeing a bright light. The problem with this view, however, is that medical tests have not shown that people who have gone through near-death experiences have less oxygen in their blood gases than other people.

Can near-death experiences be explained as a deeply embedded memory of the birth experience?

Some experts think so—especially as related to going through a dark tunnel and then seeing a bright light. The late astronomer and scientist Carl Sagan held to this view.[4]

Critics respond by noting that a memory of birth would be traumatic, not pleasant (like most near-death experiences). Further, in the birth experience the baby's face is pressed against the birth canal, conflicting with the rapid transit of going through a dark tunnel. Also, critics argue that the baby's brain is not developed enough to retain such memories.

Can near-death experiences be explained in terms of trauma to the brain?

Some say it is possible. It is suggested that severe psychological stress—such as that associated with the process of dying—may trigger the release of certain chemicals in the brain that could induce various experiences. Some also suggest the possibility that pain medications (or other types of medication) that the dying typically receive may account for some of these strange experiences.

But how are resuscitation attempts to be explained?

Some of the theories mentioned above fail to explain some of the details of the typical near-death experience. For example, these theories cannot explain how people who were brain dead at the time are later able to describe in vivid detail the attempts of medical personnel to resuscitate them.

Is satanic deception a possible explanation for near-death experiences?

It is possible. After all, Satan is the father of lies and has the ability to perform counterfeit miracles (2 Thessalonians 2:9). In support of this possibility, many researchers have noted a clear connection between near-death experiences and occultism. John Ankerberg and John Weldon, for example, note that "in large measure the NDE [near-death experience] is merely one form of the occult out-of-body experience (OBE)."[5] Also, "both the NDE and OBE have many other similarities including...spiritistic contacts, worldview changes, and development of psychic powers."[6]

What kinds of psychic powers might develop in a person who has undergone a near-death experience?

Ankerberg and Weldon note that some people experience astral travel or out-of-body experiences (that is, the soul leaves the body and travels around the so-called astral realm). Some people develop clairvoyance (the ability to perceive things that are outside the natural range of human senses). Some people develop telepathic abilities (that is, abilities to mystically communicate via thoughts alone). Many people come into contact with spirit guides, who allegedly stay with the person for the rest of his or her life.

Of course, occultism and psychic phenomena are condemned by God in Scripture. Anyone doubting this should meditate on Deuteronomy 18:10-13.

Who is the "being of light" often encountered in so-called near-death experiences? Is it Jesus Christ?

Many people have claimed it was Jesus Christ. As appealing as the idea may initially sound, this identification (at least in *most* cases) seems to be flawed in view of the fact that the so-called being of light typically says and does things contrary to the Jesus of the Bible. Since Jesus is the same yesterday, today, and forever (Hebrews 13:8), this being and the Jesus of the Bible cannot be the same Jesus. I believe that many of the individuals who go through near-death experiences actually encounter a *counterfeit* Christ (see 2 Corinthians 11:4).

What kinds of things does this "counterfeit Jesus" teach during near-death experiences?

The "Jesus" (being of light) typically encountered in near-death experiences teaches, for example, that death is good and is not to be feared. To this "Jesus," sin is not a problem. In fact, he often responds to human sin and shortcomings with humor. He claims there is no hell to worry about. All people are welcome in heaven, he says, regardless of whether one has placed faith in Christ, and he insists that all religions are equally valid.

Is it possible that the "Jesus" (being of light) of near-death experiences is actually a lying spirit?

I think it's a good possibility (see John 8:44). We must remember that Satan has the ability to appear as an "angel of light" and as a "servant of righteousness" (2 Corinthians 11:14-15). His goal, of course, is to lead people astray. He is happy to mimic a being of light if the end result is that he can lead people away from the true Christ of Scripture.

Is there such a thing as a hellish near-death experience?

Yes. Dr. Charles Garfield, who has done extensive research on near-death experiences, says that "not everyone dies a blissful, accepting death...Almost as many of the dying patients I interviewed reported negative visions (encounters with demonic figures and so forth) as reported blissful experiences, while some reported both."[7]

Dr. Maurice Rawlings wrote a book entitled *Beyond Death's Door*, in which he documented hellish near-death experiences. He said that about half the near-death experiences he has researched were hellish in nature. But most people who experience such hellish near-death experiences end up repressing the memory because it is so awful and traumatic.

Can you give an example of a so-called hellish near-death experience?

Dr. Rawlings, who was not a committed Christian, was once testing a patient on a treadmill when his patient suddenly went into cardiac arrest. Rawlings and his nurse immediately sought to revive the man by massaging his heart and doing CPR. The patient passed in and out of consciousness. Each time he revived, he screamed, "I am in hell!" He pleaded with Rawlings not to let him slip back into unconsciousness.[8]

The patient lapsed into unconsciousness again. When he revived, he said, "Don't you understand? I am in hell. Each time you quit [the CPR] I go back to hell! Don't let me go back to hell!" The man asked how to stay out of hell. Rawlings told the man what he remembered from Sunday school, and led the man in a simple prayer. The man's condition stabilized, and he was taken to a hospital.[9]

A few days later, Rawlings questioned the man about his experience and found that he had forgotten it! Rawlings thinks the experience was so unnerving to him that he repressed it. Even so, the man became a committed Christian and a regular churchgoer after his experience of hell.[10]

Whatever we are to make of such experiences, it is clear from the above account (and others like it) that hellish near-death experiences call into question the claim by many that the afterlife experienced by those who die is *always* positive, tranquil, and peaceful. Not everyone has an experience of being "unconditionally accepted" by a loving being of light.

Do these near-death experiences involve actual deaths?

I don't think so. Near-death experiences do not actually prove anything about the *final state* of the dead. After all, these experiences are near-death experiences, not once-for-all-completely-dead experiences.

The map for evaluating near-death experiences is, of course, the Bible. Scripture defines death as the separation of the spirit from the body (James 2:26). And true death occurs only once (see Hebrews 9:27).

Are there any near-death experiences in the Bible?

Some claim that near-death experiences can be found in the Bible. Acts 9:3-6 is cited as a prime example, a passage which speaks of Saul falling to the ground and seeing a light from heaven that was Jesus. Sometime later, after Saul (also known as Paul) had become a Christian, he had a discussion with King Agrippa in which he alluded to this same experience (Acts 26:12-18).

Against this interpretation are five primary points: (1) Most obviously, Paul was quite alive and was nowhere near death. By no stretch of the imagination, then, can this be called a near-death experience. (2) The light literally blinded Paul (Acts 9:8)—something completely unlike a typical near-death experience. (3) In his later discussion with King Agrippa (Acts 26:12-18), Paul never once mentioned anything remotely resembling a near-death experience.

(4) Most people are reticent about talking about their near-death experiences, but Paul spoke openly and with boldness about his encounter with the living Jesus. (5) Unlike the Jesus of a typical near-death experience, the Jesus Paul encountered commissioned him to evangelize so that people may receive forgiveness of sins by faith in Jesus and thereby escape hell.

We conclude that the book of Acts contains no references to near-death experiences. The same is true of the rest of the Bible.

Must all near-death experiences be rejected?

Many accounts of near-death experiences have clear connections with occultism and must be outright rejected. Also, many of the accounts portray a "Jesus" saying things that go against the biblical Jesus. These, too, must be outright rejected.

However, we must be cautious here. The fact that many counterfeit experiences happen does not mean no bona fide near-death experiences occur. In his discerning article on near-death experiences in the *Christian Research Journal*, researcher Jerry Yamamoto wisely suggested that since near-death experiences "are of a subjective nature, determining their source is largely a speculative venture. With divine, demonic, and several natural factors all meriting considerations, a single, universal explanation for near-death experiences becomes quite risky."[11]

Yamamoto suggests that "if the message and experience of a near-death experience does not distort or conflict with biblical teachings, then we should be careful not to speak against that which resulted in salvation and may have been a genuine work of God."[12] Yamamoto cites a case where he thinks this is in fact what occurred. The great evangelist Dwight Moody himself had a near-death experience.

Christian apologists Gary R. Habermas and J.P. Moreland, after an extensive study, concluded that "just as you can't have fake money without real money, so you can't have fake near-death experiences without real ones. You can't counterfeit what doesn't exist."[13] Their point is that even though many counterfeit near-death experiences portray a counterfeit Jesus who preaches a counterfeit message, some genuine near-death experiences occur in which people may have actually encountered the true Jesus.

So, should we accept what best-selling Christian books say about visits to heaven following alleged near-death experiences?

Here is my best advice: As we continue to live in these experiential days, let's commit to making the Scriptures our "measuring stick" of truth. Let's resolve to be wary of anything that doesn't line up with God's Word. "Test everything; hold fast what is good" (1 Thessalonians 5:21). Let's be like the Bereans and test virtually all truth claims (including truth claims made by other Christians) against our own barometer of truth—the Word of God (Acts 17:11).

When I look at some of the most current books written by Christians, in which they claim to have died and visited heaven, some red flags definitely emerge in my mind. For example, when the apostle Paul was caught up to heaven, he described a man (probably himself) who "heard things that cannot be told, which man may not utter" (2 Corinthians 12:4). Why are modern Christians allowed to reveal incredible detail about what they saw in heaven—selling millions of books in the process—when Paul was prohibited from revealing what he encountered?

Another thing that comes to mind is that Christians who are now in heaven exist as *disembodied spirits* (see 2 Corinthians 5:8; Philippians 1:21-23). They won't receive physical resurrection bodies until the future day of the rapture (1 Thessalonians 4:13-17). So how is it that the authors of some of the most current books talk about the *physical attributes* of their dead loved ones in heaven (for example, commenting on their nose, or their hair, or some other physical attribute)?

Trust me when I say that my goal is not to be cynical. My goal is simply to be biblical. So, again, let's commit to testing all things against Scripture (Acts 17:11; 1 Thessalonians 5:21). That will keep us on the correct doctrinal path.

Part 9

Questions About
Apologetic Issues

Apologetics and the Christian
Apologetics and Intelligent Design Theory
Apologetics and Danger Zone Issues
Apologetics and the Cults

33
Apologetics and the Christian

Should every Christian be involved in apologetics?

Yes, I believe so. The word *apologetics* comes from the Greek word *apologia,* which means "defense." Apologetics focuses on the defense of Christianity. All Christians should become lay-apologists in their sphere of influence—in the neighborhood, at work, at social occasions, and the like.

It is unfortunate that many Christians today seem to be what we might call secret-agent Christians who have never "blown their cover" before an unregenerate world. Sadly, many Christians have little or no impact on their world for Christ or for Christian values.

The task of apologetics begins with a single person—*you.* A great thinker once said, "Let him that would move the world first move himself."

How do we know it is God's will for all Christians to be involved in apologetics?

God calls each one of us to "contend for the faith that was once for all delivered to the saints" (Jude 3). As Christians, we are called to contend for the faith by telling it like it is.

Look at it this way: Would we have had a Reformation if Martin Luther hadn't told it like it was to the Roman Catholic Church? No, we wouldn't. Luther saw a deviation from "the faith" and he accordingly contended for the faith. We must follow Luther's example.

You and I are called by God to be prepared to give answers. First Peter 3:15 instructs us to always be "prepared to make a defense to anyone who asks you for a reason for the hope that is in you." The only way to be always prepared to give an answer is to become equipped with apologetics.

What are the benefits of apologetics?

Apologetics provides well-reasoned evidences to the nonbeliever as to why he ought to choose Christianity rather than any other religion—it can show the nonbeliever that all the other options in the "smorgasbord" of world religions are not really options at all because they are false. With apologetics, the believer can remove the mental roadblocks that prevent nonbelievers from responding to the gospel. Apologetics not only provides a defense for the faith but also gives security to Christians who need to be sure that their faith is not a blind leap into a dark chasm. It helps them understand that their faith is founded on fact by demonstrating *why* we believe *what* we believe.

Apologetics does not replace our faith. It *grounds* our faith.

Why is the relativistic view of truth wrong?

I offer four observations on the issue:

First, Christianity rests on a foundation of *absolute* truth (1 Kings 17:24; Psalm 25:5; 43:3; 119:30; John 1:17; 8:44; 14:17; 17:17; 2 Corinthians 6:7; Ephesians 4:15; 6:14; 2 Timothy 2:15; 1 John 3:19; 3 John 4,8).

Second, if all truth is relative, then one person's "truth" is just as good as another person's "truth." This ultimately means that any religion's "truth" is as good as Christianity's truth. In moral relativism, there is no way to tell which way is north and which way is south when it comes to right and wrong. As people accelerate down the road where moral relativity takes them, there is no absolute truth, no center stripe down the highway of life. Many casualties happen along this highway.

Third, the view that all truth is relative is not logically satisfying. One might understand the statement "all truth is relative" to mean that it is an absolute truth that all truth is relative. Of course, such a statement is self-defeating (since there are supposedly no absolute truths) and is therefore false. Also, one could understand this as saying that it is a relative truth that all truth is relative. But such a statement is ultimately meaningless. No matter how you understand this statement—whether you say it is an *absolute* truth that all truth is relative, or whether you say it is a *relative* truth that all truth is relative—it should be rejected.

Fourth, as Christians, we believe that absolute morals are grounded in the absolutely moral God of the Bible. Scripture tells us, "You therefore must be perfect, as your heavenly Father is perfect" (Matthew 5:48). Moral law flows from the moral Lawgiver of the universe. God stands against the moral relativist whose behavior is based on "whatever is right in his own eyes" (Deuteronomy 12:8; Judges 17:6; 21:25; Proverbs 21:2).

What are some examples of self-defeating arguments when it comes to the issue of truth?

Many today seem blissfully unaware that they are using self-defeating arguments when expressing their commitment to relativistic truth. The Christian can debunk such sloppy thinking by asking some logical questions:

If they say, "There are no absolutes," you can respond, "Are you absolutely sure about that?"

If they say, "We cannot be certain about anything," you can respond, "Are you certain about that?"

If they say, "We should doubt everything," you can respond, "Should *that* statement be doubted?"

If they say, "We cannot know truth," you can respond, "How do you know *that* is true?"

If they say, "We should never judge," you can respond, "If it is wrong to judge, then why are *you* judging?"

If they say, "It is true for you but not for me," you can respond, "Is *that* statement just true for you but not for me?"

If they say, "Truth about God is not objective," you can respond, "Is *that* an objective truth about God?"

If they say, "Words cannot express meaning," you can respond, "Do *those* words express meaning?"

If they say, "There is no rational support for what we believe," you can respond, "Is there any rational support for *that* belief?"

I can tell you from years of experience that the more adept you become at pointing out the self-defeating nature of people's truth claims, the more successful you will be in apologetics.

What is agnosticism?

The word *agnosticism* comes from two Greek words: *a*, meaning "no" or "without," and *gnosis*, meaning "knowledge." Agnosticism literally means "no knowledge" or "without knowledge." As related to the question of God's existence, an agnostic is a person who claims he is unsure—having "no knowledge"—about the existence of God. Questions about God are allegedly inherently impossible to prove or disprove.

There are two forms of agnosticism. "Soft agnostics," also called "weak agnostics," say a person *does not* know if God exists. "Hard agnostics," also called "strong agnostics," say a person *cannot* know if God exists. Another way to look at it is that soft agnosticism says the existence and nature of God are *not known*, while hard agnosticism says that God is *unknowable*, that He *cannot be known*.

What's the problem with agnosticism?

Logically, agnosticism is a self-defeating belief system. To say "one cannot know about God" is a statement that presumes knowledge about God. So the statement is self-falsifying. In other words, the statement amounts to saying, "One knows enough about God to affirm that nothing can be known about God." Ultimately, one must *possess* knowledge of God in order to *deny* knowledge of God. Put another way, to say that we cannot know anything about God is, in fact, to say *something* about God. Agnosticism is thus not a logically satisfying position to take.

What is skepticism?

The word skepticism comes from the Latin word *scepticus*, meaning "inquiring," "reflective," or "doubting." This Latin word, in turn, comes from the Greek word *scepsis,* meaning "inquiry," "hesitation," or "doubt." When it comes to the question of God's existence, a skeptic is a person who is tentative in his or her beliefs, neither denying nor affirming God's existence. He or she is hesitant, doubtful, and unsure as to whether there is a God. Even if there is a God, a skeptic is unsure as to whether a person can really know Him.

What's the problem with skepticism?

An obvious philosophical problem with this viewpoint is that the skeptic is certainly *not* skeptical that his worldview of skepticism is correct. Put another way, he is certainly *not* doubtful that his worldview of doubt is correct. In fact, the skeptic seems *quite sure* that his viewpoint of doubt must be correct. He has no hesitation in affirming that his worldview of hesitation is the correct view.

I love to ask skeptics questions: How do you explain the incredible evidence for intelligent design in our universe? What does it say to you that more than 25,000 archeological discoveries—many by non-Christian archeologists—confirm people, places, and events in the Bible? How do you explain the direct fulfillment of more than a hundred Old Testament messianic prophecies in the person of Jesus Christ? Why do you suppose the New Testament writers were willing to suffer and then die in defense of what they believed? Would you be open to a little "certainty training"?

How can we respond to critics who argue that the miracles recorded in the Bible are the fantasies of ignorant people in biblical times who did not understand the laws of nature?

Such a claim is preposterous. People in biblical times *did* know enough of the laws of nature to recognize bona fide miracles. C.S. Lewis puts it this way:

> When St. Joseph discovered that his bride was pregnant, he was "minded to put her away." He knew enough biology for that. Otherwise, of course, he would not have regarded pregnancy as a proof of infidelity. When he accepted the Christian explanation, he regarded it as a miracle precisely because he knew enough of the laws of nature to know that this was a suspension of them.[1]

Lewis also made this observation:

> When the disciples saw Christ walking on the water they were frightened: they would not have been frightened unless they had known the laws of nature and known that this was an exception. If a man had no conception of a regular order in nature, then of course he could not notice departures from that order.[2]

No one can know what a crooked line is until one first understands what a straight line is. Nothing can be viewed as "abnormal" until one has first grasped the "norm." Nothing can be viewed as supernatural until one has first grasped what is natural. People in Bible times *did* in fact understand the laws of nature.

What is the cosmological argument for God's existence?

This argument says that every effect must have an adequate cause. The universe is an "effect." Reason demands that whatever caused the universe must be greater than the universe. That cause is God (who Himself is the uncaused First Cause). As Hebrews 3:4 puts it, "Every house is built by someone, but the builder of all things is God."

What is the teleological argument for God's existence?

This argument says that the world has an obviously purposeful and intricate design. If we found a watch in the sand, the assumption would have to be that someone created the watch because, with its intricate design, it is obvious that all the parts of the watch couldn't have just jumped together to cause itself. Similarly, the perfect design of the universe argues for a Designer, and that Designer is God. (I will discuss intelligent design theory in the next chapter.)

What is the ontological argument for God's existence?

This argument says that most human beings have an innate idea of a most perfect being. Where did this idea come from? Not from man, for man is an imperfect being. Some perfect being must have planted the idea there. God can't be conceived of as not existing, for then, one could conceive of an even greater being that did exist. Thus God must in fact exist.

What is the moral argument for God's existence?

This argument says that every human being has an innate sense of oughtness or moral obligation. Where did this sense of oughtness come from? It must come from God. The existence of a moral law in our hearts demands the existence of a moral Lawgiver (see Romans 1:19-32).

What is the anthropological argument for God's existence?

This argument says that man has a personality (mind, emotions, and will). Since the *personal* can't come from the *impersonal*, there must be a personal cause—and that personal cause is God (see Genesis 1:26-27).

Are these kinds of logical arguments convincing to unbelievers?

Perhaps Reformer John Calvin's view of these arguments was the best. He said that the unregenerate person sees these evidences for God in the universe with blurred vision. It is only when one puts on the "eyeglasses" of faith and belief in the Bible that these evidences for God's existence come into clearest focus. Still, despite the blurred vision problem, these arguments for God's existence ought to remain in the apologist's arsenal, for they still bear fruit!

What can we say to the atheist who flatly asserts that there is no God?

This assertion is logically indefensible. A person would have to be omniscient and omnipresent to be able to say from his or her own pool of knowledge that there is no God. Only someone who is capable of being in all places at the same time—with a perfect knowledge of all that is in the universe—can make such a statement *based on the facts*.

Ravi Zacharias observes that in "postulating the nonexistence of God, atheism immediately commits the blunder of an absolute negation, which is self-contradictory. For, to sustain the belief that there is no God, it has to demonstrate infinite knowledge, which is tantamount to saying, 'I have infinite knowledge that there is no being in existence with infinite knowledge.'"[3] To put it another way, a person would have to *be* God in order to *say* there is no God.

What can we say to the atheist who claims there can't be a God because so much evil is in the world?

A starting point for discussion is that if one is going to claim there is no God because so much evil exists in the world, one must first ask by what criteria something is judged evil in the first place? This is a philosophical dilemma for the atheist. How does one judge some things to be evil and other things not to be evil? What is the moral measuring stick by which people and events are morally appraised?

The truth is, it is impossible to distinguish evil from good unless one has an infinite reference point that is absolutely good. Otherwise one would be like a person on a boat at sea on a cloudy night without a compass—that is, there would be no way to distinguish north from south without the absolute reference point of the compass needle (pointing north). God is our reference point for determining good and evil.

How does human free will—and the free choice to sin—explain evil in our world?

When God originally created the universe as the divine Architect, it was perfectly good in every way. Genesis 1:31 tells us, "God saw everything that he had made, and behold, it was very good." There was no evil. *Everything* was good.

Today, however, not everything is good. A great deal of evil now exists in the universe that was once entirely good. That can mean only one thing. Something dreadful has happened between *then* and *now* to cause the change. A colossal perversion of the good has occurred. To borrow a metaphor, there has been a massive termite invasion into the universe—or, more to the point, an invasion of sin.

Jimmy H. Davis and Harry L. Poe, in their book *Designer Universe: Intelligent Design and the Existence of God*, suggest that the existence of evil in our universe does not disprove the existence of God any more than termites in a house disprove the existence of an architect:

> The fact that ugliness, thorns, death, pain, suffering, and chaos are present in the world does not disprove design. *Infestation by termites* does not prove the house did not have an architect. *Vandalism* does not prove the house did not have an architect. *Arson* does not prove the house did not have an architect. *Sloppy homeowners* who do not paint or carry out the garbage do not prove the house did not have an architect. These matters simply raise questions about the situation of the house since it was built.[4]

Theologically, the Bible is clear that God exists and that He created the universe in a perfectly good state. The Bible is also clear that things have changed dramatically since God created the world. Because of human sin, rooted in human free will, things are not now as they were created to be (Genesis 3). God's original design has been corrupted by an intruder—the intruder of sin. God's "good universe" is no longer good.

Couldn't God have created human beings so that they never would have sinned?

This would have necessitated that people no longer have the capacity to make choices and to freely love. This scenario would require that God create robots who act only in programmed ways—like one of those chatty dolls where you pull a string on its back and it says, "I love you." Paul Little notes that with such a doll, "there would never be any hot words, never any conflict, never anything said or done that would make you sad! But who would want that? There would never be any love, either. Love is voluntary."[5]

Christian apologists have observed that love is the highest value in the universe, and in a world of robots, such love would be entirely absent. "Real love—our love of God and our love of each other—must involve a choice. But with the granting of that choice comes the possibility that people would choose instead to hate."[6]

The truth is, unless human beings can freely choose *not to* love, they cannot freely choose *to* love. The possibility of the one necessitates the possibility of the other.[7]

God wanted Adam, Eve, and all humanity to show love by freely choosing obedience. That is why God gave human beings a free will. Yet, a free choice always leaves the possibility of a wrong choice. As one Christian thinker put it, "Evil is inherent in the risky gift of free will."[8]

Since God gave human beings free will, isn't God then responsible for evil?

Simply because God gave us the gift of free will does not mean He is responsible for how we *use* that free will. From a scriptural perspective, it seems clear that God's plan—from the very beginning—had the *potential* for evil when He bestowed upon humans the freedom of choice. Evil became *actual*, however, when man directed his will away from God and toward his own selfish desires.[9] "Whereas God created the *fact* of freedom, humans perform the *acts* of freedom. God made evil *possible*; creatures make it *actual*."[10] We are in no position to blame God.

Theologians Gordon R. Lewis and Bruce A. Demarest give us an illustration in the person of Henry Ford: "Henry Ford is the final cause of all Ford cars, for there would not be any if he had not invented them to provide transportation. But Henry Ford, who could well have envisioned misuses of his automobiles, apparently felt it wiser, in a kind of benefit-evil analysis, to invent them than not."[11]

When a person who has had one too many drinks gets in a Ford car and ends up in a head-on collision that kills innocent people,

Henry Ford does not thereby become guilty of a crime. By analogy, we cannot blame the evil in the world on God simply because God gave humans a free will, for it was the creatures' wrong use of free will that has caused such evil.

Wouldn't a good God get rid of all evil right now?

One would be wise to rethink the idea that God should simply get rid of all evil immediately. Choosing this option would have definite and fatal implications for each of us. As Paul Little put it,

> If God were to stamp out evil today, he would do a complete job. His action would have to include our lies and personal impurities, our lack of love, and our failure to do good. Suppose God were to decree that at midnight tonight all evil would be removed from the universe—who of us would still be here after midnight?[12]

Let us be clear on this: Desiring a universe in which God brings about instant justice has the definite downside of yielding a people-less universe. Absent the cross, you and I and everyone else would be absolute "goners." *Show over!* God would be the only one left! After all, each of us has committed some evil, whether it is by commission or omission, by word, deed, or thought.[13] In the interest of self-preservation, I am glad God does not wipe out all evil immediately!

When will God deal with evil definitively?

God is not finished yet! It is simply wrong to conclude that God is not dealing with the problem of evil because He has not dealt with it once-for-all *in the present moment.* God's definitive dealing with evil is yet future.

As one Christian philosopher put it, "Since the solution is future, it is *not yet.* We are in a story, and only the end of the story explains the rest of it, just as only the conclusion of an argument explains why the premises are selected as they are."[14] When we read a good novel, we often do not understand everything that has taken place in the story until the very end of the book. That is when our perspective on the story becomes complete. That is when we say, "Oh, I get it now!" Likewise, one day in the future we will come to the last chapter in the "human story," and all will become clear.

Stay tuned for the second coming and the events that follow.

Is our discontent with the problem of evil partially rooted in our limited understanding?

I think so. Look at it this way: We can compare each of our lives to a single thread in the tapestry of life. As single threads, we cannot see the entire tapestry, and are therefore ignorant of the overall scheme of things. God, however, is the master-craftsman, weaving each thread just as He sees fit, bringing about an eventual masterpiece.

In this scenario, "the transcendent and sovereign God sees the end of history from its beginning and providentially orders history so that His purposes are ultimately achieved through human free decisions."[15] We, as finite human beings, however, are completely ignorant of the vast complexities involved in God working among free agents to sovereignly bring history to its ordained end. One day, once we are in heaven, I believe we will see that tapestry. Then, and only then, will we say, "Ahhh, I get it now!"

As God weaves the circumstances in our lives, which will eventually yield a masterpiece in heaven, He sometimes purposefully allows us to experience short-range pains because of the long-range benefits that eventually come about. Biblically, God may bring about quite a number of "goods" through His allowance of suffering.

Can God strengthen a Christian's faith through evil and suffering?

Yes indeed. As a backdrop, great Christian thinkers have often compared faith to a muscle. A muscle has to be repeatedly stretched to its limit of endurance in order to build more strength. Without increased stress in training, the muscle will simply not grow.

In the same way, faith must be repeatedly tested to the limit of its endurance in order to expand and develop. Very often, I think God allows His children to go through trying experiences in order to develop their faith muscles (1 Peter 1:7). This learning process takes place in the school of real life—with all of its difficult trials and tribulations.

This is illustrated in the life of Joseph, who was sold into slavery by his own brothers (see Genesis 38–39). While it seemed painful at the time, God was still in control. God ended up using these negative circumstances to bring Joseph to Egypt, where He elevated Joseph to a position of great authority (Genesis 41). What we have to realize, however, is that during the time of suffering itself, Joseph had no idea what God's intentions were. He did not know that God was using these dire circumstances to bring him to a position of prominence.

This is why it is so important to trust God, no matter what the circumstances. In Joseph's case, God truly did bring about a greater good through the pain he suffered. Joseph summarized the matter when he later told his brothers, "You meant evil against me, but God meant it for good" (Genesis 50:20). Our faith in God must ever rest upon the belief that God can bring a greater good out of any evil that befalls us.

Can God bring about saving faith in many people by allowing evil and suffering?

Suffering often *does* bring people to saving faith in God. People often do not turn to God until they feel their need for Him.

Interestingly, studies have proved that nations that are going through intense suffering are experiencing the most rapid growth in evangelical Christianity.[16] One must wonder whether there would be *any* growth in Christianity if suffering simply did not exist. If a world of suffering is necessary in order to bring people to eternal life in Jesus Christ, then such suffering is worth it, for the glories of the afterlife are beyond what any human can fathom.

Christian scholar Os Guinness communicates this insight about faith:

> It is often said that after Auschwitz there cannot be a God—evil is so overwhelming that it is the "rock of atheism." But as Viktor Frankl pointed out, those who say that [about evil] were not in

Auschwitz themselves. Far more people deepened or discovered faith in Auschwitz than lost it. He then gave a beautiful picture of faith in the face of evil. A small and inadequate faith, he said, is like a small fire; it can be blown out by a small breeze. True faith, by contrast, is like a strong fire. When it is hit by a strong wind, it is fanned into an inextinguishable blaze.[17]

Does God sometimes allow evil and suffering as a means of engaging in character development in our lives?

I believe so. We humans often tend to interpret events in our lives from a strictly earthly perspective. Evil often feels devastating to us because of our assumption that God's purpose for us is happiness. Since that is God's purpose, we reason, then why is this horrible thing happening to me?

We must come to understand that God is operating from the perspective of eternity. He cares more about *holiness* than He does about *happiness*.[18] Christian author Paul Powell suggests that "God's goal is not primarily to make us comfortable but to conform us to the image of His Son, Jesus Christ. And in the pursuit of that goal He can and does use all of life's experiences."[19]

God may therefore allow us to go through a season of hurt that has no apparent earthly benefit, but has immense benefit in terms of our eternal future with God. God is involved in our character development (1 Peter 1:6-7; James 1:2-4). Miles Stanford writes that "God does not hurry in His development of our Christian life. He is working from and for eternity."[20]

Meanwhile, what is God doing to keep evil from mushrooming out of control?

God has put boundaries on the spread of evil. God has even now taken steps to ensure that evil does not run utterly amok. After all, He has given us human government to withstand lawlessness (Romans 13:1-7) and founded the church to be a light in the midst of the darkness, to strengthen God's people, and even to help restrain the growth of wickedness in the world through the power of the Holy Spirit (see, for example, Acts 16:5; 1 Timothy 3:15).

God has given us the family unit to bring stability to society (see, for example, Proverbs 22:15; 23:13). Also, God has, in His Word, given us a moral standard to guide us and keep us on the right path (Psalm 119). God has promised a future day of accounting in which all human beings will face the divine Judge (Hebrews 9:27). For Christians, this future day serves as a deterrent to committing evil acts.

34
Apologetics and Intelligent Design Theory

What is intelligent design theory?

Intelligent design is a theory which seeks to explain the "irreducible complexity" of the universe—that is, it seeks to uncover signs of intelligence that lie behind the complex nature and apparent design of our universe. It appears that the universe has been specifically designed with optimal conditions for the existence of life.

Are there any verses in the Bible that support the idea of the universe being created by intelligent design?

Yes, I believe so. Of course, Genesis 1:1 tells us, "In the beginning, God created the heavens and the earth." Likewise, Hebrews 3:4 tells us, "Every house is built by someone, but the builder of all things is God." We can complement this with Psalm 19:1-4, where we read:

> The Heavens declare the glory of God, and the sky above proclaims his handiwork. Day to day pours out speech, and night to night reveals knowledge. There is no speech, nor are there words, whose voice is not heard. Their measuring line goes out through all the earth, and their words to the end of the world.

In keeping with this, Romans 1:20 tells us that God's "invisible attributes, namely, his eternal power and divine nature, have been clearly perceived, ever since the creation of the world, in the things that have been made. So they are without excuse."

The Bible quite obviously affirms that the universe was designed and created by an intelligent God. The Bible also affirms that human beings can detect the existence of this invisible God by the visible universe He has made.

Toward this end, intelligent design theory utilizes scientific methodology to uncover evidence that the universe was designed by an intelligent being. The evidence is massive, beginning at the molecular level and reaching into the deep recesses of interstellar space.

Can we really recognize signs of intelligence in the universe?

I believe so. Think about it. Human beings have become adept at recognizing signs of intelligence in many fields of endeavor. Sometimes signs of intelligence are obvious—such as the four presidents chiseled into the granite cliff at Mount Rushmore, or words in the sky like "Free Concert in the Park Tonight."

Other times, signs of intelligence must be uncovered. Today various job professions seek clues of "intelligent design" and intentionality— that is, clues that indicate that an intelligent being intentionally engaged in a particular action, as opposed to a chance occurrence.

For example, crime scene investigators look for intentionality at crime scenes. Insurance investigators look for clues of intentional fraud. Archeologists uncover evidences of intentional design among ruins. Cryptographers seek to distinguish random signals from intelligently encoded messages. And copyright offices examine claims of purposeful plagiarism.

Here is the point to remember: The same kind of evidence that shows crime scene investigators, archeologists, cryptographers, copyright offices, and people who see words in the sky that an intelligent being was involved are also clearly seen in the universe around us. We have *substantive* evidence that an intelligent being intentionally brought our universe into existence. The evidence is also clear that the universe was not the result of random chance or a cosmic accident. We are discovering God's fingerprints all over the universe.

What is "irreducible complexity," and how does it help us recognize signs of intelligence in the universe?

From a scientific perspective, we infer that an item is intelligently designed if it is "irreducibly complex." An irreducibly complex mechanism is composed of a number of well-matched, interacting parts that contribute to the functioning of that mechanism. If any of these well-matched, interacting parts is removed, the mechanism will no longer function.

A good example is a mousetrap. All the components to this mechanism are necessary to its functioning. If any component is missing, it no longer functions correctly. If it's missing a spring, hammer, or platform, for example, it will not work. That is why we categorize it as irreducibly complex. We therefore infer that the mousetrap was designed by an intelligent being.

What is an example of something in the world of nature that is "irreducibly complex," thereby pointing to the existence of an intelligent designer?

The irreducible complexity of the eye is evident in that it is a mechanism with many well-matched, interacting parts that contribute to the function of sight. If any of these well-matched, interacting parts is removed, the eye will no longer see. Among these parts are the sclerotic, the cornea, the aqueous humor, the vitreous humor, the choroid, the retina, rods and cones, and the pupil, all of which function together in harmony with the brain to facilitate sight.

Evolution cannot explain this mechanism. A piece-by-piece development of this incredibly complex organ—resulting from infinitesimally small Darwinian improvements over an unimaginably long period of time, requiring untold thousands of random positive mutations—is virtually impossible to fathom.

An objective examination of the eye indicates that an incredibly knowledgeable engineer (God) planned the eye from beginning to end.

Is there another good example from the world of nature that illustrates "irreducible complexity"?

Another example is the wing of a bird. At the very least, a functioning wing requires a specific bone structure, a specific muscle structure, precise symmetrical positioning on a body (one wing on each side), wings proportionally large enough (relative to the size of the animal's body) to facilitate "lift off," bodily coordination, and a synergistic relationship with the brain to make it all happen.

The irreducibly complex wing gives every indication of being designed.

What kind of irreducible complexity do we see at the molecular level?

It is amazing to ponder that scientists have discovered cells that contain ultra-sophisticated molecular machines. The existence of complex, information-rich structures at the molecular level cannot be explained by Darwinism but rather calls for the existence of an intelligent designer (God).

At the molecular level scientists witness such things as information storage and transfer, sorting and delivery systems, and self-regulation.

Scientists have also discovered complex molecular mechanisms that contain well-matched, interacting parts that contribute to the functioning of that mechanism. For example, at the molecular level one witnesses what might be likened to rotary engines that contain components such as a rotor, stator, and drive shaft. The complexity witnessed at the molecular level is every bit as high-tech as gadgets created by human beings. Observations at the molecular level virtually beg for an explanation— an explanation that Darwinism cannot provide.

Is intelligent design evident in DNA?

Absolutely yes. DNA is an abbreviation for *deoxyribonucleic acid*. It is a nucleic acid that carries genetic information in the cell that is capable of self-replication.

The volume of information contained in DNA staggers the mind. A single human cell has enough capacity to store the *Encyclopedia Britannica*—all 30 volumes—three or four times over. The information capacity in a pinhead's volume of DNA is equivalent to a pile of paperback books 500 times as tall as the distance from Earth to the Moon.

Where did this staggering amount of information—similar to computer software code—come from? Naturalistic evolution cannot explain it. Computer programs do not write themselves. A programmer is always involved. Even if you provide plenty of time (millions of years), a computer program still cannot write itself.

The same is true regarding the information in DNA. Somebody (God) had to program that complex information into DNA.

What is the anthropic principle, and how does it relate to intelligent design?

The anthropic principle—from the Greek word *anthropos*, meaning "man"—recognizes that conditions on the earth are ideal, apparently by design, for the existence of human (and other) life. An objective examination of the universe indicates that it is fine-tuned—*tweaked with precision*—for the existence of complex life.

What are some examples of how things are fine-tuned for life on the earth?

Below is a small sampling of factors related to how fine-tuned things are for life on the earth:

Earth is just the right distance from the sun for life to survive. If the earth were too close to the sun, everything would burn up. If the earth were too far from the sun, everything would freeze.

Just enough oxygen is on the earth—comprising 21 percent of the atmosphere—for life to exist. If there were too much oxygen (25 percent or more), things would catch on fire too easily. If there were not enough oxygen (say, 15 percent), living beings would suffocate.

The level of water vapor in the atmosphere is just right for life on the earth. Too much water vapor in the atmosphere would cause a runaway greenhouse effect, and it would get too hot to allow for human life on the earth. Too little water vapor in the atmosphere would yield an insufficient greenhouse effect, and it would get too cold.

Some volcanoes are necessary for the spreading of soil nutrients. Too many volcanoes, however, would cause critical energy from the sun to be blocked by clouds of volcanic ash.

We have one moon that is just the right size. If earth had more than one moon, or if our one moon were much larger, there would be tidal instability on the earth. In fact, a much larger moon might cause tidal waves to engulf the land.

Jupiter, a giant planet with a phenomenally strong gravitational pull, attracts asteroids and comets that otherwise might strike the earth.

What can we conclude from such fine-tuning of our universe?

The reality is, numerous highly improbable factors have to be *precisely* in place in a *balanced* fashion for the survival of life on earth. Without any one of these factors, life would not be possible. Life, however, has emerged precisely because these conditions are *just right* for life.

One scholar puts it this way: "One could think of the initial conditions of the universe...as a dartboard that fills the whole galaxy, and the conditions necessary for life to exist as a small one-foot wide target: unless the dart hits the target, life would not be possible."[1] Amazingly, life has emerged on earth because the dart "hit the target."

The conclusion is inescapable: An Intelligent Designer brought it all into existence.

Have any scientists come to faith as a result of evidence for intelligent design?

Yes. Astronomer Robert Jastrow, author of *God and the Astronomers*, comments, "If the universe had not been made with the most exacting precision we could never have come into existence. It is my view that these circumstances indicate the universe was created for man to live in."[2]

Astronomer Frederick Hoyle suggests that "a super-intellect has monkeyed with physics, as well as with chemistry and biology." Indeed, a super-intellect has fine-tuned our universe for the existence of life.[3]

Astronomer George Greenstein comments, "As we survey all the evidence, the thought insistently arises that some supernatural agency—or, rather, Agency—must be involved. Is it possible that suddenly, without intending to, we have stumbled upon scientific proof of the existence of a Supreme Being? Was it God who stepped in and so providentially crafted the cosmos for our benefit?"[4]

These three scientists are representative of a far larger group.

Answering Objections

Does intelligent design theory stifle scientific inquiry by attributing what may not yet be understood to an unknowable cause (that is, God)?

Intelligent design theorists *do not* stifle scientific inquiry. Rather, they use a well-defined scientific method based on irreducible complexity that enables them to empirically detect signs of intelligence in the universe. Just as a forensic detective would infer an intelligent cause of a crime he was investigating by using scientific techniques, so design can be rationally inferred in the universe by using scientific techniques. More specifically, intelligent design theory has grown out of our scientific knowledge of irreducibly complex cells and organs, as well as evidence for the anthropic principle.

If intelligent design—which requires the miraculous—is true, does this dependence on the miraculous rob the universe of regularity and uniformity, thereby making true science impossible?

Creationists do not disagree with the idea that the general cosmos has some uniformity. God created the universe with regularity and order. But creationists *do* take exception to the notion that the universe is a self-contained closed system with absolute laws that are inviolable.

Creationists believe the laws of nature are *observations* of uniformity or constancy in nature. They are not *forces* which initiate action. They simply describe the way nature behaves when its course is not affected by a superior power. God, however, is not prohibited from taking action in the world if He so desires.

When a miracle occurs, the laws of nature are not violated but are rather superseded by a higher (supernatural) manifestation of the will of God. The forces of nature are not obliterated or suspended, but are only counteracted *at a particular point* by a force superior to the powers of nature. Put another way, miracles do not *go against* the regular laws of cause and effect. They simply have a cause (God) that *transcends* nature.

Note that uniformity in the world of nature *remains*. By definition, miracles are out of the norm. Unless there were a "norm" to begin with, miracles would not be possible. A miracle is a unique event that stands out against the background of ordinary and regular occurrences. So the possibility of miracles does not rob the universe of uniformity, nor does it disrupt the possibility of doing real science.

Do those who hold to intelligent design theory have a creationist bias in their examination of the data?

All people have *some* biases, including secular scientists. Astronomer Robert Jastrow admits that scientists become irritated when evidence uncovered by science conflicts with their preconceived scientific biases.[5] Physicist Fritjof Capra, author of *The Tao of Physics*, once admitted, "My presentation of modern physics has been influenced by my personal beliefs and allegiances."[6]

Let us be honest in admitting that the accusation of bias is a sword that can cut both ways. While skeptics might accuse creationists of a bias toward intelligent design, such skeptics in *their own* biases may be blinding themselves to the existence of real patterns of intelligent design in the natural world.

This is the key question that should concern all of us: *What does the evidence truly reveal?* Creationists believe the evidence is on the side of intelligent design.

Does the reality that the universe has apparent design flaws prove that an Intelligent Designer does not exist?

This line of argumentation is flawed. A person might look at a particular model of a car and think of various ways the car could have a better design. But that does not mean the car itself did not come from the hands of a designer.

A person might look at the floor plan of a house and decide that the plan could be better in some ways. But that does not mean the floor plan did not come from the hands of a designer.

So it is with the universe. Just because someone might imagine how a structure in the universe might have had a better design does not mean the structure did not come from an intelligent designer.

It is wise to consider that even in regard to humanly designed structures, we might think we have a better design for an item, but upon talking to the designer, we discover variables we had not previously considered that casts the design in a different (more favorable) light.

For example, I might think a computer encasing would have a better design if it were much smaller. Upon talking to the design engineer, however, I discover that the larger size better accommodates the internal cooling system for the components that generate heat. This new information adjusts my thinking so that I now know my idea is not necessarily a better design.

In the same way, we may think we can come up with better designs for structures in the universe. But there are likely variables that we know nothing about, and that the Intelligent Designer is fully aware of.

Maybe we do not know as much as we think we do.

35
Apologetics and Danger Zone Issues

Is it okay for Christians to get hypnotized?

I wouldn't advise it. When a person is hypnotized, he goes into what is called an "altered state of consciousness." During such a mystical state, when the rational mind recedes, it is possible for demonic powers to afflict the Christian in various ways. The Christian may end up compromising his faith, or perhaps he may open himself up to spiritual oppression.

Besides, the founder of hypnotism, Franz Anton Mesmer, bought into many unbiblical ideas. He taught that health and illness are determined by the flow of "universal fluids" or "heavenly tides" in the body. When these properties are out of balance, a person allegedly becomes sick. By readjusting these properties, he said, one returns to health.[1] Such an idea fits right in with current New Age medicine. *Christians, beware!*

What is "holistic" health care?

The word "holistic," when applied to health care, refers to an approach that respects the interaction of mind, body, and environment. Holistic health focuses on the *whole* person and his surroundings.

Many proponents of holistic health care criticize Western medicine as being reductionistic in its approach. As Fritjof Capra put it, "By concentrating on smaller and smaller fragments of the body, modern medicine often loses sight of the patient as a human being, and by reducing health to mechanical functioning, it is no longer able to deal with the phenomenon of healing."[2] It is claimed that reductionistic medicine is disease-centered, not person-centered, and treats *only* the parts of the body that are ailing (the heart, for example).

A holistic approach to health is said to be a "multidimensional phenomenon involving interdependent physical, psychological, and social aspects."[3] The holistic approach seeks to treat the *whole* person—body, mind, and spirit—and also considers the social aspects of the patient's life as a factor to health. Holistic health claims to be person-centered, not disease-centered.

Is there a danger to "holistic" health care?

We can all agree that some aspects of holistic health sound reasonable enough and can be accepted by the Christian. The thing to watch out for is that in many cases holistic health care practitioners have (and promote) an anti-Christian worldview. Their holistic health therapies are often based on a mystical conception of *energy*, not matter. They see the universe "as a unified field of energy that produces all form and substance."[4]

This energy is not a visible, measurable, scientifically explainable energy. Rather, it is said to be a "cosmic" or "universal" energy based on a monistic (all is one) and pantheistic (all is God) worldview. To enhance the flow of "healing energy" in the body, one must allegedly *attune* to it and realize one's unity with all things.[5] Many holistic health therapies are based on this premise.

This monistic and pantheistic worldview is entirely at odds with a Christian worldview. Scripture is clear that God the Creator is eternally distinct from the creation (Genesis 1; Isaiah 44:24; Colossians 1:16). *So, Christians, beware!*

Is it okay for Christians to practice meditation?

No and *yes*. Allow me to explain.

Christians are not to practice eastern forms of meditation. In Eastern meditation, the primary goal is to empty the mind so that one experiences a sense of oneness with all things. Proponents of this type of meditation call this sense of oneness "cosmic consciousness." Most such proponents are pantheists—that is, they believe that God is all and that all is God. Their worldview contradicts the biblical distinction between God the Creator and His creatures (see Isaiah 44:6-8; Hebrews 2:6-8).

It is also important to recognize that the kinds of altered states of consciousness characteristic of eastern meditation can open one up to spiritual affliction and deception by the powers of darkness. This alone should serve to dissuade any Christian from participating in this type of meditation.

Having said all this, we as Christians ought to practice meditation as defined in the Bible. In this type of meditation, the individual believer objectively contemplates and deeply reflects upon God's Word (Joshua 1:8; Psalm 1:2; 19:14) as well as His Person and faithfulness (Psalm 119; see also 19:14; 48:9; 77:12; 104:34; 143:5). There is no subjective emptying of the mind.

The Hebrew word for *meditate* carries the idea of "murmuring." It pictures an individual reading and concentrating so intently on what he's reading in Scripture that his lips move as he reads. Such Christian meditation fills our minds with godly wisdom and insight. Scripture affirms, "Blessed is the man...[whose] delight is in the law of the LORD, and on his law he meditates day and night" (Psalm 1:1-2).

Is it okay for Christians to read horoscopes?

No. In fact, it's off-limits.

As a backdrop, astrologers believe that humanity's evolution goes through progressive cycles corresponding to the signs of the zodiac. Each of these cycles allegedly lasts between 2,000 and 2,400 years. It is believed that humanity is now moving from the Piscean Age (the age of intellectual humankind) into the Aquarian Age (the age of spiritual humankind).

Astrology can be traced back to the religious practices of ancient Mesopotamia, Assyria, and Egypt. It is a form of divination—an attempt to seek counsel or knowledge by occultic means—that was very popular among the people of these nations. As such, astrology (including reading horoscopes) is strictly off-limits for the Christian.

In Isaiah 47, we find a strong denunciation of astrologers and their craft. Verse 15 explicitly states that "they wander about each in his own direction," and "there is no one to save you." The book of Daniel confirms that astrologers lack true discernment, and that the only source of accurate revelation is God Almighty (Daniel 2:2,10).

What's wrong with "positive thinking" or "possibility thinking"?

Those who subscribe to the "positive thinking" teachings have redefined many key biblical concepts. For example, many people in this camp view sin as any act or thought that robs people of their self-esteem. The core of sin is viewed as a lack of self-esteem. Being "born again" is viewed as a transformation from a negative to a positive self-image. The way of the cross is viewed as pursuing possibility thinking. Unbelief is redefined to mean a deep sense of unworthiness. Hell is redefined to mean the loss of pride that leads to a sense of separation from God. The person "in hell" is one who has lost self-esteem. Obviously, this is not just a distortion of biblical Christianity—it bears no resemblance to it!

Of course, there's nothing wrong with having a positive outlook on life. Nor is it wrong, for example, to positively imagine yourself hitting the ball out of the ballpark when you're playing baseball with your friends. My only point is that any "positive thinking" theology that redefines biblical concepts must be avoided.

Is the phenomenon known as "holy laughter" biblical?

I don't believe it is. The Bible admonishes us to test all things against Scripture (Acts 17:11; 1 Thessalonians 5:21). I don't see anything that even remotely resembles holy laughter in Scripture.

One fruit of the Holy Spirit is self-control (Galatians 5:23). In the holy laughter phenomenon, people laugh uncontrollably, even when there is nothing funny to laugh about. I've heard of people laughing at meetings even when the preaching was on hell. But Scripture tells us that God takes no joy at the perishing of the wicked (Ezekiel 18:23,32), so to say that God was inspiring such laughter in this context is absurd.

In 1 Corinthians 14:33 the apostle Paul speaks of the need for order in the church. In outbreaks of holy laughter all order is lost in the church. Paul flatly states, "All things should be done decently and in order" (1 Corinthians 14:40).

I don't know of a single verse in the Bible that says that when the Holy Spirit comes upon a person, he breaks out into uncontrollable laughter. There are good passages on joy in the Bible (like Psalm 126), but holy laughter proponents who cite such "joy" passages in support of this phenomenon are reading something into the text that simply is not there.

During the ministry of our Lord Jesus (who had the Holy Spirit without measure), the New Testament mentions not a single instance of people breaking out into uncontrolled laughter. Neither was there any laughter when the apostle Paul or the apostle Peter ministered in the book of Acts.

Is it okay for a Christian to become a Mason?

I know this is a controversial issue among many Christians, but I must advise against becoming a Mason. These are some of the reasons I say this:

Masons typically teach that the Bible is one of many holy books. They teach that Jesus is just one of many ways to the Supreme Being or the "Great Architect of the Universe" (but see John 14:6; Acts 4:12; 1 Timothy 2:5). They teach that God is known by many names—including Jehovah, Krishna, Buddha, and Allah. Masonry teaches a works-oriented system of salvation, which is a direct contradiction of salvation by grace (Ephesians 2:8-9). Further, they require every member to take oaths that no Christian in good conscience should ever take (such as admitting that they are in spiritual darkness and have come to the Masonic Lodge for light).

Further, some rituals in the Masonic Lodge are directly rooted in occultism, pagan religion, and the mystery religions.[6]

What do you think about the appearances of the Virgin Mary in such places as Fatima, Lourdes, Guadalupe, and Medjugorje?

I do not believe these were genuine appearances of the Virgin Mary. I say this not because I have anything against Mary. (I have nothing against her at all, for she is truly blessed among women. See Luke 1:28.) I say this because of the scriptural teaching that contact with the dead *in any form* is forbidden by God (Deuteronomy 18:11). We should not expect that God would allow Mary to do something that He has expressly forbidden. From a scriptural perspective, we will be reunited with the Christian dead *only* at the future rapture (see 1 Thessalonians 4:13-17) and not before.

Some reputable evangelical scholars who have studied the issue have suggested that people who claim they've seen Mary may have actually encountered a demonic impersonation of Mary.[7] Certainly the powers of darkness are capable of such deceptive acts (see 2 Corinthians 11:14-15). The goal, of course, is to distract people away from the Christ of Scripture.

Was Nostradamus a Christian prophet?

By no means. Nostradamus was a sixteenth-century French astrologer and physician. If anything, he was an occultic prophet, not a biblical prophet. He relied quite heavily on horoscopes and other occult methods of divination.[8] His brand of prophecy thus stands condemned by Scripture (Deuteronomy 18:9-14).

Many of Nostradamus's predictions are esoteric, vague, and open-ended. This is why his predictions have been interpreted in so many different ways by Nostradamus enthusiasts. This is unlike the biblical prophecies, which are much more straightforward and precise. Micah 5:2, for example, predicted the Messiah would be born *in Bethlehem.* Isaiah 7:14 predicted He would be born *of a virgin.*

How do we account for the *appearance* of Nostradamus having predicted certain events accurately? There are a number of possible explanations. It may be that Satan inspired these predictions, and even though Satan is not omniscient (all-knowing) as God is, he is a good guesser. Or, it may be that Satan inspired Nostradamus to utter a prophecy and then Satan worked in the world in such a way to bring about some semblance of a fulfillment, thereby lending credence to Nostradamus as a "prophet." Perhaps Satan's goal was to use Nostradamus as a means of drawing other people into occultism. Clearly, though, he was not a biblical prophet.

Understanding UFOs

Is it possible that there is life on other planets?

I can't be dogmatic about this. But it seems to me that the absolute centrality of the earth in Scripture might be one reason to question the claim of life on other planets.

Though atheistic scientists would scoff at this, Scripture points to the centrality of the earth and gives us no hint that life exists elsewhere. To the naturalistic astronomer, the earth is but an astronomical atom among the whirling constellations, only a tiny speck of dust among the ocean of stars and planets in the universe. It is just one of many planets in our small solar system, all of which are in orbit around the sun.

But the earth is nevertheless the center of God's work of salvation in the universe. *On it* the Highest presents Himself in solemn covenants and divine appearances. *On it* the Son of God became man. *On it* stood the cross of the Redeemer of the world. And *on it*—though indeed on the new earth, yet still on the earth—will be at last the throne of God and the Lamb (Revelation 21:1-2; 22:3).

The centrality of the earth is also evident in the creation account, for God created the earth before He created the rest of the planets and stars. One possible reason for this is that in this way God has emphasized the supreme importance of the earth among all astronomical bodies in the universe. Despite its comparative smallness of size, even among the nine planets, to say nothing of the stars themselves, it is nonetheless absolutely unique in God's eternal purposes.

Why would God create such a vast universe if He didn't intend to populate other planets?

I think Psalm 19:1 gives us the answer: "The heavens declare the glory of God, and the sky above proclaims his handiwork." The sheer vastness of the physical universe points us to the greater vastness and infinity of God Himself.

How could unfallen aliens live in the same universe as fallen earthlings?

This might sound like a strange question. But it's actually a good philosophical question.

Scripture reveals that the effects of Adam's sin *pervade the entire universe* (Romans 8:19-22). The entire cosmos has been affected. (The second law of thermodynamics—which says that all things tend toward disorganization and death—may be considered the scientific description of the curse God pronounced on creation in Genesis 3:14-19.) It does not seem likely that God would allow the effects of sin to impact a world of unfallen creatures or aliens (Revelation 21:4).[9] This might then be some supportive evidence that there cannot be life on other planets.

Does Ezekiel 1 make reference to a UFO landing?

No. This is not a reference to a UFO but is rather a vision of the glory of God. This is evident for several reasons. First, the text states clearly that this was "the appearance of the likeness of the glory of the LORD" (Ezekiel 1:28). Moreover, the very first verse of the chapter reveals that what Ezekiel beheld involved "visions of God."

It is clear from the context that the "living creatures" were angels, since they had "wings" (Ezekiel 1:6) and flew in the midst of heaven (see Ezekiel 10:19). They are comparable to the angels mentioned in Isaiah 6:2 and especially the "living creatures" (angels) that are described as being around God's throne (Revelation 4:6).

The message from these beings was from the "Sovereign Lord" of Israel to the prophet Ezekiel (Ezekiel 2:1-4), not one from "the mother ship." The context was a message from the God of Israel through the Jewish prophet Ezekiel to His "rebellious nation" (2:3-4; see also 3:4).

What are some of the natural explanations of UFO sightings?

Many UFO sightings have a natural explanation. Sometimes military jets fly high in the atmosphere. Sometimes sunrays reflect off of satellites floating around the earth. Also, over 7,000 pieces of space junk are floating around the earth. If the sunlight hits one of these objects in the right way, it could appear as a UFO high in the atmosphere. There is also a phenomenon known as ball lightning, in which the lightning is oval-shaped, can hover above ground, can dart around the sky at incredible speeds, and can appear to be a bright-looking craft. Of course, some sightings of UFOs may involve deliberate hoaxes (for example, there have been many doctored photographs or videos of alleged flying saucers).

Do some people today claim to receive messages from "space brothers" aboard UFOs?

Yes. The problem is, though, that these messages are not being transmitted by radio. Rather, New Age psychics are claiming that the space brothers have been in psychic contact with them. And the messages that come from the "space brothers" always contradict the Bible and align with New Age teaching. One is naturally inquisitive as to why "aliens" would travel billions of miles to planet earth only to communicate ideas that New Agers have been teaching for decades. One is also surprised to learn that these "aliens" are occultists with a bias against the Bible. I detect the demonic!

Is it true that many alleged UFO abductees have been or are presently involved in the occult?

Yes. Christian UFO researchers have noted that individuals who claim to be contacted by (or become abducted by) aliens often have a strong prior involvement in some form of occultism. Brooks Alexander of the Spiritual Counterfeits Project said that "many of the reported cases show some kind of occult involvement prior to initial UFO contact."[10] John Weldon likewise notes that "UFO contactees often have a history of psychic abilities or an interest in the occult."[11]

John Keel, a respected authority on UFOs, has noted that "the UFO manifestations seem to be, by and large, merely minor variations of the age-old demonological phenomenon." Indeed, "the manifestations and occurrences described in [the literature of demonology] are similar, if not entirely identical, to the UFO phenomenon itself. Victims of [demon] possession suffer the very same medical and emotional symptoms as the UFO contactees."[12]

Christian UFO investigator David Wimbish has suggested that interest in UFOs can actually draw one into the occult: "Many UFO investigators have followed a path that has taken them directly into the world of the occult. They believe they are rediscovering ancient spiritual truths and uncovering new realities about the universe. It's more likely that they are getting involved with some ancient deceptions."[13] Indeed, the UFO phenomenon "has led many to experiment with astral projection, to believe in reincarnation, and to get involved in other practices that directly oppose the historic teachings of the Christian church."[14]

Let us not forget that the apostle Paul sternly warned, "Even Satan disguises himself as an angel of light. So it is no surprise if his servants, also, disguise themselves as servants of righteousness" (2 Corinthians 11:14-15). Appearances can be deceiving. These so-called "space brothers" may in reality be manifestations of evil spirits bent on deceiving us.

36
Apologetics and the Cults

What is a cult?

The term *cult* is not intended as a pejorative, inflammatory, or injurious word. The term is used simply as a means of categorizing certain religious or semireligious groups in modern America.

A cult may be defined from both a sociological and a theological perspective. Sociologically speaking, a cult is a religious or semireligious sect or group whose members are controlled or dominated almost entirely by a single individual or organization. A sociological definition of a cult generally includes (but is not limited to) the authoritarian, manipulative, and sometimes communal features of cults. Cults that fall into this category include the Hare Krishnas, the Children of God (today called "the Family"), and the Unification Church.

Theologically speaking, a cult is a religious group that emerges out of a parent or host religion, and often claims to be the true form of that religion, but in fact denies one or more of the essential doctrines of that religion. So, for example, Mormonism and the Jehovah's Witnesses are cults because they emerged out of the parent religion of Christianity, they both claim to be the true form of Christianity, and yet both deny essential doctrines of Christianity. Some cults emerge out of the parent religions of Islam (such as the Baha'i Faith) and Hinduism (such as the Hare Krishnas).

What do cults teach about new revelations from God?

Many cult leaders claim to have a direct pipeline to God. The teachings of the cult often change. Therefore, they need new "revelations" to justify such changes. For example, when the founder of Mormonism, Joseph Smith, introduced polygamy into the cult, he allegedly received a new revelation to the effect that his original wife, Emma, was to submit without complaint to this new state of affairs. Another example relates to how Mormonism once excluded African-Americans from the priesthood. When social pressure was exerted against the Mormon church for this blatant form of racism, the Mormon president (the "living prophet" of the church) received a new "revelation" reversing this decree.[1]

What are some examples of cults that deny the sole authority of the Bible?

Many cults deny the sole authority of the Bible. Christian Scientists, for example, elevate Mary Baker Eddy's book *Science and Health with Key to the Scriptures* to supreme authority. Members of the Unification Church elevate Reverend Moon's *Divine Principle* to supreme authority.[2] Many New Agers prefer books like *The Aquarian Gospel of Jesus the Christ* and *A Course in Miracles*. Mormons elevate the Book of Mormon.

What are some examples of cults that distort the doctrines of God and Jesus Christ?

Many cults set forth a distorted view of God and Jesus. For example, the Jehovah's Witnesses deny both the Trinity and the absolute deity of Christ. They claim that Christ was created as the archangel Michael and is a lesser God than the Father (who is God Almighty). The Mormons say Jesus was the first and greatest spirit child born to the heavenly Father and is one of his wives. He is allegedly the spirit-brother of Lucifer.

The Jesus of the spiritists is just an advanced medium.[3] The Jesus of the Wiccans is a witch, and his disciples are members of his coven. New Agers say Jesus was just a human being who embodied the cosmic Christ (a divine spirit). UFO cults claim Jesus was a hybrid being—half human and half alien. (An alien allegedly had sexual relations with Mary.)

What are some examples of cults that deny salvation by grace?

Cults, almost without exception, deny salvation by grace, thus distorting the purity of the gospel. They typically feature a works-oriented system of salvation. The Mormons, for example, emphasize the necessity of becoming more and more perfect in this life. The Jehovah's Witnesses emphasize the importance of distributing Watchtower literature door-to-door as a part of "working out" their salvation. Moonies must render perpetual obedience to the teachings of Reverend Moon.

What are some examples of how cults can be authoritarian?

Authoritarianism involves the acceptance of an authority figure who often uses mind-control techniques on group members. As prophet and/or founder, this leader's word is considered ultimate and final. The late David Koresh of the Branch Davidian cult in Waco, Texas, is a tragic example. Members of this cult followed Koresh to the point of death. The same was true of those who followed Jim Jones, the leader of the Jonestown cult.

What are some examples of how cults can be exclusivist?

Cults often believe, "We alone possess the truth." For example, the Mormons—as the alleged "restored church" with a "restored priesthood" and a "restored gospel"—believe they are the exclusive community of the saved on earth. The Jehovah's Witnesses likewise believe *they* are the exclusive community of Jehovah on earth.[4]

What are some examples of how cults engage in extreme dogmatism?

Closely related to the above, many cults are extremely dogmatic—and this dogmatism is often expressed institutionally. The Jehovah's Witnesses, for example, claim that the Watchtower Society is the sole voice of Jehovah on earth.[5] We are told that without the Watchtower and its vast literature, no one on earth would be able to understand the Bible. Jehovah's Witnesses are thus expected to render complete obedience and submission to the Watchtower Society.

In other cults, members are instructed that they must interpret the Bible according to the unique insights of the cult leader. An example of this is the Children of God, whose members interpret the Bible according to the writings of David Berg (also known as "Moses"), the cult's founder.

What are some examples of cults that are isolationist?

The more extreme cults sometimes create fortified boundaries, often precipitating tragic endings, such as the disaster in Waco, Texas, with the Branch Davidian cult. Another example is the Fundamentalist Church of Jesus Christ of Latter-Day Saints (the polygamous FLDS Church), under the leadership of the controversial Warren Jeffs. Jonestown, under the leadership of Jim Jones, was the same way.

Do cults sometimes threaten satanic attack for offenders?

Yes. The Watchtower Society is typical of many cults in that it warns new followers that friends and relatives may very well be used by Satan to try to dissuade them from remaining with the Jehovah's Witnesses.[6] Then, when a friend or relative *actually does* try to dissuade a new member in this way, it makes the Watchtower Society appear to be a true prophet. This, in turn, encourages the new convert to be even more loyal to the Watchtower Society. The Watchtower's warning consequently serves as an effective way of keeping new converts so they can be thoroughly indoctrinated into the cult.

Cult members are also warned that if they leave the group, both they and their families may become the target of satanic attack. This type of fear motivates cult members to be compliant.

Are sincere cultists lost?

Yes, they are. A person can sincerely take a pill that is unknowingly laced with cyanide. All the sincerity in the world is not going to stop that cyanide from killing the person. In the same way, a person can participate in a cult that, unknown to him, teaches all kinds of deadly doctrines. All the sincerity in the world won't prevent him from going into eternity without the true Christ. Never forget: If you believe in a *counterfeit Christ* that preaches a *counterfeit gospel*, you end up with a *counterfeit salvation.*

Let this be a motivation for you to always be willing to share the truth when you find a cultist on the doorstep. In fact, when they ring your doorbell, you should consider them to be a "kingdom assignment." (My books *Reasoning from the Scriptures with Jehovah's Witnesses* and *Reasoning from the Scriptures with Mormons* can help you a great deal in being an effective witness to them.)

Does Scripture say we should never let cultists into our houses?

The verse generally appealed to in support of this idea is 2 John 10: "If anyone comes to you and does not bring this teaching, do not receive him into your house or give him any greeting." This verse, however, does not prohibit Christians from allowing cultists into their homes in order to witness to them. Rather it is a prohibition against giving cultists a platform from which to teach false doctrine.

The backdrop to this is that in the early days of Christianity, there was no centralized church building where believers could congregate. Instead, many small house churches were scattered throughout the city. The early Christians are seen "breaking bread in their homes" (Acts 2:46; see also 5:42) and gathering to pray in the house of Mary, the mother of Mark (Acts 12:12). Churches often met in houses (Colossians 4:15; 1 Corinthians 16:19). The use of specific church buildings did not appear before the end of the second century.

Apparently, then, John is here warning against (1) allowing a false teacher into the church, and (2) giving this false teacher a platform from which to teach. Seen in this way, this prohibition guards the purity of the church. To extend hospitality to a false teacher would imply that the church accepted or approved of his or her teaching. If the church were to extend hospitality to a false teacher, he would be encouraged in his position and take this action as an acceptance of his doctrine. This should never be.

Do the Scriptures teach that human beings are (or can become) "little gods"?

No. If it were true that human beings are "little gods," then one would expect them to display qualities similar to those known to be true of God. This seems only logical. However, when one compares the attributes of humankind with those of God, we find more than ample testimony for the truth of Paul's statement in Romans 3:23 that human beings "fall short of the glory of God."

After all, God is all-knowing (Isaiah 40:13-14), but man is limited in knowledge (Job 38:4). God is all-powerful (Revelation 19:6), but man is weak (Hebrews 4:15). God is everywhere present (Psalm 139:7-12), but man is confined to a single space at a time (John 1:50). God is holy (1 John 1:5), but even man's "righteous" deeds are as filthy garments before God (Isaiah 64:6). God is eternal (Psalm 90:2), but man was created at a point in time (Genesis 1:26-27). God is truth (John 14:6), but man's heart is deceitful above all else (Jeremiah 17:9).

God is characterized by justice (Acts 17:31), but man is lawless (1 John 3:4; see also Romans 3:23). God is love (Ephesians 2:4-5), but man is plagued with numerous vices like jealousy and strife (1 Corinthians 3:3).

If man is a god, one could never tell it by his attributes!

Doesn't human ignorance of alleged divinity prove that human beings are not God?

Yes indeed. If human beings are essentially God, and if God is an infinite and changeless being, then how is it possible for human beings (if they are a manifestation of divinity) to go through a changing process of enlightenment by which they discover their divinity? "The fact that a man 'comes to realize' he is God proves that he is not God. If he were God he would never have passed from a state of unenlightenment to a state of enlightenment as to who he is."[7] To put it another way, "God cannot bud. He cannot blossom. God has always been in full bloom. That is, God is and always has been God."[8]

Controversial Issues Related to Cults

Is it wrong to wear a cross, as the Jehovah's Witnesses claim?

No. As a backdrop, the Jehovah's Witnesses teach that the cross is a pagan religious symbol. Christians adopted this pagan symbol, we are told, when Satan took control of ecclesiastical authority in the early centuries of Christianity. Jehovah's Witnesses say that Christ was not crucified on a cross but on a stake.[9] That's the correct meaning of the Greek word *stauros,* they say. So for people to wear crosses today dishonors God.

Actually, the Greek word *stauros* was used to refer to a variety of wooden structures used for execution in ancient days. The *stauros* as a wooden structure took on a variety of shapes, including that of the letter T, a plus sign (+), two diagonal beams (X), as well as (infrequently) a simple upright stake with no crosspiece. To argue that *stauros* always referred to an upright beam, as the Jehovah's Witnesses do, contradicts the actual historical facts.

In support of the idea that Jesus died on a cross is the fact that "nails" were used (John 20:25). If Jesus was crucified not on a cross but on a stake, then only a single nail would have been used. It is also significant that when Jesus spoke of Peter's *future* crucifixion, He indicated that Peter's arms would be outstretched, not above his head on a stake (John 21:18-19). Further, in keeping with a cross crucifixion instead of a stake crucifixion, we read in Matthew 27:37 that a sign saying "King of the Jews" was put above Jesus' *head,* not above His *hands.*

Interestingly, an early edition of the Jehovah's Witnesses' *Watchtower* magazine has a sketch on the cover of Jesus crucified upon a cross. It was later that they had a change in doctrine.

Is it wrong to celebrate birthdays, as some cultists claim?

No. Cultists (such as the Jehovah's Witnesses) argue that the Bible makes reference to birthday celebrations in only two passages—

Genesis 40:20-22 and Matthew 14:6-10. In both cases, they argue, birthdays are presented in an extremely negative light. Indeed, both individuals (Pharaoh in the Old Testament, Herod in the New Testament) were pagans and both had someone put to death on their birthdays. In view of this, it is concluded that no follower of God should ever celebrate a birthday.[10]

Cultists are here using the logical fallacy "guilt by association." Concluding that a particular day is bad and evil simply because something bad or evil *happened* on that day is truly warped logic. Genesis 40:20-22 proves only that the Pharaoh was evil, not that birthdays are evil. Likewise, Matthew 14:6-10 proves only that Herod was evil, not that birthdays are evil. Certainly Scripture never commands the celebration of birthdays, but there is no warrant for saying that celebrating birthdays is forbidden from these passages or any other passage.

Against the cultic view, aren't birthdays portrayed in a positive light in the book of Job?

A number of scholars believe birthdays are mentioned in Job 1:4: "His [Job's] sons used to go and hold a feast in the house of each one *on his day*, and they would send and invite their three sisters to eat and drink with them" (see also Job 3:1-3). It is likely that a birthday festival is here intended. When the birthday of one arrived, he invited his brothers and sisters to feast with him, and each observed the same custom.

Nothing in the text indicates that Job's children did evil things on this day. Their celebration is not portrayed as a pagan practice. And certainly Job does not condemn the celebration. If such celebrations of birthdays were offensive to God, then Job—a man who "was blameless and upright, one who feared God and turned away from evil" (Job 1:1)—would have done something to prevent this practice among his own children.

There is no reason a birthday cannot be celebrated, like everything else, to the glory of God who created us (1 Corinthians 10:31). Nothing is wrong with giving proper honor to another human being. The Bible says we should give respect to him who is due respect and honor to him who is due honor (Romans 13:7). Since a typical birthday does not worship another human being, there is no reason we cannot honor him or her on this occasion.

Do the Jehovah's Witnesses teach that it is wrong to receive a blood transfusion?

Yes. They try to argue that references to "eating blood" in the Bible prohibit receiving blood via transfusion. They typically cite Leviticus 7:26-27: "You shall eat no blood whatever, whether of fowl or of animal, in any of your dwelling places. Whoever eats any blood, that person shall be cut off from his people" (see also Genesis 9:4; Leviticus 17:11-12; Acts 15:28-29).[11]

Why did God prohibit the eating or drinking of blood?

Some of the pagan nations surrounding Israel had no respect for blood. Such pagans ate blood on a regular basis. Sometimes they did this as part of the worship of false gods. At other times they did this because they thought it might bring them supernatural power. In any event, the prohibition against eating blood set Israel apart from such ungodly nations.

Is "eating" blood the same as a blood transfusion?

No. Evangelical Christians agree that Genesis 9:4 and other such passages prohibit the "eating" of blood, but this is not the same as a blood transfusion. A transfusion simply replenishes the supply of essential, life-sustaining fluid that has in some way been drained away or has become incapable of performing its vital tasks in the body. In this context, blood does not function as food. A transfusion simply represents a transference of life from one person to another, and as such, it is an act of mercy.

Christian apologist Norman Geisler further points out that even though a doctor might give food to a patient "intravenously" (that is, through a vein) and even call this procedure "feeding," it is simply not the case that giving blood intravenously is the same as eating blood. This is clear from the fact that blood is not received into the body as "food." Geisler explains this distinction as follows:

> To refer to the giving of food directly into the blood stream as "eating" is only a figurative expression...Eating is the *literal* taking in of food in the normal manner through the mouth and into the digestive system. The reason intravenous injections are referred to as "feeding" is because the ultimate result is that, through intravenous injection, the body receives the nutrients that it would normally receive by eating.[12]

In view of these facts, Genesis 9:4, Leviticus 7:26-27; 17:11-12, Acts 15:28-29, and other such passages cannot be used to support a prohibition on blood transfusions, since it is not a form of "eating." Interestingly, even orthodox Jews who hold to a strictly literal interpretation of the books of Genesis and Leviticus will accept blood transfusions.

Is it against God's will for Christians to celebrate Christmas?

There's not a single commandment in Scripture that instructs us to celebrate Christ's birth. But this doesn't mean it is wrong to do it. Scripture indicates that anything is permitted so long as it does not violate biblical principles, and so long as it is done in faith, with love, and in a manner that edifies people (see Romans 13:10; 14:4,5; 1 Corinthians 6:12; 10:23; Colossians 2:20,22).

Is Christmas based on the date of a pagan ritual?

Some have objected that Christ wasn't born on December 25. That's probably true. His birth likely occurred at a different time of year altogether. Nevertheless, it is perfectly appropriate for Christians to celebrate the incarnation, the most incredible event of human history. And it's fine to do it on December 25, even though Christ probably wasn't born that day. (After all, Americans commemorate Washington's birthday on the third Monday of February, even though his real birthday was February 22.)

It is true that Christmas is celebrated on a day that in the ancient Roman Empire was a pagan holiday linked to the mystery religions. But this doesn't make Christmas a pagan holiday. The fact is, the early Christians refused to participate in this pagan ritual. Their attitude was that if the pagans were going to celebrate their false religion, Christians should celebrate the one true religion. And what better way to celebrate than to focus attention on the incarnation, the event in which eternal God became a man?

Personally, I think it brings a smile to Christ's face when Christians celebrate His birth. On the other hand, I think it must sadden Him when He sees Christians focusing exclusively on exchanging gifts with one another, focusing little or no attention on Him.

Part 10

Questions About Ethics

Ethics and the Christian Life
Ethical Issues Related to Death

37
Ethics and the Christian Life

What does the Bible say about charity?

In Old Testament times, the Mosaic Law encouraged charity among the people. For example, Leviticus 25:35 instructs, "If your brother becomes poor and cannot maintain himself with you, you shall support him as though he were a stranger and a sojourner, and he shall live with you." Likewise, Deuteronomy 15:7 encourages, "If among you, one of your brothers should become poor, in any of your towns within your land that the LORD your God is giving you, you shall not harden your heart or shut your hand against your poor brother" (see also Psalm 41:1). Old Testament law stipulated that farmers should leave the corners of their fields unharvested, so that poor people who walked by could pick some food to eat (see Leviticus 19:9-10; Deuteronomy 15:11; Ruth 2:2).

The New Testament is replete with admonitions to freely give unto others. Hebrews 13:16 instructs us to do good and share with others. We are admonished to give to the poor (Matthew 19:21; Luke 11:41; 12:33; 1 John 3:17) and to give to those who ask (Matthew 5:42). We are called to share food with the hungry (Isaiah 58:7,10), to share money generously (Romans 12:8), and to use money for good (1 Timothy 6:17-18). The early church certainly showed charity as an evidence of Christian love (Acts 9:36; 10:2,4; Romans 12:13; Ephesians 4:28; 1 Timothy 6:18; Hebrews 13:16; 1 John 3:17-19). Jesus advises us to give to others secretly instead of openly in order to win the praise of men (Matthew 6:1-2).

The New Testament often describes such generous activities as almsgiving. The word "alms" derives from the Greek word *eleos*, which means "mercy." "Almsgiving" thus means "mercy-giving." We are called to show mercy and kindness to others whenever the opportunity arises.

Is it ever right for the Christian to lie?

Yes—but I need to carefully qualify what I mean. On the one hand, Scripture forbids lying (Exodus 20:16). Lying is a sin (Psalm 59:12) and an abomination to God (Proverbs 12:22). God never lies (Numbers 23:19). Righteous men hate lying (Proverbs 13:5).

On the other hand, some Scriptures indicate that under certain circumstances, lying is not condemned. For example, though the Hebrew midwives were commanded by the Egyptian Pharaoh to let newborn baby boys die, the midwives disobeyed the Pharaoh and lied to him when questioned about it (Exodus 1:15-19). To the Hebrew midwives, *lifesaving* was higher on the ethical scale than *truth-telling*. Not only did God refrain from condemning the midwives for lying— He was kind to them for their merciful act (see verse 20).

A more recent example would be the numerous Christians who lied to the Nazis in order to protect Jews from being captured and exterminated. In such cases lying is not condemned because lifesaving is a higher ethic than truth-telling.

What does Scripture teach about obedience to the government?

The apostle Paul commanded believers to be submissive to the government because authority is ordained of God (Romans 13:1-7). In Paul's argumentation, resistance to government is, in the final analysis, resistance against God (verse 2). Government, Paul says, resists evil (verse 4).

It is noteworthy that some eight years later, after having been imprisoned a number of times by the Roman government, Paul had not changed his mind. He still taught that Christians should obey the government. Maltreatment at the hands of the Roman government had not caused him to alter his view.

Peter, too, wrote about the need to obey the government (1 Peter 2:13-17). Like Paul, he says that obeying government shows our obedience to God Himself. All this is significant in view of the fact that both Paul and Peter wrote what they did while living under the reign of the cruel emperor Nero (AD 54–68).

Is it ever right to disobey the government?

We must answer this question very carefully. I think the biblically balanced answer is that believers must obey the government unless the government explicitly commands them to go against one or more of God's commands. In that case, one must obey God rather than the government.

We find this principle illustrated in both the Old and New Testaments. For example, after being commanded by the Sanhedrin (Jewish government) not to preach any further, "Peter and the apostles answered, 'We must obey God rather than men'" (Acts 5:29). God commanded Peter and the others to preach. The Jewish leaders commanded them not to preach. So they chose to obey God rather than human government.

We see the same thing illustrated in the book of Daniel in the Old Testament. Shadrach, Meshach, and Abednego righteously disobeyed the king when they were commanded to worship the golden image (Daniel 3). Daniel also righteously disobeyed the government when it commanded him to go against God's revealed will (Daniel 6). In both cases, God confirmed that they had made the right choice by delivering them from the punishment that was afflicted upon them.

Of course, Christians must guard against abusing this principle in Scripture. Scripture indicates that we are to disobey government *only* when it commands us to violate God's commands, not just when we feel the government has personally violated our rights.

What does Scripture say about drinking?

Drunkenness is forbidden by God all throughout Scripture. It is simply not an option for the Christian. In Ephesians 5:18, the apostle Paul explicitly instructs, "Do not get drunk with wine, for that is debauchery, but be filled with the Spirit." Paul is telling us to be controlled by the Spirit, not by wine.

While drinking wine *in moderation* is permissible in Scripture (see John 2:9; 1 Timothy 3:3,8), many wine-drinking Christians today are wrongly assuming that what the New Testament means by wine is identical to the wine used today. This, however, is not correct.

Today's wine is by biblical definitions "strong drink." What the New Testament meant by wine was basically purified water. The beverage that was drunk in ancient times was generally 20 parts water and one part wine. Twenty-to-one water is essentially wine-flavored water. Sometimes in the ancient world they would go as strong as one part water and one part wine—and this was considered strong wine.

Anyone who drank wine unmixed was looked upon as a Scythian, a barbarian. So anyone who would take wine unmixed, even the Greeks thought was a barbarian. That means the Greeks would look at our culture today and say, "You Americans are barbarians—drinking straight wine."

What principles can guide us regarding whether or not we should drink wine?

Every Christian adult must decide for himself whether or not to drink. We all must ask ourselves this question: While drinking may be *permissible,* is it *beneficial* for me to do so?

In 1 Corinthians 6:12, Paul wrote, "'All things are lawful for me,' but not all things are helpful. 'All things are lawful for me,' but I will not be enslaved by anything" (1 Corinthians 6:12). He also wrote, "It is good not to eat meat or drink wine or do anything that causes your brother to stumble" (Romans 14:21).

At the same time, he also insisted, "So, whether you eat or drink, or whatever you do, do all to the glory of God" (1 Corinthians 10:31). Also, he says, "Let each of you look not only to his own interests, but also to the interests of others" (Philippians 2:4).

My personal choice is not to drink at all.

Are there any commandments in the Bible against smoking cigarettes?

No. But the Scriptures do indicate that the Christian's body is a temple of the Holy Spirit, and as such, we should seek to glorify God in our body (1 Corinthians 6:19-20). Of course, this also applies to eating the right kind of food and making sure we stay fit.

Though smoking will not keep you out of heaven, it will probably get you there much quicker. Another thing to keep in mind is that your "secondhand smoke" might end up sending others into eternity—believers *and* unbelievers—much earlier than otherwise would have occurred.

What does Scripture say about premarital sex?

God created human beings as sexual beings. But God intended sexual activity to be confined to the marriage relationship. Unfortunately, as is true with so many other things, many people have taken that which God intended for good and have perverted its use. The result: *sexual enslavement.*

Scripture has a lot to say about human sexuality. It is consistent in its emphasis that a sexual relationship can only be engaged in within the confines of marriage—that is, a marriage between a male and a female (1 Corinthians 7:2). The apostles urged all Christians to abstain from fornication (Acts 15:20). Paul said that the body is not for fornication and that a man should flee it (1 Corinthians 6:13,18).

Adultery is condemned in Scripture (Exodus 20:14). In the Old Testament adulterers were to be put to death (Leviticus 20:10). Jesus pronounced adultery wrong even in its basic motives (Matthew 5:27-28). Paul called adultery an evil work of the flesh (Galatians 5:19). John envisioned in the lake of fire some of those who practiced adultery (Revelation 21:8).

Sex within marriage, however, *is good* (see Genesis 2:24; Matthew 19:5). Sex was a part of God's "good" creation. Indeed, God created sex and "everything created by God is good" (1 Timothy 4:4). But it is good *only* within the confines of the marriage relationship, which He Himself ordained (see Hebrews 13:4).

Is homosexuality acceptable to God?

No, it is not. The Bible explicitly warns that "men who practice homosexuality" will not inherit the kingdom of God (1 Corinthians 6:9-10). The Scriptures consistently condemn homosexual practices (for example, see Leviticus 18:22; Romans 1:26). God loves all persons, including homosexuals, but *He hates homosexuality.* The Bible condemns *all* types of fornication, which would therefore include homosexuality (Matthew 15:19; Mark 7:21; Acts 15:20,29; Galatians 5:19-21; 1 Thessalonians 4:3; Hebrews 13:4).

The good news is that the apostle Paul speaks of the possibility of complete liberation from homosexual sin in 1 Corinthians 6:9-11: "Do not be deceived: neither the sexually immoral, nor idolaters, nor adulterers, nor men who practice homosexuality...will inherit the kingdom of God. And *such were some of you. But you were washed, you were sanctified, you were justified in the name of the Lord Jesus Christ and by the Spirit of our God.*"

Is it permissible for the Christian to get divorced?

This is a difficult issue. Scripture is clear that God Himself created the institution of marriage, and He intended it to be permanent (Matthew 19:4-6). Divorce was never a part of God's original plan. In fact, God hates divorce (Malachi 2:16). The marriage relationship was intended to be dissolved only when one of the marriage partners dies (Romans 7:1-3).

When sin entered the world, this affected God's ideal in marriage and many other things. Scripture tells us that even though divorce was not God's ideal, He nevertheless allowed it because of human sinfulness (Matthew 19:7-8; Deuteronomy 24:1-4).

From a biblical perspective, divorce is allowed only under two circumstances: (1) One of the marriage partners is unfaithful (Matthew 19:9). (2) The unbelieving partner deserts the believing partner (1 Corinthians 7:15-16). Divorce for any other reason is a violation of God's ideal.

Even in cases in which a person clearly has biblical grounds for divorce, God's desire is that the person, if at all possible, forgive the offending spouse and be reconciled to him or her. This follows from God's command to forgive others of their wrongs toward us (Ephesians 4:32; Colossians 3:13).

Of course, God forgives us of all our sins—including the sin of divorce (Colossians 2:13). However, simply because God forgives us does not remove the painful consequences of our actions on ourselves or on others. There is a heavy price to pay for violating God's ideal.

Does the Bible support slavery?

No. From the very beginning, God declared that all humans are created in the image of God (Genesis 1:26-27). The apostle Paul also declared that we are "God's offspring" (Acts 17:29), and that God "made from one man every nation of mankind to live on all the face of the earth" (verse 26).

Moreover, despite the fact that slavery was countenanced in the Semitic cultures of the day, the law in the Bible demanded that slaves eventually be set free (Exodus 21:2; Leviticus 25:40). Likewise, servants had to be treated with respect (Exodus 21:20,26). Israel, itself in slavery in Egypt for a prolonged time, was constantly reminded by God of this (Deuteronomy 5:15), and their emancipation became the model for the liberation of all slaves (see Leviticus 25:40).

Further, in the New Testament, Paul declared that in Christianity "there is neither Jew nor Greek, there is neither slave nor free, there is neither male nor female, for you are all one in Christ Jesus" (Galatians 3:28). All social classes are broken down in Christ; we are all equal before God.

Though the apostle Paul urges, "Slaves, obey your earthly masters" (Ephesians 6:5; see also Colossians 3:22), he is not thereby approving of the institution of slavery, but simply alluding to the de facto situation in his day. He is simply instructing servants to be good workers, just as believers should be today, but he was not thereby commending slavery. Paul also instructed all believers to be obedient to government (even if unjust) for the Lord's sake (Romans 13:1; see also Titus 3:1; 1 Peter 2:13). But this in no way condones oppression and tyranny which the Bible repeatedly condemns (Isaiah 10:1; Exodus 2:23-25).

38
Ethical Issues Related to Death

What does the Bible say about suicide?

Suicide is a particularly difficult issue to address, primarily because of the pain left behind for the loved ones of the deceased. The truth is, people sometimes lose the will to live, or they become emotionally imbalanced, or they become hopeless in the face of a catastrophic situation. Some people are just prone to severe depression and they give up. Some people get despondent over a relationship gone bad. For these and many other reasons, people sometimes tragically choose suicide.

Below are a few theological insights on the issue. I pray that the communication of these theological facts won't come across as "cold orthodoxy." I say this because I suspect that some of my readers may have personally experienced the loss of a loved one due to suicide. If that has happened, my heart goes out to you. If I were sitting next to you, I'd speak to you more as a friend and less as a theologian. For the purposes of this book, however, a summary of theological facts is appropriate.

From a biblical perspective, we begin by noting that issues of life and death properly lie in the sovereign hands of God alone. Job said to God that man's "days are determined, and the number of his months is with you, and you have appointed his limits that he cannot pass" (Job 14:5). David said to God, "In your book were written, every one of them, the days that were formed for me, when as yet there were none of them" (Psalm 139:16). God is sovereign over life and death.

How does the sixth commandment (of the Ten Commandments) relate to the issue of suicide?

Some theologians suggest that suicide goes against the commandments of God—particularly, the sixth commandment: "You shall not murder" (Exodus 20:13). This command is based on the sanctity of human life, and the fact that human beings are created in the image of God (Genesis 1:26-27).

Theologians point out that the command, "You shall not murder," has no direct object. That is, it doesn't say, "You shall not murder *someone else*," or "You shall not murder *your fellow human being*." It simply says, "You shall not murder." The prohibition would thus seem to include even the murder of oneself.

Did people in Bible times ever think about suicide?

Yes. The lives of certain biblical saints are instructive on the issue of suicide. In the Bible, sometimes certain servants of God were so severely tested and distressed that they wished for their own death (see 1 Kings 19:4). But these individuals did not take matters into their own hands and kill themselves. Instead, in these cases, they cast themselves upon God, and He delivered them.

The apostle Paul certainly went through tough times. Indeed, in 2 Corinthians 1:8, Paul reflected on his past: "We do not want you to be ignorant, brothers, of the affliction we experienced in Asia. For we were so utterly burdened beyond our strength that we despaired of life itself."

Nevertheless, Paul did not succumb to breaking God's commandment against murder and commit suicide. He depended on God, and God came through and gave him all the sustenance he needed to make it through his ordeal (1 Corinthians 1:9-10).

Is suicide an unforgiveable sin?

No. Nothing in Scripture even remotely hints that suicide is unforgiveable. If your Christian loved one has committed suicide, I believe you will be reunited with him or her in the afterlife in a grand and glorious reunion in heaven (see 1 Thessalonians 4:13-17). So keep your hope strong in the Lord (see Psalm 33:18,20,22; 39:7; 43:5; 71:5; 130:7; Isaiah 49:23; Colossians 3:1-4; 1 Peter 1:3). Take comfort in this.

Is capital punishment supported by the Bible?

Yes. In Genesis 9:6 we find that capital punishment was instituted in view of the sanctity of human life. The underlying basis for this severe punishment is the fact that human beings are made in the image of God (Genesis 1:26-27). Human beings are so valuable as individuals that anyone who tampers with their sacred right to live must face the consequences of losing his or her own life. The worth of the individual is so great that the highest penalty is attached to those who tamper with the life of even one person. This was true in Bible times and it is true today. When a human being is murdered, this ultimately amounts to an outrage against God.

Certainly the death penalty was incorporated into the Mosaic code (see Exodus 21:12; Numbers 35:16-31). And in Romans 13:1-7 the apostle Paul taught that human government has a God-given right to use force in its resistance of evil. Romans 13:4 in particular indicates that the government has the right to take the life of a criminal.

It is true that one of the Ten Commandments says we are not to murder (Exodus 20:13). But murder by a citizen and execution by the government are viewed as two different things in Scripture. One is a premeditated crime; the other is a deserved punishment. And since government is set up by God (Romans 13:1-7), it would seem that capital punishment may be viewed as the enacting of divine judgment through the instrumentality of the government.

Is cremation following death permissible for Christians?

In the Bible cremation is portrayed only as an exceptional method of disposing of bodies. Most often cremation took place in the midst of unusual circumstances. For example, in 1 Samuel 31:11-12 we read about the "inhabitants of Jabesh-gilead" (verse 11) who burned the corpses of Saul and his sons in order to prevent desecration of their bodies at the hands of the Philistines.

We don't find cremation mentioned in the New Testament. Burial is the normal method. Moreover, the church fathers preferred "the ancient and better custom of burying in the earth."[1]

But Scripture contains no actual prohibition against cremation in its pages. And if a Christian does get cremated, this poses no problem for God in resurrecting that person's body from the dead (1 Corinthians 15:42-44).

We read in 2 Corinthians 5:1, "We know that if the tent, which is our earthly home, is destroyed, we have a building from God, a house not made with hands, eternal in the heavens." It does not matter how our earthly "tent" (body) is destroyed; all that matters is that God will raise it from the dead. Even those who are buried eventually dissolve into dust and bones. So, regardless of whether we're buried *or* cremated, we can all look forward to a permanent resurrection body that will never be subject to death and decay.

Christian Views of War

What is the case for the activist view of war?

Activism is the view that Christians should participate in all wars in obedience to their government. This is based on the belief that all government is ordained by God. "Let every person be subject to the governing authorities. For there is no authority except from God, and those that exist have been instituted by God" (Romans 13:1; see also Titus 3:1; 1 Peter 2:13-14).

In view of such verses, activists suggest that Scripture makes a connection between obedience to government and obedience to God. Whoever resists government is, in the end, resisting God. As a duty to God, Christians are duty-bound to obey their government. If one's government issues the command to go to war, one must obey the government as an expression of one's underlying obedience to God.

What's the problem with activism?

Some Christians believe that activism does not adequately deal with Scripture verses that call for peace and nonresistance (for example,

Matthew 5:38-48). Neither does it account for the fact that one's country might engage in an *unjust* war.

Christian activists respond that activism is still justifiable. Even if one's country is in the wrong in a war, a citizen should nevertheless obey the government in going to war, for the *evil of war* is lesser than the *evil of anarchy* or *revolution*. It is better to maintain order by obeying a government in the wrong than to participate in societal disorder.

What is the case for the pacifist view of war?

Some Christians espouse pacifism—the idea that it is *always* wrong to injure or kill other humans, no matter what the circumstances. This view is usually based on the exemplary life and teachings of Jesus.

Jesus set forth a biblical mandate to *turn the other cheek* when encountering evil and violence (Matthew 5:38-42). He instructed, "Do not resist the one who is evil" (Matthew 5:39). He urged, "Love your enemies" (Luke 6:35). He said the kingdom was not to be advanced by physical force (John 18:36).

One of the Ten Commandments instructs, "You shall not murder" (Exodus 20:13). War is nothing but mass murder. The prohibition against murder is rooted in the fact that human beings are created in the image of God (Genesis 1:26-27). Because vengeance belongs to God (Deuteronomy 32:35), Christians should never retaliate—that is, we should not be overcome by evil but rather overcome evil by good (Romans 12:19-21).

Paul urged, "If possible, so far as it depends on you, live peaceably with all" (Romans 12:18).

What's the problem with pacifism?

Some Christians criticize pacifism as not reflecting the whole of Scripture. For example, the New Testament commends Old Testament warriors for their military acts of faith (Hebrews 11:30-40). None of the New Testament saints—nor even Jesus—ever instructed a military convert to resign from his commission (Matthew 8:5-13). Jesus instructed the disciples to sell their outer garments in order to purchase a sword for self-defense (Luke 22:36-38).

Moreover, Christian activists sometimes ask Christian pacifists, "What if your wife is attacked? What would you do?" Some pacifists respond that they would not kill the attacker. After all, the wife would go straight to heaven if she were killed. The attacker, however, would go straight to hell. The avoidance of killing the attacker leaves open the possibility of winning him to Christ. Other pacifists understandably fudge a bit, and suggest that *some* force could be used in an attempt to wound or disarm the attacker.

What is the case for the selectivist view of war?

Selectivism is the view that Christians may participate in *just* wars, but not *unjust* wars. While Paul urged Christians to be at peace with all men if possible (Romans 12:18), such peace *is not always possible*, especially in circumstances where an evil bully—or evil nation, like Nazi Germany—attacks others. Paul said Christians are not to be overcome by evil but are to overcome evil by good (Romans 12:19-21), but sometimes overcoming evil by good necessitates good people *justly* using force against evil terrorists.

Selectivists emphasize that nonresistance is not the essential point of Christ's *turn-the-other-cheek* teaching in Matthew 5:38-42. Contextually, Jesus was saying only that Christians should not retaliate *when insulted* (see also Romans 12:17-21).

Selectivists do not absolutely equate *life-taking* with *murder* (Exodus 20:13). When God instituted human government during Noah's time, He delegated authority to the government to take human life—capital punishment (Genesis 9:6). This was not viewed as murder. Paul approvingly speaks of capital punishment in Romans 13.

The selectivist recognizes cases will arise in which a war sponsored by his government may be unjust. In this situation, the selectivist declines participation. Scripture teaches it is not always right to obey one's government—especially when the government issues a command that violates a higher command from God (Exodus 1:17-21; Daniel 3; 6; Acts 4–5). The selectivist thus feels justified in declining participation in a war if it is judged to be unjust in view of the teachings of Scripture.

Is there a case for self-defense in the Bible?

Yes. In fact, self-defense may result in one of the greatest examples of human love. Jesus said, "Greater love has no one than this, that someone lays down his life for his friends" (John 15:13). When protecting one's family or neighbor, a Christian is unselfishly risking his or her life for the sake of others.

To *not* engage in self-defense (or defense of others) is morally wrong. To allow murder to take place when one could have prevented it is morally wrong. To permit a young girl to be raped when one could have hindered it is an evil. To watch a child be treated with cruelty without intervening is morally reprehensible. *Not* resisting evil is *an evil of omission* (see James 4:17).

The principle of self-defense is applicable on a broader scale to the concept of just wars and selectivism. To *not* respond to a bully nation seeking to destroy or injure a less powerful nation or group of people is to fail morally. This principle is illustrated in Abraham's battle against the kings of Genesis 14, in which Abraham sought to rescue Lot from these unjust aggressors (see 1 Samuel 23:1).

When Paul's life was in great danger of being unjustly taken, he engaged in self-defense by appealing to his Roman citizenship. He appealed to the military might and protection of the Roman army (Acts 22:25-29). Nothing in the text indicates that Paul thought anything wrong with such military defense.

What are the principles of a "just war"?

War is justifiable *only* under certain circumstances. Seven principles have been suggested to guide our thinking. Augustine of Hippo (AD 354–430) enunciated many of these early in the fifth century.

First, *there must be a just cause*. Defensive wars are a just cause. Wars of unprovoked aggression and wars designed to plunder are not. Second, *there must be a just intention*. War must not be carried out for the purposes of revenge, conquest, economic gain, or mere ideological supremacy. Just wars are fought to rescue those who have been attacked by a hostile power, or to protect those in danger of such an attack.

Third, *war must be a last resort.* War is to be entered into only after all methods of solving disputes nonviolently have been exhausted. Fourth, *a nation must make a formal declaration of war.* Terrorists who live in a nation cannot declare war. Militias cannot declare war. Mercenaries cannot declare war.

Fifth, *the war must have limited objectives.* The war should not have as its goal the complete destruction of the opposing nation. The war should be waged such that hostilities cease as soon as the objectives have been reached. Sixth, *the war must utilize proportionate means.* Only the level of force necessary to secure victory over opposing combatants should be utilized. Annihilation is out of the question.

And seventh, *every effort must be made to ensure that noncombatants remain immune from danger.*

Responding to the Arguments for Abortion

How can we respond to the claim of abortionists that the baby in the womb is not really human until it is born?

Scripture is clear that everything God has created reproduces *after its own kind* (Genesis 1:21,24). This means that at the moment of conception, what is in the womb is truly human. Certainly Scripture portrays the baby in the womb as a human being (see Psalm 139:13-15; Jeremiah 1:5; Exodus 21:22-24).

One must raise the question of how premature births relate to this issue. Some babies are born months before their due date, and even though they may need medical life support to survive, it is very clear that the baby is a human being. (In some cases, even babies born in their fourth month have survived!)

Would the abortionist say that a simple change in location is what makes the baby a human being? Such an idea is absurd. The only difference between born and unborn babies is their size and location, not their essential nature as a human being.[2]

How can we respond to the claim of some abortionists that because the unborn baby is not conscious, abortion is acceptable?

Medical science has proven that the baby has brain-wave activity at one and a half months following conception. Moreover, the baby responds to external stimuli (which indicates brain activity) at three months.[3]

Beyond these facts, the very idea of "consciousness" as an argument is flawed. Even if we granted that the unborn baby is not conscious, in view of the fact that it is not right (or legal) to kill a *sleeping* person or a *comatose* person, it is not right to kill a baby in the womb. The issue of consciousness is irrelevant to the issue of the morality of abortion.

How can we respond to the claim of some abortionists that because abortions are going to occur anyway, whether we like it or not, we might as well legalize them?

Such a view is the height of folly. Incest is going to happen in our society anyway, but does that mean we should legalize it? Child snatching in our society is going to occur anyway, but does that mean we should legalize it? Murder in our society is going to occur anyway, but does that mean we should legalize it? Theft in our society is going to occur anyway, but does that mean we should legalize it? Of course not. To be consistent, if we legalize abortion, we should also legalize all these other crimes because they're all going to happen anyway.

How can we respond to the claim that having an abortion is more merciful than giving birth to a child with birth defects?

The real issue is whether or not the unborn fetus is a human being. If it is, then no one has the right to snuff out that life, regardless of whether birth defects occur. From a scriptural perspective, the unborn baby is most certainly a human person (see Psalm 51:5; 139:13; Jeremiah 1:5). To abort the baby therefore amounts to murder.

We can illustrate the absurdity of this position by addressing the situation of an already-born child who has birth defects. Should we execute this child simply because of a missing limb?

You see my point. If it is true that the unborn baby is a human person, then to kill the unborn baby is really no different than killing a young child.

One must also keep in mind the scriptural teaching that a person born with a physical deformity may end up glorifying God in a great way. The blind man of John 9 was born blind, and some of the disciples thought it may have been because of sin. But Jesus said, "It was not that this man sinned, or his parents, but that the works of God might be displayed in him" (John 9:3). This situation led to glorifying God.

How can we respond to the claim of abortionists that because women have the right to control their own bodies, they can therefore have an abortion if the baby is unwanted?

The baby in the womb is not part of the woman's body. The baby has his or her *own* body *within* the womb of the mother's body. It is true that the mother's body sustains the baby's body with nutrients and a protective environment, but it is nevertheless a distinct body from her own. Therefore, for her to have an abortion is not just an operation on her own body but amounts to killing another human being whose body is within her body.

Is abortion okay in the case of rape?

No, it is not. While rape is a terrible indignity, two wrongs never make a right. In fact, the sin of a mother murdering an unborn baby is greater than the sin of the rapist violating a woman. Having an abortion in this situation amounts to punishing an innocent party. It is the rapist who deserves punishment, not the unborn child.

The raped woman who has an abortion must now emotionally deal with two terrible events—the horrible and crushing indignity of being raped *and* the guilt over killing an innocent human being. Babies who are conceived by rape have every bit as much right to live as any other human being. And to have that life snuffed out is a crime against them and against God.

Notes

Chapter 1—Scripture: From God to Us

1. Norman Geisler and William Nix, *A General Introduction to the Bible* (Chicago, IL: Moody, 1978), p. 28.
2. Craig Blomberg, "The Seventy-Four 'Scholars': Who Does the Jesus Seminar Really Speak For?" *Christian Research Journal,* Fall 1994, p. 36.

Chapter 2—The Trustworthiness of the Bible

1. Donald J. Wiseman, "Archaeological Confirmation of the Old Testament," cited in Norman L. Geisler, *Christian Apologetics* (Grand Rapids, MI: Baker, 1976), p. 322.
2. Nelson Glueck, *Rivers in the Desert* (Philadelphia, PA: Jewish Publications Society of America, 1969), p. 31.
3. William F. Albright; cited in Josh McDowell, *Evidence That Demands a Verdict* (San Bernardino, CA: Campus Crusade for Christ, 1972), p. 68.
4. Randall Price, *The Stones Cry Out* (Eugene, OR: Harvest House, 1997), pp. 46-47.
5. F.F. Bruce, *The New Testament Documents: Are They Reliable?* (Downers Grove, IL: InterVarsity, 1984), p. 19.
6. J. Harold Greenlee, *Introduction to New Testament Textual Criticism* (Grand Rapids, MI: Baker, 1993), p. 68.
7. Gleason Archer, *A Survey of Old Testament Introduction* (Chicago, IL: Moody, 1964), p. 19, emphasis added.
8. Dan Story, *Defending Your Faith: How to Answer the Tough Questions* (Nashville, TN: Thomas Nelson, 1992), p. 35.
9. Greg L. Bahnsen, "The Inerrancy of the Autographa," cited in Norman L. Geisler, ed., *Inerrancy* (Grand Rapids, MI: Zondervan, 1980), p. 161.

Chapter 3—The Books That Belong in the Bible

1. Norman L. Geisler and Ronald M. Brooks, *When Skeptics Ask* (Wheaton, IL: Victor Books, 1989), pp. 155-56.

Chapter 5—Interpretation of Scripture: Sense and Nonsense

1. "The Westminster Confession," in Bruce Milne, *Know the Truth* (Downers Grove, IL: InterVarsity Press, 1982), p. 46.
2. Gordon L. Lewis, *Confronting the Cults* (Phillipsburg, NJ: P & R Publishing, 1985), p. 137.
3. Benjamin B. Warfield, *Biblical and Theological Studies* (Phillipsburg, NJ: P & R Publishing, 1968), p. 30.

Chapter 6—Common Questions About the Old Testament

1. Gleason L. Archer, *Encyclopedia of Bible Difficulties* (Grand Rapids, MI: Zondervan, 1982), p. 80.
2. See Ken Ham, *The Lie* (El Cajon, CA: Creation-Life Publishers, 1987), pp. 123-30.
3. Charles Caldwell Ryrie, ed., *Ryrie Study Bible* (Chicago, IL: Moody, 1994), p. 15.

Chapter 7—Common Questions About the New Testament

1. Walter C. Kaiser, *Hard Sayings of the Old Testament* (Downers Grove, IL: InterVarsity, 1988), p. 167.
2. *Reasoning from the Scriptures* (Brooklyn, NY: Watchtower Bible and Tract Society, 1989), p. 76.

Chapter 8—The Trinity

1. Robert M. Bowman, *Why You Should Believe in the Trinity* (Grand Rapids, MI: Baker, 1989), p. 43.
2. Benjamin B. Warfield, *The Person and Work of Christ* (Philadelphia, PA: Presbyterian and Reformed, 1950), p. 66.
3. Robert L. Reymond, *Jesus, Divine Messiah: The New Testament Witness* (Phillipsburg, NJ: Presbyterian and Reformed, 1990), p. 84.
4. Lewis Sperry Chafer, *Systematic Theology,* vol. 1 (Wheaton, IL: Victor Books, 1988), 1:181.

Chapter 9—Common Errors About God

1. Norman L. Geisler and Jeff Amano, *The Infiltration of the New Age* (Wheaton, IL: Tyndale House, 1990), p. 20.
2. Norman Geisler and Thomas Howe, *When Critics Ask* (Wheaton, IL: Victor Books, 1992), p. 31.
3. Geisler and Howe, p. 31.
4. Walter C. Kaiser, *Hard Sayings of the Old Testament* (Downers Grove, IL: InterVarsity, 1988), p. 167.
5. F.F. Bruce, *The Gospel of John* (London: Pickering, 1983), p. 234.

Chapter 10—Understanding the Holy Spirit

1. William F. Arndt and F. Wilbur Gingrich, *A Greek-English Lexicon of the New Testament and Other Early Christian Literature* (Chicago, IL: The University of Chicago Press, 1957), p. 874.
2. Arndt and Gingrich, p. 146.

Chapter 11—The Humanity of Jesus

1. Robert Lightner, cited in John F. Walvoord and Roy B. Zuck, ed., *The Bible Knowledge Commentary: New Testament* (Wheaton, IL: Victor, 1983), p. 654.

Chapter 12—Jesus and the Father: Equally Divine

1. Robert M. Bowman, *Why You Should Believe in the Trinity* (Grand Rapids, MI: Baker, 1989), p. 60.
2. *The Watchtower,* 1 July 1986, p. 31.
3. Benjamin B. Warfield, *The Person and Work of Christ* (Philadelphia, PA: Presbyterian and Reformed, 1950), p. 56.
4. Leon Morris, *The Gospel According to John* (Grand Rapids, MI: Eerdmans, 1971), p. 658.
5. Cited in Bowman, *Why You Should Believe in the Trinity,* pp. 14-15.
6. Robert L. Reymond, *Jesus, Divine Messiah: The New Testament Witness* (Phillipsburg, NJ: Presbyterian and Reformed, 1990), p. 247.
7. David Reed, *Jehovah's Witnesses Answered Verse by Verse* (Grand Rapids, MI: Baker, 1992), p. 97.
8. Reed, p. 97.
9. J.B. Lightfoot, *Paul's Epistles to the Colossians and to Philemon* (Grand Rapids, MI: Zondervan, 1979), p. 147.
10. Spiros Zodhiates, *The Complete Word Study Dictionary* (Chattanooga, TN: AMG Publishers, 1992), p. 260.
11. William F. Arndt and F. Wilbur Gingrich, *A Greek-English Lexicon of the New Testament and Other Early Christian Literature* (Chicago, IL: The University of Chicago Press, 1957), p. 112.
12. Zodhiates, *The Complete Word Study Dictionary,* p. 261.
13. Bowman, *Why You Should Believe in the Trinity,* p. 65.
14. Bowman, *Why You Should Believe in the Trinity,* p. 66.

Chapter 13—Evidence for the Deity of Christ

1. James Oliver Buswell, *A Systematic Theology of the Christian Religion* (Grand Rapids, IL: Zondervan, 1979), 1:105.
2. Charles C. Ryrie, *Basic Theology* (Wheaton, IL: Victor Books, 1986), p. 248; compare with Robert Reymond, *Jesus, Divine Messiah: The New Testament Witness* (Phillipsburg, NJ: Presbyterian and Reformed, 1990), p. 68.

3. See John F. Walvoord, *Jesus Christ Our Lord* (Chicago, IL: Moody Press, 1969), pp. 22-25.

Chapter 14—Christ in the Old Testament

1. C.F. Keil and F. Delitzsch, *Commentary on the Old Testament,* vol. 6 (Grand Rapids, MI: Eerdmans, 1986), pp. 273-78; A.R. Fausset, *A Commentary—Critical, Experimental, and Practical—on the Old and New Testaments* (Grand Rapids, MI: Eerdmans, 1973), p. 508.
2. Norman Geisler, *To Understand the Bible Look for Jesus* (Grand Rapids, MI: Baker, 1979), p. 67.
3. Francis Brown, S.R. Driver, and Charles A. Briggs, *A Hebrew and English Lexicon of the Old Testament* (Oxford, England: Clarendon Press, 1980), p. 521.

Chapter 15—The Resurrection of Christ

1. Robert Gundry, *Soma in Biblical Theology* (Cambridge, England: Cambridge University Press, 1976), p. 168.
2. See Norman Geisler and Ronald Brooks, *When Skeptics Ask* (Wheaton, IL: Victor, 1989), p. 124.

Chapter 16—Errors About Christ

1. *Gospel Principles* (Salt Lake City, UT: The Church of Jesus Christ of Latter-day Saints, 1986), p. 9.
2. See David Spangler, *Reflections on the Christ* (Forres, Scotland: Findhorn, 1981).
3. Shirley MacLaine, *Out on a Limb* (New York, NY: Bantam Books, 1984), pp. 233-34.
4. Albert Barnes, *Notes on the Old Testament—Isaiah* (Grand Rapids, MI: Baker, 1977), p. 193.
5. Barnes, p. 193.
6. J.F. Stenning, *The Targum of Isaiah* (London, England: Oxford Press, 1949), p. 32.

Chapter 17—The Origins of Humankind

1. *Science: Order and Reality*, eds. Laurel Hicks, Delores Shimmin, Gregory Rickard, Ed Rickard, Julie Rickard, Barbara Porcher, Cindy Froman (Pensacola, FL: A Beka Book, 1993), p. 392.
2. See Robert Lightner, *Evangelical Theology: A Survey and Review* (Grand Rapids, MI: Baker, 1986), p. 180.

Chapter 20—The Gospel That Saves

1. John Blanchard, *Whatever Happened to Hell?* (Durham, England: Evangelical Press, 1993), p. 113.
2. Norman Geisler and Ralph MacKenzie, *Roman Catholics and Evangelicals* (Grand Rapids, MI: Baker, 1995), pp. 221-48.

3. John F. Walvoord and Roy B. Zuck, eds., *The Bible Knowledge Commentary: New Testament* (Wheaton, IL: Victor, 1983), p. 851.

4. Kenneth Barker, ed., *The NIV Study Bible* (Grand Rapids, MI: Zondervan, 1985), p. 1894.

Chapter 21—The Security of the Christian's Salvation

1. John F. Walvoord and Roy B. Zuck, eds., *The Bible Knowledge Commentary: New Testament* (Wheaton, IL: Victor, 1983), p. 825.

Chapter 22—God's Part and Man's Part

1. John Calvin, *Commentary on John's Gospel* (Grand Rapids, MI: Baker, 1949), vol. 1, p. 64.

2. Millard J. Erickson, *Christian Theology* (Grand Rapids, MI: Baker, 1985), p. 834.

3. John Calvin, *Commentary on Romans* (Grand Rapids, MI: Baker, 1949), p. 211.

4. Walter Elwell, "Atonement, Extent of the," *Evangelical Dictionary of Theology* (Grand Rapids, MI: Baker, 1984), p. 99.

5. Erickson, *Christian Theology,* p. 832.

Chapter 24—Christians as Witnesses

1. See Erwin Lutzer, *Christ Among Other Gods* (Chicago, IL: Moody, 1994).

2. Some years ago, I read an article by Stuart Dauermann in which he outlined how to witness to Jews. I've since lost that article, and have no idea what magazine it was published in. But I do want to credit him for the overall strategy.

3. See Geoffrey Parrinder, ed., *World Religions* (New York, NY: Facts on File Publications, 1971), pp. 485-90.

4. *Draper's Book of Quotations for the Christian World* (Wheaton, IL: Tyndale House, 1992), p. 106.

5. *Spurgeon Quotes,* electronic media, HyperCard database.

6. Eric Stuyck, "Can Children Be Saved?" Child Evangelism Fellowship of Frederick County, Maryland.

Chapter 25—All About the Church

1. Barnabas, "The Epistle of Barnabas," Chapter 15, 1670-1671, insert added.

2. Ignatius, "The Epistle of Ignatius to the Magnesians," in Philip Schaff, *The Apostolic Fathers with Justin Martyr and Irenaeus* (Grand Rapids, MI: Eerdmans, 2001), Chapter 9, p. 682.

3. Justin Martyr, "The First Apology of Justin," in Schaff, *The Apostolic Fathers with Justin Martyr and Irenaeus,* Chapter 67.

Chapter 26—Angels Among Us

1. David Connolly, *In Search of Angels: A Celestial Sourcebook for Beginning Your Journey* (New York: Perigee, 1993), p. 78.

2. Kenneth L. Woodward, "Angels: Hark! America's Latest Search for Spiritual Meaning Has a Halo Effect," *Newsweek,* 27 December 1993, p. 57.

3. Woodward, p. 57.

4. Connolly, p. 57.

5. C. Fred Dickason, *Angels, Elect and Evil* (Chicago, IL: Moody, 1978), p. 86.

6. John Calvin, *Institutes of the Christian Religion,* ed. John T. McNeill, trans. Ford Lewis Battles (Philadelphia, PA: The Westminster Press, 1960), 1.14.11.

Chapter 27—The Devil and His Fallen Angels

1. Charles C. Ryrie, cited in Paul Enns, *The Moody Handbook of Theology* (Chicago, IL: Moody, 1989), p. 298.

Chapter 29—The Wonder of Heaven

1. R.C. Sproul, *Now, That's a Good Question* (Wheaton, IL: Tyndale, 1996), p. 291.

Chapter 30—The Judgment of Humankind

1. Cited in Charles C. Ryrie, *Basic Theology* (Wheaton, IL: Victor, 1986), p. 513.

Chapter 31—Erroneous Views of the Afterlife

1. Alan Gomes, "Evangelicals and the Annihilation of Hell," Part Two, *Christian Research Journal,* Summer 1991, p. 11.

2. Shirley MacLaine, *Out on a Limb* (New York, NY: Bantam, 1984), p. 233.

Chapter 32—Near-Death Experiences

1. Jerry Yamamoto, "The Near-Death Experience," *Christian Research Journal,* Spring 1992, p. 2.

2. Yamamoto, p. 2.

3. Yamamoto, pp. 2-3.

4. See Doug Groothuis, *Deceived by the Light* (Eugene, OR: Harvest House, 1995), pp. 165-79.

5. John Ankerberg and John Weldon, *The Facts on Life After Death* (Eugene, OR: Harvest House, 1992), p. 10.

6. Ankerberg and Weldon, p. 11.

7. Ankerberg and Weldon, p. 28.

8. Recounted by Doug Groothuis, *Deceived by the Light* (Eugene, OR: Harvest House, 1995), pp. 70-71.

9. Groothuis, pp. 70-71.

10. Groothuis, pp. 70-71.

11. Jerry Yamamoto, "The Near-Death Experience," *Christian Research Journal,* Spring 1992, p. 5.

12. Yamamoto, p. 5.

13. Gary R. Habermas and J.P. Moreland, *Immortality: The Other Side of Death* (Nashville, TN: Thomas Nelson, 1992), p. 93.

Chapter 33—Apologetics and the Christian

1. C.S. Lewis, *God in the Dock* (Grand Rapids, MI: Eerdmans, 1972), p. 26.
2. Lewis, p. 26.
3. Ravi Zacharias, *The Real Face of Atheism* (Grand Rapids, MI: Baker, 2004), p. 36.
4. Jimmy Davis and Harry Poe, *Designer Universe: Intelligent Design and the Existence of God* (Nashville, TN: Broadman & Holman Publishers, 2002), p. 221, emphasis added.
5. Paul Little, *Know Why You Believe* (Downers Grove, IL: InterVarsity Press, 1975), p. 81.
6. Peter Kreeft, cited in Lee Strobel, *The Case for Faith* (Grand Rapids, MI: Zondervan, 2006), p. 37.
7. Gregory Boyd, *Is God to Blame? Beyond Pat Answers to the Problem of Suffering* (Downers Grove, IL: InterVarsity Press, 2003), p. 63.
8. Little, p. 87.
9. Ken Boa and Larry Moody, *I'm Glad You Asked: In-Depth Answers to Difficult Questions* (Colorado Springs, CO: David C. Cook, 1995), p. 131.
10. Norman Geisler and Jeff Amanu, "Evil," in *New Dictionary of Theology*, eds. Sinclair Ferguson and David Wright (Downers Grove, IL: InterVarsity Press, 1988), p. 242.
11. Gordon Lewis and Bruce Demarest, *Integrative Theology* (Grand Rapids, MI: Zondervan, 1996), I:322.
12. Little, p. 81.
13. Millard Erickson, *Christian Theology* (Grand Rapids, MI: Baker, 1987), p. 425.
14. Peter Kreeft, *Making Sense Out of Suffering* (Ann Arbor, MI: Servant Books, 1986), p. 123.
15. William Lane Craig and Walter Sinnott-Armstrong, *God? A Debate Between a Christian and an Atheist* (Oxford: Oxford University Press, 2004), pp. 116-17.
16. "The Craig-Jesseph Debate: Does God Exist?" Transcript posted at www.leaderu.com.
17. "Os Guinness Looks Evil in the Eye," Interview with Os Guinness by Stan Guthrie, *Christianity Today*, March 10, 2005, Internet.
18. William Lane Craig, *No Easy Answers* (Chicago, IL: Moody Press, 1990), p. 90.
19. Paul Powell, *When the Hurt Won't Go Away* (Wheaton, IL: Victor Books, 1986), p. 62.
20. Miles Stanford, *Principles of Spiritual Growth* (Lincoln, NE: Back to the Bible, 1976), p. 11.

Chapter 34—Apologetics and Intelligent Design Theory

1. Robin Collins, "The Fine-Tuning Design Argument," *Reason for the Hope Within*, September 1, 1998, Discovery Institute web site.

2. Robert Jastrow, *God and the Astronomers* (New York, NY: Norton, 1992), p. 118.

3. Frederick Hoyle, "The Universe: Past and Present Reflections," *Annual Reviews of Astronomy and Astrophysics* 20 (1982), p. 16.

4. George Greenstein, *The Symbiotic Universe* (New York, NY: Morrow, 1988), pp. 26-27.

5. Jastrow, p. 16.

6. Fritjof Capra, *The Turning Point* (New York, NY: Simon and Schuster, 1984), p. 96.

Chapter 35—Apologetics and Danger Zone Issues

1. George Mather and Larry Nichols, eds., *Dictionary of Cults, Sects, Religions, and the Occult* (Grand Rapids: Zondervan, 1993), p. 184.

2. Capra, p. 123.

3. Capra, p. 322.

4. Rick Fields, et al., eds., *Chop Wood, Carry Water* (Los Angeles, CA: J.P. Tarcher, 1984), p. 186.

5. Elliot Miller, *A Crash Course on the New Age Movement* (Grand Rapids, MI: Baker, 1988), p. 187.

6. John Ankerberg and John Weldon, *The Facts on the Masonic Lodge* (Eugene, OR: Harvest House, 1989), pp. 17.

7. Elliot Miller and Kenneth R. Samples, *The Cult of the Virgin* (Grand Rapids, MI: Baker, 1992).

8. Documented in Ron Rhodes, *The Culting of America* (Eugene, OR: Harvest House, 1994), pp. 205-07.

9. Elliot Miller, "Questions and Answers," *Christian Research Newsletter,* July/September 1992, p. 4.

10. Brooks Alexander, "Machines Made of Shadows," *SCP Journal,* 17:1-2, 1992, p. 11.

11. John Weldon with Zola Levitt, *UFOs: What on Earth Is Happening* (Eugene, OR: Harvest House, 1975), p. 101.

12. John Keel, *UFOs: Operation Trojan Horse* (New York: G.P. Putnam's Sons, 1970), pp. 215, 299.

13. David Wimbish, *Something's Going On Out There* (Old Tappan: Revell, 1990), p. 158.

14. Wimbish, p. 164.

Chapter 36—Apologetics and the Cults

1. Bruce R. McConkie, *Mormon Doctrine* (Salt Lake City, UT: Bookcraft, 1966), pp. 526-28.

2. Documented in Ron Rhodes, *The Culting of America* (Eugene, OR: Harvest House, 1994), pp. 97-98.

3. Walter Martin, *The Kingdom of the Cults* (Minneapolis, MN: Bethany House, 1985), pp. 377-85.

4. *Your Will Be Done on Earth* (Brooklyn, NY: Watchtower Bible and Tract Society, 1985), p. 362.

5. See, for example, *The Watchtower,* 15 January 1917, p. 6033.

6. David Reed, *How to Rescue Your Loved One from the Watchtower* (Grand Rapids, MI: Baker, 1989), pp. 23-24.

7. Norman L. Geisler and Ronald M. Brooks, *Christianity Under Attack* (Dallas, TX: Quest Publications, 1985), p. 43.

8. Norman Geisler and Jeff Amano, *The Infiltration of the New Age* (Wheaton, IL: Tyndale House, 1990), p. 18.

9. *The Imperial Bible Dictionary,* 1:376; cited in Reasoning from the Scriptures (Brooklyn, NY: Watchtower Bible and Tract Society, 1989), p. 89.

10. David Reed, *Jehovah's Witnesses Answered Verse by Verse* (Grand Rapids, MI: Baker, 2002), pp. 11, 25.

11. *Reasoning from the Scriptures* (Brooklyn, NY: Watchtower Bible and Tract Society, 1989), p. 75.

12. Norman Geisler and Thomas Howe, *When Critics Ask* (Wheaton, IL: Victor, 1992), p. 434.

Chapter 38—Ethical Issues Related to Death

1. Carl F.H. Henry, *Baker's Dictionary of Christian Ethics* (Grand Rapids, MI: Baker, 1973), p. 149.

2. I am indebted to the work of Norman Geisler on the issue of abortion. His class notes from an ethics class at Dallas Theological Seminary in the early 1980s have proved to be invaluable.

3. See Frank Beckwith, *Politically Correct Death* (Grand Rapids, MI: Baker, 1995).

**To access a bibliography for this book,
go to www.ronrhodes.org and check on the Odds & Ends tab.**

Subject Index

Primary Verse Index

Other Great Harvest House Books by Ron Rhodes

Books About the Bible
Bite-Size Bible® Answers
Bite-Size Bible® Definitions
Bite-Size Bible® Handbook
Bite-Size Bible® Charts
Commonly Misunderstood Bible Verses
Find It Fast in the Bible
What Does the Bible Say About...?

Books About the End Times
The Coming Oil Storm
Cyber Meltdown
The End Times in Chronological Order
Northern Storm Rising
The Topical Handbook of Bible Prophecy
Unmasking the Antichrist

Books About Other Important Topics
5-Minute Apologetics for Today
1001 Unforgettable Quotes About God, Faith, and the Bible
The Complete Guide to Christian Denominations
The Truth Behind Ghosts, Mediums, and Psychic Phenomena
The Wonder of Heaven

The 10 Most Important Things Series
The 10 Most Important Things You Can Say to a Catholic
The 10 Most Important Things You Can Say to a Jehovah's Witness
The 10 Most Important Things You Can Say to a Mason
The 10 Most Important Things You Can Say to a Mormon

The Reasoning from the Scriptures Series
Reasoning from the Scriptures with Catholics
Reasoning from the Scriptures with the Jehovah's Witnesses
Reasoning from the Scriptures with the Mormons
Reasoning from the Scriptures with Muslims
Reasoning from the Scriptures with Masons

Quick Reference Guides
Five Views on the Rapture: What You Need to Know
Halloween: What You Need to Know
Is America in Bible Prophecy?: What You Need to Know
Islam: What You Need to Know
Jehovah's Witnesses: What You Need to Know